A Life of My Own

The Life and Death of Mary Wollstonecraft
Shelley and His World
Katherine Mansfield: A Secret Life
The Invisible Woman: The Story of Nelly Ternan and
Charles Dickens
The Winter Wife (play)
Mrs Jordan's Profession
Jane Austen: A Life
Several Strangers: Writing from Three Decades
Samuel Pepys: The Unequalled Self
Thomas Hardy: The Time-Torn Man
Charles Dickens: A Life
Poems of Thomas Hardy (selected and introduced)
Poems of John Keats (selected and introduced)
Poems of John Milton (selected and introduced)

A Life of My Own

CLAIRE TOMALIN

PENGUIN BOOKS

PENGUIN BOOKS

UK | USA | Canada | Ireland | Australia
India | New Zealand | South Africa

Penguin Books is part of the Penguin Random House group of companies
whose addresses can be found at global.penguinrandomhouse.com.

Penguin
Random House
UK

First published by Viking 2017
Published in Penguin Books 2018
001

Copyright © Claire Tomalin, 2017

Photograph on page 87 copyright © Newnham College, Cambridge; sketch on page 143
copyright © David Gentleman; photographs on pages 181 and 275 copyright © Frank Herrmann.
All other photographs courtesy of the author.

Set in 12.5/15.25 pt Bembo Book MT Std
Typeset by Jouve (UK), Milton Keynes
Printed in Great Britain by Clays Ltd, St Ives plc

A CIP catalogue record for this book is available from the British Library

ISBN: 978–0–241–97483–4

www.greenpenguin.co.uk

Contents

List of Illustrations

Introductory Note

Writing about myself has not been easy. I have tried to be as truthful as possible, which has meant moving between the trivial and the tragic in a way that could seem callous. But that is how life is. Even when you are at the worst moments and would like to give all your attention to grief, you still have to clean the house and pay the bills; you may even enjoy your lunch. One of my aims in writing was to insist on the seamlessness of life – something I saw presented by Pepys in his diaries, in which he gives the texture of the days as he lived them, work and play mixed together, never pretending that he felt as he should, or behaved better than he did.

I set out to describe as best I could my experience of the world, how it was for a European girl growing up in mid-twentieth-century England, how I got my education, how I made friends and related to different families who were good to me, how I was carried along by conflicting desires to have children and a worthwhile working life; and how long it took me to get going with the work I most enjoy and value: researching and writing historical biographies.

In taking on this self-imposed task, I was driven partly by curiosity: what would I learn about myself? Through the process of examining my life, I thought I might understand myself better. One thing I have learnt is that, while I used to think I was making individual choices, now, looking back, I see clearly that I was following trends and general patterns of behaviour which I was about as powerless to resist as a migrating bird or a salmon swimming upstream. And I was driven to make progress in my career by my first husband's not infrequent decisions to abandon the family. For me the Sixties did not always swing cheerfully.

✳

How reliable is memory? Mine brings many scenes from my childhood, scenes I can visualize clearly and in some cases hear, and I believe these to be true memories. They are hard to check, though, because neither of my parents was inclined to talk about those early years, and my sister and I were not close to one another as adults. My mother talked to me a great deal about aspects of her life before I was born but had little to say of the years of my childhood. My father's long memoir has helped me write this book, as will be obvious, since it starts with an account of my parents' ill-starred marriage. All three of them are now dead.

To my surprise I found after my father's death that he had kept almost every letter I wrote to him from the age of eleven. So here was an aide-mémoire that gave me both the facts and the feelings that had gone with them, insofar as I had been prepared to tell him about them. I did not tell all, but I have been surprised to find how much I did reveal to him — maybe because my letters were written as much to my stepmother, whom I liked, and whose opinion I valued. Almost none of my letters to my mother have survived.

There was no doubt of my love for her or hers for me, but by my teens I had learnt to censor what I told her of my feelings, behaviour and ambitions.

My copious early diaries disappeared during the years I was moving between Paris and Cambridge. From 1960, when I was twenty-seven, I kept basic diaries, mostly giving little more than appointments although expanding into commentary, cheerful, sad or angry, from time to time. I was surprised to find how much they brought back to me. At various points in my life I also wrote private accounts of episodes I wanted to record for myself.

My children are of course at the heart of my life, but I decided to say the minimum about them, not wanting to intrude on them or attribute feelings or remarks to them. I have asked them for their memories and been helped by them, especially in writing about their father and our life in Gloucester Crescent. My son Tom figures more largely for this reason: I believe it is important for people to know what it is like to be a disabled child growing up, and what is involved in being the parent of such a child. These are common experiences but still little understood. Tom has now lived longer than his father's lifespan and his courage always amazes me.

My story should be cheering to anyone who is finding it hard to establish a career they find congenial. I spent my girlhood convinced that poetry was my vocation – I wrote hundreds of poems and was encouraged even at Cambridge to believe that I was a poet. But my poems always related more to literature than to life. I saw this as I left Cambridge and, although producing poems had given me the greatest pleasure I knew, I resolved to write no more. It left me rather stranded: what was I to do? With an English degree I found literary work, in publishing, mostly reading manuscripts, then in reviewing, occasional broadcasting and literary editing. Only in the early 1970s, as I approached forty, did I start working on my first historical biography, but I still had to earn my living by working as a literary editor. It was 1986 and I was in my mid-fifties before I could concentrate on full-time research and writing. I found great happiness in this work, and for the next twenty-five years I researched and wrote steadily. So at last I found my true vocation.

※

I am a Londoner, born here and settled here, and my first chapter is about how this came about. Both my parents had gifts which brought them to study in London, my father from the Alps of the Haute-Savoie, my mother from Liverpool in north-west England. London was the city of their dreams, and also where they met and married. The book begins with my father, still a schoolboy, arriving in London in 1921.

I

A London Romance

To begin with my father, Émile Delavenay: here he is, a slight, eager boy of fifteen from the mountains of Savoy, with thin arms, curly hair above a high brow, spectacles for his short sight, arriving at Victoria Station on a hot July day in 1921. I have a clear picture of him as he was, elated to be travelling abroad for the first time, as chaperone to his elder sister Hélène. She had just recovered from scarlet fever and been offered the trip as a treat by their parents, and they made the long train journey – from their home in Savoy, through Paris and on to London – by themselves. An exchange had been organized for them by Émile's young English teacher, and she had already fired him with a determination to seize the opportunity to make progress in the language: he had brought his dictionary with him. Soon they were standing in the Marylebone Road, opposite Madame Tussauds, looking up at the large five-storey house in which their hosts, the Macarthurs, were waiting to receive them.

They were warmly greeted and were to be generously entertained for the month of their visit. The Macarthurs were from Glasgow and spoke with a rolling *r*, and there was much invoking of the auld alliance between Scotland

and France. Mr Macarthur was a chiropodist, but no ordinary chiropodist, since he treated royal feet – the Duke of York was mentioned – and the feet of the famous, Rudyard Kipling and the polar explorer Shackleton among them. The doctors in Harley Street nearby sent him many patients. Mrs Macarthur and her sister-in-law were both chiropodists too – this was a hard-working family. Isa and John, their teenage children, sometimes helped out as well, but they were now in charge of showing Émile and Hélène the sights of London.

They made a very thorough job of it: Hampton Court and Windsor, all the South Kensington museums, Victoria & Albert, Natural History and Science; then the Tate, the Wallace Collection, the National Gallery. There were trips on the Thames, a visit to the theatre – Émile had never seen a live performance before and was entranced – and meals in restaurants. They visited Madame Tussauds across the road. English magazines and novels were on offer in the house, Anthony Hope and Conan Doyle. They were taken to church, and attended family prayers, activities entirely unknown to the unbaptized children of atheist French schoolteachers.

Émile enjoyed every moment, even being woken at dawn by the sound of hooves, as processions of great horses hauled their loaded carts to Euston and King's Cross. It was a sight and sound he never forgot. He was encouraged to explore the streets of Marylebone for himself and took pride in familiarizing himself with the district – when he was in his nineties I saw him retracing the walks he had made then with intense satisfaction, although the

Macarthurs' house and garden had long been replaced by a block of flats.

Émile had scarcely seen a large town in his life, because, although Geneva was close to home, and he had cousins there, it was cut off from Savoy throughout the First World War and until 1919. The nearest town to his native village of Ayse was Bonneville, with a population of a few thousand, and in winter he sledged down the mountain daily to the Bonneville lycée, pulling his sledge back up in the afternoon. What he saw in London – the life of a great city with a rich culture – made an overwhelming impression on him. He realized that the English language was opening a door into a world that offered possibilities he had never imagined, and he resolved to master its pronunciation, vocabulary and grammar as fast as he could. Carrying his dictionary with him wherever he went, listening and questioning, he made dramatic progress during the month of his stay. While his sister managed hardly a word of English, he could understand a good deal and talk in simple sentences by the time they went home to Savoy. They took the Macarthur children with them, and he insisted on speaking English with them throughout their stay in Savoy. He was soon able to read Dickens – his mother's old copy of *David Copperfield*, which she had studied in English at her girls' school in Grenoble – and contemporary writers. He read Henry James's *Roderick Hudson*, the story of a brilliant young American who falls in love with Europe and flies too far, too fast; and H. G. Wells's novels describing modern English life, which he found especially attractive. England became a promised land to him.

He told me once that speaking English made him feel he was a different person, and he began to prefer to be that second, alternative man. Whatever constraints and shyness he felt in France dropped away in England, and he could communicate freely and easily with people of all kinds and classes. Later, I found for myself that even having a foreign name – his name, Delavenay – gave me a special sort of freedom, because the English could not easily place me.

All the same, he was French, and he had to make his way through the brutally tough stages of French education, with his parents' support, if he were to achieve his ambitions. First, he gained entry to the most prestigious school in France, the Lycée Louis-le-Grand in Paris, an intellectual forcing house with a relentless programme of work. The day's studies started at 6.30 in the morning and sometimes went on till midnight. This was pretty regularly the case for him, since he was there to prepare the entrance examination for the École Normale Supérieure. The École Normale in the rue d'Ulm is one of the pinnacles of the French educational system: a college of higher education set up by Robespierre in 1794 and refounded by Napoleon, it has maintained its excellence throughout the centuries. France is a meritocracy, and, after four years of graduate study at Normale, a Normalien is assured of a prestigious career. My father told me that before he took the entrance examination he had nightmares of failure, dreaming he might have to become a bus driver rather than a scholar. In fact his two years at Louis-le-Grand culminated in a notable success, and he became the first Savoyard to go to Normale.★

He did not forget his English persona, and had even managed to make another brief summer visit to the Macarthurs in 1924, getting to hear Sybil Thorndike play Saint Joan at the Old Vic, and working in the University College Library. And, since his chosen subject at Normale was English Literature, he was now obliged by his tutors to spend much of his time in England, studying and teaching in London and Cambridge. Meanwhile he had acquired another interest through attending summer schools on international intellectual cooperation in Geneva, where an aunt put him up, and witnessing early sessions of the Assembly of the League of Nations. He was effectively bilingual by now, but his tutor at Normale warned him that he would not be properly bilingual until nobody in England complimented him on his good English. The advice was good, and his English became so easy and natural to him that he always spoke it with his own children, and could indeed pass as an Englishman.

★ In January 1999 I was in Paris, and described in a letter to a friend how 'I walked through the Luxembourg Gardens to the Panthéon and down the rue d'Ulm and went boldly to the entrance of Normale, where I announced, "Mon père est normalien." And I was waved in with, "Entrez, madame," and a polite welcoming gesture. My father was ninety-three that year. I stood in the courtyard with its modest fountain and grey walls bearing the sculpted heads of great Frenchmen, and thought of him arriving, so young, so long ago, and blinked back a filial tear' (from my letter to Betsy Dworkin, 17 January 1999).

Normale sent him to England in October 1925. He was just twenty years old. His schoolteacher parents had brought him up with the expectation that he would live by their strict moral standards, and his brain was trained and sharpened by one of the most demanding and rigorous educational systems ever devised, but in every aspect of human feeling and behaviour he was as innocent as a child.

The pleasure of going to London was the greater when he found he could have a room at the recently established French Institute in South Kensington, near Hyde Park and Kensington Gardens. He saw the grand houses of Queen's Gate as being inhabited by real-life Forsytes, perfect specimens of those depicted in Galsworthy's *Forsyte Saga*, his current reading. Reading was his chief occupation, and long days were spent in the British Museum studying modern writers, Meredith, Kipling, Barrie and Hardy, as well as the classics; and attending lectures at the London School of Economics and King's College. When he could afford to, he took himself to the Old Vic to hear Shakespeare, never failing to read the text of the play beforehand to prepare himself. At the Institute he was among contemporaries from Normale, linguists, philosophers, historians, scientists, mostly, like him, from the French provinces, and socialists too, all eager to talk about politics, women, their work and their hopes as they embarked on new experiences. Together they found cheap places to eat: ABCs, Lyonses, the Express Dairy at Marble Arch, where they teased the waitresses and speculated among themselves about their sex lives. Marcel Mathieu, an X-ray crystallographer working at the Royal Institution's Davy-Faraday

Research Laboratory, became Émile's closest friend, serving him tea made over a Bunsen burner, carrying him off to concerts – he was a passionate music lover and amateur violinist – and telling him about his love for a rich French girl, Alice, who was doing a little teaching in a private school in London. She enjoyed his attentions, he said, but had warned him that her family would never allow her to marry a poor man. Mathieu invited her to a dance to be held at the French Institute in January, and she agreed to find a partner for Émile. She chose a colleague who taught piano, harmony and counterpoint at her school, and brought her to be inspected over tea at the Institute.

The music teacher was my mother, Muriel Herbert. She was not quite five foot tall, black-haired, dark-eyed, very pretty. When Mathieu invited her to try the Institute piano, she surprised them by playing and singing her own songs. Remarkably, she was already a published composer. The friendship was made, and the date for the dance agreed.

Looking back at what I know about only from their accounts, I see my young father advancing towards a fate that will change his prospects and character, driving him close to madness. And my mother too will be transformed, crushed and partly destroyed. Yet things began simply and happily between these two gifted and attractive creatures when they met and were drawn to one another. For both of them, reaching London was a reward won through hard work. It was the place Émile most desired to be, where he could imagine his dreams and ambitions reaching fulfilment. Muriel had also arrived from a provincial town she had no wish to return to, and was already enjoying success.

But neither was a Londoner and neither had any family or solid base in London. Each was flying alone in unknown territory.

✼

My mother's story was this. She was born in October 1897, the youngest child and only daughter in the family after five boys. Her mother told her how, as she was born upstairs, the family doctor, a musical friend, sang Schubert downstairs, accompanying himself on the piano, to welcome her. She was named Muriel Emily Herbert and brought up in Liverpool, then a flourishing city with a powerful cultural tradition. Her mother led a church choir and was a dedicated reader, and their house was full of music and books. Her brother Percy, ten years older than her and intensely musical, encouraged her very early interest in piano, singing and making up her own songs, and they read poetry together. In 1908 he went up to Oxford to read Mathematics, spending much of his spare time making music with another undergraduate, Adrian Boult. So far so good, but their father was now ill with diabetes and the following year he died, leaving the family impoverished. At the same time, her aunt's husband, Frank Hornby, was becoming a millionaire through marketing his invention Meccano as a children's toy. While the Hornbys grew richer, their Herbert cousins struggled. On finishing at Oxford, Percy felt he must take a job offered in the Colonial Office and served abroad, first in the West Indies, where he was for much of the First World War, and then Nigeria.

Widowhood and poverty wore their mother down. Life in Liverpool was harsh without money. They had to move into a smaller house. Muriel remembered that her bicycle was stolen and could not be replaced, and that she was not allowed to join the Girl Guides because the uniform was too expensive. The flowers she grew in their small front garden were broken or stolen, and the headmistress of her girls' school, who came from the South, told the Liverpool girls they must lose their ugly accents. Muriel needed no scolding on this account, since her mother spoke the required genteel English, as did Percy, and she naturally copied them. But she may have had two voices. Her Hornby uncle spoke Scouse and stuck to it, even when he became a Conservative MP.

Music was her refuge. A self-appointed surrogate father appeared on the scene, Hugh Farrie, a journalist and novelist with his own literary column in the *Liverpool Daily Post*, who watched over her education, found music teachers and paid for her lessons, supplied her with books and encouraged and adored her. I have a volume of poetry he gave her, inscribed 'Love Poems to a little love poem'. He was married, childless, romantic and generous. He hoped she might become a concert pianist – she played Chopin with impressive dash – but composition was her real interest. She studied harmony and began to absorb the songs of Debussy, Ravel, Fauré and Richard Strauss as well as the Schubert and Schumann of her childhood, and to write down her own songs.

The war came in 1914, taking the young men away to fight and be killed. But, with all its horrors, it meant that women found their chances of higher education improved, and in 1917 Muriel won the Liverpool scholarship in composition to the Royal College of Music in London. Her mother, proud of her success, took her to London to settle her in the room the college gave her in Queen Alexandra's House in South Kensington, close to the College and the Albert Hall. From the start, she found friends among her fellow students, friendships that deepened and lasted, several lifelong. She was invited to visit their families, who made much of her, and of her surprising musical skills. A new life was opening. It was just as well, because before the end of the war, early in 1918, Hugh Farrie died and she lost her second father figure.

At college she was taught by Charles Villiers Stanford, the most eminent British composer of his generation. He was now in his sixties, horrified by the war, the injuries and deaths at the front of so many of his pupils, and the air raids on London. His teaching methods were described by one of his pupils as being without method or plan, his criticism mostly a matter of 'I like it, my boy' or 'It's damned ugly, my boy.' He could be bad-tempered, he was not disposed to like women students, and he gave my mother a hard time. Almost at their first encounter he challenged her to play a Beethoven symphony arranged for two pianos with him, at sight, in front of the other students; to her relief she saw that it was one she had played with Percy, and got through it well enough. In any case, she was thoroughly grounded in piano playing and musical theory and could hold her own. She was told she must learn a second instrument for her course of study, and the double bass was suggested. A full-sized double bass was considerably larger than she was, but she saw the joke and took it on happily. In spite of the war, being in London, at college and finding herself surrounded by affectionate friends filled her with pride and happiness.

She made music with violinist friends and learnt to write for the violin: two of her short pieces for piano and violin were included in one of Barbirolli's concerts, and published. When she showed Stanford a first attempt at a violin sonata, he grumbled, 'Ever heard of Elgar?', whom he disliked; still the sonata was performed in 1922 by her friend Gertrude Newsham. Stanford should probably have pushed her towards orchestral writing, but she went no further than a few orchestral accompaniments for her songs. She was happiest with the simple voice and piano, and here she was doing well, with settings of Housman, Bridges, Alice Meynell and a 'Cradle Song' by Swinburne.

Among her new London musical friends were the Hess sisters, Dorothy the pianist, Stefany the violinist, Alice the music teacher; and the Hess family, entertaining in their large flat in Earls Court, introduced her to Roger Quilter, at the height of his renown as a song writer. He offered to look at her work and thought her songs good enough to recommend to Augener's, prestigious music publishers. He then escorted her to their offices to introduce her, and finally witnessed the contract they drew up to publish five songs. It was a strikingly generous act by an established composer to an unknown young woman. He was good-looking and kind, with perfect manners, and he believed in her talent. In November 1922 she wrote to her mother to tell her, 'Mr Quilter is allowing me to dedicate some of my songs to him! I asked him to choose which he would like and he asked for Renouncement, the Cradle Song and When Death to Either.' 'Renouncement', a striking setting of Alice Meynell's passionate sonnet about renouncing an impossible love but living it in her dreams at night, was a surprisingly apposite choice, because Muriel fell in love with Quilter, in her innocence not understanding that he was a homosexual. When he realized the situation, he was aghast and backed away sharply from any further friendship. She did not see him again, and carried a wound, never forgetting him or the pain of the experience.

Another surprising friendship had been formed when Maud, Marchioness of Douro, asked the College to recommend someone who might help her to develop her interest in music. They sent Muriel. Maud was the beautiful daughter of Lord Glentanar, a multimillionaire whose money came from cotton. She moved in high society, was painted by Sargent and married in 1909 a man of ferociously right-wing views, more interested in military matters than in music or books; whereas she had a real interest in both. It seems likely that he married her chiefly for her money and she took him chiefly to become Duchess of Wellington when he should succeed to the title. He fought in the war; they had a son who was not clever enough to get into Eton, and a delicate daughter. Maud was lonely. Ten years older than Muriel, she warmed to her at once and was soon treating her like a younger sister. If Muriel was at first dazzled by being taken up by the aristocracy, she responded to Maud's affection and gave many hours to working on music with her. It became a true friendship, important to both of them.

She was often invited to stay at Stratfield Saye, the Wellingtons' country house in Hampshire. This continued after she was married, and even when she had children. I can just remember being handed over to a Stratfield Saye nanny and taken upstairs to the nursery. Maud was generous in practical ways, passing on silk and satin evening gowns to Muriel (she kept them, and I was able to wear two of them twenty-five years later). She had Muriel photographed by a professional. She sent her to her own nursing home to have her first child. She gave her books, and discussed private problems with her.

Early in their friendship, Maud introduced Muriel to her brother Tom Glentanar, also a music lover, who gave Christmas house parties on his estate in Scotland, putting on operas – Mozart one year, Gilbert and Sullivan another – with a mixture of professional and amateur singers and players. For several years Muriel took the lead soprano parts and joined in the weeks of luxury, hard work and fun while they rehearsed, sang and acted, dancing in the evening, taking country walks when they could, and enjoying the good food and comfortable life of the very rich. When Émile appeared on the scene, he was invited too. The last time they went was in 1931, married and with a child. The Glentanars remained such good friends that they offered to send Muriel's children to Canada with their own daughter when war came, to escape bombing or invasion. My mother was grateful, but decided it would be better for us all to stay together.

Émile was treated to the political opinions of the Duke over port in the evening. He had succeeded to the title in 1934, and become strongly pro-German, and personally friendly with Ribbentrop. When, after Pétain's submission to the Nazis, Émile thought briefly of applying for British nationality, he wrote to the Duke asking if he would consider sponsoring him. The Duke replied that there were enough socialists in England already and he should not count on him to increase their number. Émile was advised by wiser friends that he could do more for France by remaining French. In 1941 the Duke died. His son was already serving in the army when he became Duke, and in 1943 he was killed fighting in Italy. I remember how upset my mother was when the grieving Duchess wrote asking her opinion of a design for a memorial. She died in 1946: more sorrow.

✿

When I think about my mother's life in these early years, I wonder how she managed at all. She had no family in London, and once she had finished at college she needed to earn her own living. Music was at the centre always, and composition requires time and quiet. She visited her mother regularly in Liverpool but had no wish to return to live in the North. Her young Hornby cousin, only daughter of her aunt and uncle, died suddenly in her teens, and they offered in their grief to adopt Muriel, making it a condition that she should give up her music and share their life. She refused their offer unhesitatingly. They dropped her for a time, then decided to forgive the slight. Her aunt presented her with a fur coat, and she was invited to dine with them when they were in London. She did not enjoy dancing with her uncle ('pressed to his fat stomach', she said with a shudder) or their games of bridge.

She found teaching work and was invited to share a flat in Maida Vale with a pianist friend, Jessie Cormack, and her husband Kenneth Wright, a Vickers engineer who was involved in setting up something new, the first broadcasting at Savoy Hill, off the Strand. He had to plan programmes of live music and Muriel became an occasional broadcaster of her own work: she had her voice trained and performed well. All her life she sat at the piano as though this was the most natural place for her to be, with perfect command when she played and sang.

Émile was made welcome at the Wrights' weekend parties in their Maida Vale flat, where there was much impromptu music-making. These evenings were a revelation to him and greatly enjoyable. He saw them as representing a true *vie de bohème*, centred on artistic aspiration and achievement, and far removed from conventional bourgeois life. He was captivated by Muriel: they went dancing together, they walked in Kew Gardens and at Hampton Court, and attended many concerts. They gave each other volumes of poetry: I have the neat edition of the *Oxford Book of English Verse* she gave him in May 1926, and a Rupert Brooke in October that year. Walter de la Mare's volume *The Listeners* was inscribed by him to her 'Euston Station, Nov. 1926!', the exclamation mark because she had told him that her first idea for a setting of Yeats's 'Lake Isle of Innisfree' came to her while waiting at Euston Station. He wondered at her musical gifts, admired her independence and was irresistibly drawn by her physical beauty – soft skin and shape, dark eyes now welcoming, now sad. She told me that he had once said to her that if he ever left her he would always see her reproachful eyes looking at him.

For the moment they were equals, both poor, both ambitious, neither with any definite idea of the future. He knew he would be returning to Paris for further study and examinations. She must have hoped to build on her small but significant success with her song writing. But teaching took time and energy, and when Jessie and Kenneth Wright's marriage broke down and they left their flat she had to find lodgings by herself. She chose a boarding house in North London where she would have meals provided, to keep time free for composing.

She and Émile were both feeling their way. Neither of them had support or advice at hand. They wrote home, but Muriel's mother was in decline, her brother Percy was now in Nigeria, administering education for the Colonial Office, and her college friends were embarking on adult lives as she was, getting married, or returning to their families far from London. Émile too was a long way from his austere and high-principled parents in Savoy, who valued scholarship and the intellect alongside socialist ideas – his father was invited to stand as a Deputy but declined – and expected their son to build great things on his brilliant studies, after he had finished them.

His scholarship money was meagre but he earned something by giving conversation classes at King's and the

London School of Economics, where many of his students were training to become journalists. They studied in the evening and worked in the City by day, and he found the best way of getting them to talk was to discuss politics. In May 1926 the failure of the General Strike, called to back the miners, whose pay was being cut to starvation level, filled the students with anger. Émile sympathized – he had been reading a history of the miners – but he could not help being impressed by the calm of the English when he found there were no barricades and no violence – and that the miners gave way.

His own life was suddenly in turmoil. In May 1926 he and Muriel became engaged. By his own account this allowed them to exchange their first passionate kiss, an overwhelming experience for them both. You can judge what puritans they were, how much they had suppressed, how much they longed to make love and how sternly they denied themselves before marriage. He was twenty, she twenty-eight. She had taken a year off her age, and when he discovered this by looking at her passport, she at once offered to release him from their engagement. Naturally he refused. He wanted to be married. By French law he could not marry without the consent of his parents before the age of twenty-five. They responded discouragingly to the news of his engagement, as he might have expected, given his age and the fact that he had more years of study to get through. He became all the more determined to show his independence. For the next two years he divided his time between Geneva, Paris, London and Cambridge, where Caius College offered him two years' teaching. Muriel

Émile Delavenay   Muriel Herbert

visited him chastely in Geneva, Paris and Cambridge, and
slowly his parents came round. She learnt to speak reasonably good French, and they became fond of her. The
wedding was set for June 1928. They were married in St
Mary's, Kilburn. The church wedding was at her mother's
and Aunt Hornby's insistence, and against his wishes. None
of his family came to London for the occasion, but they
prepared to receive the new couple on their honeymoon.

Émile was of course much too young to marry, as well
as being still in the middle of his studies. Muriel, by
marrying a Frenchman, forfeited her British nationality
automatically. They left for France at once. On 14 June
they were in Paris and he inscribed her new married name,
Muriel Delavenay, in a volume of James Joyce poems he

bought for her, *Chamber Music*. Then on to Geneva, and on 12 July she was setting Joyce's poem 'I hear an army charging' to music – the date is pencilled in her copy of *Chamber Music*. The poem is troubled, and her setting, strikingly beautiful as it is, is tempestuous as well as sad – not what you might expect from a young woman on her wedding journey. She set several more of Joyce's poems, and later on their honeymoon they visited Joyce in his flat in Paris, introduced by an Irish friend of Émile, Thomas Mac-Greevy, a poet who taught at Normale. Joyce listened carefully to her playing and singing her settings, asked her to repeat them, said how much he liked them and gave her permission to publish. Tea was served, Joyce's woman doctor arrived and asked him to remove his shirt at the tea table so that she could listen to his chest. My mother was taken aback by such informality, but charmed by Joyce, who gave her signed copies of his *Pomes Penyeach* and *Chamber Music*, and told her that her music was better than his words. She misunderstood, thinking he'd said the opposite, and agreed, then realized her mistake and everyone laughed to cover her embarrassment. They parted good friends and Joyce wrote later to give her permission to broadcast her settings. MacGreevy had also written to Yeats, telling him he must give Muriel permission to publish her setting of 'The Lake Isle of Innisfree'. Yeats obliged, and it was immediately and lastingly successful.

All this made for a thrilling honeymoon. There was the matter of sex too, and they had taken precautions – the same sort of barrier contraceptive, known as a Dutch cap, I would use a generation later. She told me how they laughed at her difficulty in inserting it, so they must have had some fun; but for her sex was a disappointment. And soon, in spite of their precautions, she was pregnant. Émile faced a demanding year ahead, with examinations to be sat in Paris in April, the month the baby was due. Lady Douro sent Muriel to her obstetrician, who presided over his patients in a smart nursing home. It worked out badly. Muriel wanted to be conscious for the birth, but the doctor ignored her wishes and anaesthetized her over her protest. This increased the dislike and distrust of the medical profession she had already begun to feel under the influence of Dorothy Hess, who was a Christian Scientist. To make things worse, Émile had to leave for Paris two days after the birth of their daughter Marguerite, to sit for those important examinations, and, although he achieved the necessary results, he did less well than had been hoped.

The expected course for him now would be to take a teaching post in France, arranged through Normale, and start work on a thesis. Instead he resolved to stay in England and find teaching in London. It was a step so crucial that it suggests he now felt more at home in England than in France. Times were hard everywhere with the worldwide depression, but at least in England the election of 1929 brought in a coalition headed by a Labour prime minister, Ramsay MacDonald. It was the first election to give young women the vote, but ironically Muriel had lost hers along with her British nationality. Another of Émile's reasons for choosing England was that her musical contacts were all there, and he felt he should not take her away from them; she earned little, but her earnings made a significant contribution.

He could not find a full-time teaching post and had to accept more part-time teaching, hard work and poorly paid. Things improved slightly when in 1930 he was taken on by Frederick Attenborough, principal of the Borough Road Training College in Isleworth, but still for only three mornings a week. Better still, he also now agreed with Normale on a subject for his thesis: it was to be on D. H. Lawrence, who had just died of tuberculosis in the South of France. A senior colleague suggested the idea, Émile sat down to read *Sons and Lovers*, saw its greatness at once, went on to the stories and more of the novels, and made his decision. He knew it would be the work of many years.

Their income at this time was about £400 a year, of which a quarter came from Muriel's earnings. This gave them enough to employ a maid, and to move to St Peter's Square in Hammersmith, where the houses were handsome and the rents low, attracting artists, poets, intellectuals, journalists and writers. With this congenial touch of *Bohème*, it was also close to the Thames – no motorway then – and laid out around a garden where children could play. Muriel and Émile shared Number 27 with two women: the artist Gertrude Hermes, separated from her husband and with a son and a daughter, and Barbara Weekley, a name my father responded to with interest, knowing her to be the daughter of D. H. Lawrence's widow by her first husband. Gertrude and Muriel agreed to share some of the childcare.

It seemed as though they were entering into a productive and happy time. Their daughter Marguerite, a bright and active child, was a joy to them both, and they soon took her proudly to meet her French grandparents, who were now entirely won over by Muriel. Yet Émile was already repenting his marriage. Muriel's distrust of medicine and interest in Christian Science infuriated him. She was irrational, he decided, and at the same time too respectful of convention. She had mood swings that were difficult to deal with. They quarrelled fiercely. Her friends loved her, and many of them were interesting to Émile, but there were days when he found himself disliking her. Feeling his dislike was terrible to Muriel, worse than a lovers' quarrel because it led to a cold and disdainful withdrawal. She became jealous. Their love-making gave her little pleasure and, I suppose, not much more than temporary relief to him. So they grew angry and ashamed, each ready to blame the other for their failure.

While he agonized about how he could escape from what he had desired for so long, she also formed a wish, to have another child. If she mentioned it to him he did not respond. Long after I was grown up and my mother was dead, my father wrote a memoir in which he described how, in September 1932, on holiday in Cornwall with her and walking in silence on a high cliff path, he felt such hatred for her that he thought seriously of killing her. He reasoned that if he pushed her over the cliff edge no one would ever know it was not an accident. It was the only time in his life he had a murderous intention, he wrote, but he never forgot it.

He did not act on it. Instead, that night, still without exchanging a word, she set out to end their estrangement and I was conceived. It was her will that brought this about, using his reluctant submission to sexual need, not only without love but with the gritted teeth of murderous loathing. I learnt about this in 1991, when he showed me the text of his autobiography. It is such an upsetting story that I ask myself why he chose to write it down and publish it for me to read. Did he think I ought to know? Did he feel some obligation to make all things clear to me, perhaps to explain why he had been so hostile to me when I was a small child? Was he ridding himself of the guilt of having had a murderous thought by making this secular confession?

At least my mother was spared the knowledge. And I never asked him about it: why not? He must have been confident that our relationship was good enough to bear the revelation. It was. But it was not deep enough for me to question him. I did not complain. I was in my late fifties by then, preoccupied with my own life, my children and a grandchild, and busy writing. Still, it puzzles me. I knew he had concealed other things in his memoir – adulterous love-affairs that would have upset his second wife – so why not this? Over the years since, I have thought about this odd beginning of my existence a good deal. While the conception of a child is often a random event, mine seems to have been very much against the odds, my mother's strong intention pitted against my father's hatred. Do I feel differently about myself? Perhaps I have developed a stronger sense of the randomness of things.

From my mother I always heard a different and happy story of my birth as a much desired child, arriving on the exact day I was expected, and born, as she wished, at home, with minimum fuss. There was only a monthly nurse in attendance, and I made my appearance before the doctor arrived. Gertrude Hermes came to sculpt the newborn baby, my mother breastfed me happily. The person who suffered most was my four-year-old sister Marguerite, who had been invited to stay with friends, the kindly Attenboroughs, whose sons Richard, David and John were a little older than her. She hated being sent away, and returning to find a supplanter in her mother's arms. Our relationship started badly.

I was born because my mother was determined to have a second child. She was my friend, and she loved both me and my sister, but as soon as I was aware of anything I knew my father disliked me. He did his best to make my sister his ally against me. We became a divided family, although his anger was sometimes directed against Marguerite too: when he saw she had put up a copy of the Lord's Prayer on the wall of her bedroom he became enraged and tore it down.

My mother's unconditional love gave me confidence, and was stronger than my father's unkindness. In 1937 he proposed to my mother that they should formally separate, he taking Marguerite, she keeping me. She turned down this plan. By his own account the marriage was dead for him, but even then his feelings were not entirely fixed, because in that same year he gave her for her fortieth birthday a book, Helen Waddell's *Mediaeval Latin Lyrics*, three of which she set to music memorably. He wanted her to compose, and he still occasionally hoped to please her. Precise as he always was, he inscribed the book 'with love'.

When he did finally leave her, four years later, he asked the family doctor if he should be worried about my future, and she assured him there was no need to worry because I was an intelligent child, at which point he began to revise his view of me. Later in life, when my stepmother Kath became my friend, we were on much better terms, and he was proud of my scholastic achievements. But he kept some element of doubt about me: when my husband Nick walked out on me, my father wrote to him saying he had not been able to live with my mother and so understood why Nick could not live with me. It may have been meant as a piece of male solidarity but it was not the act of an affectionate father.

As I look back, it seems to me that the failure of the marriage drove him to the brink of madness, and something similar happened to her. He records a moment when she reproached him for turning her from a gentle and lovable creature into a hellcat, as she knew she had become, unable to deal sensibly or calmly with the misery and rage his coldness and disdain provoked. She was uncontrollably jealous of contacts he had with other friends, especially women, that excluded her. She made scenes, embarrassed him in front of other people, threw things at him, threatened suicide. The onset of the war, the invasion of France, the bombing of London and the threat of worse put them both under enormous extra strain. Yet, as soon as they were separated, she pulled herself together and behaved with admirable courage and good sense, setting up a new life, helped by friends, and finding herself a routine office job at which she worked steadily, uncongenial as it was. As long as they were together they poisoned one another; apart, they were restored to sanity.

※

This is to run ahead. In 1934, as the world was moving towards another war, Émile accepted an invitation to join Havas, the French news agency, in their London office. It meant setting aside his thesis for the moment. He found he enjoyed journalism and was good at it, and it was well paid. During the five years he was with Havas we left St Peter's Square for flats closer to Kensington, ending in Stanhope Gardens, at the top of one of the large houses there. Our French grandmother came to London to see the coronation in 1937, for which the Duchess gave Muriel some good seats, and I was taken out by our maid against strict orders, to be lifted on to the shoulders of a friendly policeman. I don't remember much, but I formed a favourable impression of the police.

A memory of 1938: my parents are disagreeing about Munich. My father holds up a glass and says, 'Down with Chamberlain!' My mother answers, 'Oh poor man, he is only trying to do his best . . .' Also in 1938 my mother published a set of children's songs, wistful and light-hearted, which I learnt to sing with her. In July 1939 my father joined the BBC, where he worked throughout the war, in charge of programmes relating to France, among them *Les Français parlent aux Français*, with its famous 'V for Victory' Morse Code sound signal: dot-dot-dot-dash. The war meant we children were sent out of London. In October

1941 our parents separated. Nothing was left but exasperation, jealousy and wretchedness. Émile abandoned their flat and started divorce proceedings, alleging that Muriel was of unsound mind. She, supported by friends, steadied her nerve, moved out of London and found office work to prove that she was sane and could cope. She succeeded admirably. Her jealousy was not all fantasy, because Émile had found a soul-mate in Katharine, his Oxford-educated secretary at the BBC. I understood nothing of what was happening, but our parents never spoke to one another again. He moved back into the Stanhope Gardens flat with Katharine once they were married. Our family life, such as it was, was over.

2
States of Grace

Aged four

My mother told me early that whatever happens to you, however unhappy you may be, you can escape into a book. She was right. Before I could read for myself she read poetry to me as I settled down for the night. It was more sound than sense for me then, but poetry and music were part of our life from the start. I used to sit under her black grand piano while she played and sang or worked at a manuscript. Both parents were deeply involved with writing on different sorts of paper: hers ready printed with five-line staves to take the crotchets and quavers; my father's blank, thin and white, which he made into sandwiches with black carbon paper for his typewriter. When my fingers were nimble enough, I was sometimes allowed to put together the sandwiches. His typewriter covered the paper with letters. I pretended I could produce letters too, as children do, scribbling across the white paper before I could write.

The first book I remember being given came from a nurse in the London Homoeopathic Hospital at Christmas 1937. It was *The Tale of Tom Kitten*, and it pleased me so much that I quickly memorized the words read to me and had the illusion I could read for myself. I liked Beatrix Potter's formal language and use of words new to me: 'Mrs Tabitha was affronted' by the behaviour of her kittens. She was also shown to be a liar, which adults were not meant to be, telling her friends that the kittens were ill when in fact she had sent them upstairs as a punishment. I enjoyed the drama and the successful rebellion of the kittens. I knew nothing of the drama of my own situation, which had arisen as I was rushed to hospital in a taxi with an ear infection. My mother said later that the two consultants in the hospital offered conflicting advice, one telling her I might die if they did not operate on the ear, the other that an operation was likely to kill me. She opted for inaction and I recovered. Christian Science had scored a point, she felt, and I went home unscarred.

The next book I was given that became a favourite was an anthology of poetry for children: *For Your Delight*, which I still have, heavily marked with underlinings and ticks of approval. It offered Stevenson, Christina Rossetti, Harold Monro, De la Mare, a sprinkling of Shakespeare, Milton, Shelley and Keats, as well as mysterious Anon. I was keen on jokes too, *A Dog Day*, Winnie-the-Pooh and Doctor Dolittle. We were not supposed to read comics, but my sister was resourceful enough to get hold of one occasionally and let me look at it. I can still see a picture that frightened me, done in sinister red and black, showing a man dropping a sack containing a body over the edge of a rowing boat. It made me less eager for comics. I read *Just William* and school stories by the dozen.

I was given *Black Beauty* at Christmas 1938, and fell on it with passionate enthusiasm, my first full-length novel, to be read and reread: not many jokes, but love and loss and cruelty. There were French children's books I enjoyed too. André Maurois's *Patapoufs et Filifers*, written in 1930 as a pacifist fable about the hostility between French and Germans, and a great children's story. Maurois makes the Patapoufs idle and greedy pleasure-lovers and pits them against super-efficient, pencil-thin organizers, and they go foolishly to war over a pointless dispute. Even better were the books about Babar the Elephant. Little Babar runs away from the jungle when his mother is shot and discovers an exciting new world. I read Babar to my children, and five-year-old Susanna was inspired to write a poem which adds a chill to the story:

> Mrs Elephant lived in the jungle
> She loved to run and tumble
> And when the hunter came
> She thought it was a game.

In the second volume of the stories, Babar and his bride Céleste go honeymooning in a yellow balloon, and for years I half believed that a honeymoon is necessarily a trip in a yellow balloon. Later the ideal new town of Céleste-ville is built for the elephants, on good socialist principles.

❧

My father's lack of religious beliefs meant that as a young child I knew nothing about the concept of God. I suppose we celebrated Christmas, but if we did it was with very little ceremony. Later I learnt that he had been brought up without any Christian formation or knowledge, and that his mother had taught him to regard nuns with suspicion. She had been educated by French Protestant women teachers in a boarding school in Grenoble, and had emerged neither Catholic nor Protestant. My French grandfather, reared in a fervently Catholic family, entered the seminary only to reject its teachings. He removed himself and became a schoolteacher in the state system, which is entirely secular in France. My father, educated in the traditions of the French Enlightenment, was a rationalist to his bones and shocked by any departure from strictly rational thought. He enjoyed verbal jokes and was good at making them, and he had to have the last word in any argument. And he could quickly become angry, and cruel.

My mother was not an atheist. I have described how she was drawn to the ideas of Christian Science, through friends such as Dorothy Hess. She did not take us to church but she owned a Bible which she sometimes read and which I understood to be a special book with stories and messages that were different from the stories in other books. My sister and I were not christened, and we were sent to the Lycée français de Londres in Kensington – secular, like all French state schools. I enjoyed my year in the Jardin d'enfants, where we spent more time singing, dancing and acting than working at our desks. With the war the Lycée was moved out of London, and there was a period of confusion when it was sent to Cambridge and then further away. So at seven I arrived with Marguerite at a small private boarding school in Hertfordshire, run by a friend of our mother and Miss Hess. This was Miss Roberts – Margaret Noel Roberts – an ardent believer in Christian Science and a good woman, stout, warm-hearted and cultivated. Looking back, I think she suffered from asthma, but she would never concede an inch to illness and soldiered on, wheezing. She came from Wales, had an Oxford degree and was an inspiring teacher, and she set up her school in September 1940 in a roomy country villa with a large garden and a swimming pool. The Hertfordshire woodlands were all around us, and the school was called Oaklands. There were two dozen or so girl pupils and one boy, Robin Denniston, squeezed in among the girls because it was wartime and his father was engaged in secret work at Bletchley. Robin was thirteen but seemed to me almost one of the grown-ups, so sensible and kind he was. He went on to Westminster School and Oxford, became a publisher – he was involved in the publication of my first book – and then a clergyman. We had no religious services at Oaklands, but Miss Roberts sometimes read to us from her Bible. When measles struck and five of us were lying in a darkened room feeling wretched with fever, she appeared magisterially and told us off quite sharply: she was disappointed in us, she said, for failing to make a demonstration against the measles. We were too ill to reply.

Soon we were all better. Life was good, and my mother was there, teaching music. The war made everything odd: mothers became teachers, children arrived from other countries or because their parents were unable to look after them. One day a newly arrived pupil threw a stone at me in the garden, quite unexpectedly and for no reason that I could think of. It hit me on the head, and I was frightened but not really hurt. Still, I found someone to complain to, who explained that Trixie had just come from a country where people threw stones at her, and I must understand that she had suffered and was disturbed. Nothing more was said. Miss Roberts presided serenely. She put on plays, finding parts for us all in scenes from *A Midsummer Night's Dream* and *Alice in Wonderland*. I was Puck and put a girdle round the earth in forty minutes. As a Lily in *Alice* I disgraced myself, forgetting to say my single line because I was in such a dream that I had to be prompted several times, everyone laughing and then shouting, before I realized I had missed the moment. I was no actress, but I had discovered that I could make patterns with words. I began to write poems and fell into a tranced state, walking round the garden alone whenever I could, allowing words and rhythms to come into my head to be shaped into verses.

In the hot weather, the swimming pool, with its greenish murky water, drew us all. My sister was a good swimmer. I had not yet been taught to swim, but I had been reading *Tom Brown's School-Days* and learnt there that, if you simply threw yourself into some deep water, you would find yourself swimming automatically. Trustingly, I put on my bathing suit and leapt into the pool. I have a clear memory of sinking through the water, beginning to choke, hitting the bottom and starting to come up again – only to find that I was not emerging into the air but still choking, and descending again to the green depths. Then at last I was seized and pulled out on to the edge of the pool, a wet, gasping heap. The relief was enormous, just being able to breathe. Julia Aston, a strong, quick-witted girl with golden hair, had noticed me sinking, dived in, taken hold of me as I struggled, and managed to lift me out of the water and haul me on to the surrounding concrete. To me she seemed a big girl, but she was only twelve when she saved my life – a true heroine. She came from South Africa, which was why she swam so well, having lived by a warm sea, and her name has stayed with me ever since, although I have never been able to track her down and have no idea what became of her.

I was very happy at Oaklands. The lessons were informal and good; Robin put together a school magazine and
printed some of my poems. This was the beginning of self-
consciousness, I suppose. At the age of eight I thought I
was growing up and I longed to become an adult. Grown-
ups were in control of their own lives, it seemed to me. A
young American woman visiting the school gave me a pair
of sandals with wooden platform soles that added an inch
to my height, and I wore them all through that summer,
possessed by the sense that they were glamorous objects
and made me into a different, and much older, person.

But I was not in control of my own life. At the end of a
year Miss Roberts decided that my sister and I ought to go
to a bigger school with more formal teaching, and advised
my parents to apply to Hitchin Girls' Grammar School,
which had a small boarding department and a distinguished
headmistress, Miss Chambers, who had raised the reputation of the school so effectively that girls came daily by
train from all over Hertfordshire to be taught there.

Taken to be interviewed by Miss Chambers – not wearing
my platform sandals – I found her a formidable person. She
had a very straight back, a commanding eye and immacu-
lately tidy white hair drawn back into a bun. After a few kind
words, she asked me, 'Can you tell me seven times nought?' I
disgraced myself by answering 'seven'. In spite of this, I was
given a place. My sister and I were to be boarders.

My first formal encounter with religion came in the evening of the day I arrived to board. I was taken to a large
bathroom where there were several bath tubs and a group of
girls about my age – I was now eight – being helped to

undress and get into the baths to be washed. The matron, Miss Davies, asked me as I sat in the bath, 'Are you a Roman Catholic?' I had no idea what she meant and didn't know how to answer her. She whispered with the young under-matron, who was helping her bathe us, and I heard something about my foreign name and French father, which surely indicated that I must be a Roman Catholic. Someone went off to ask my sister, who told them that we were not Catholics. So the matter was solved and I was able to join the others, all members of the Church of England. This was important, because on Sunday morning the boarders – about twenty-five of us – put on our best dresses, navy-blue wool with white collars for winter, flowered Liberty silk for summer – and our hats and coats, formed a crocodile and walked down the hill on which the school had been built in 1908, to the parish church, St Mary's, for the morning service.

St Mary's cast a spell over me from the first Sunday. I had never been inside a church before, and this was a large and beautiful building of grey stone and mellow brick. (It was built in the fourteenth and fifteenth centuries with the prof-its of the wool trade, but I knew nothing of that.) It stands in the centre of Hitchin, near the river, with a porch and a sturdy tower, and on both sides of the nave were five of the widest windows I had ever seen, magnificently shaped, and so big that the inside of the church was filled with light. We took our places in wooden pews and there was music as well as light. Men and boys in robes processed up the central aisle of the church as the organ played. Sometimes we joined in; sometimes we listened to the robed singers performing a curious rhythmical chant made of words – they were from the Psalms, as I learnt in due course. Sometimes a leading man – the vicar – spoke, mostly reciting or reading formal and occasionally strange words. I watched what the girls around me did, kneeled when they kneeled, stood or sat as they did, and after a few Sundays was able to join in some of the words: 'We have left undone those things which we ought have done; And we have done those things which we ought not to have done; And there is no health in us . . .' This I partly understood, but 'Glory be to the Father, and to the Son, and to the Holy Ghost; As it was in the beginning, is now, and ever shall be: world without end' seemed purely ornamental, as did 'I believe in the Holy Ghost; The Holy Catholic Church; The Communion of Saints; The Forgiveness of Sins; The Resurrection of the Body; And the Life Everlasting . . .'

The words carried almost no meaning for me. But chanting fixes words in the memory, giving them power – which is the point of the chanting. I knew the Lord's Prayer pretty well from Oaklands, and I picked up hymns, psalms, the words of the Nunc dimittis and the Creed quickly. Those Sunday mornings in the light-filled church, with the music, the words, the formality and peace, gave me a delight in church architecture and the words and music of an Anglican service that has stayed with me. When, years later, as an undergraduate, I read the poetry of George Herbert and Henry Vaughan, I found their expressions of faith so perfectly worded that I was briefly drawn into becoming an Anglican worshipper. I did not become a believer, and I soon gave up, but have kept my gratitude for the good work done by the Church.

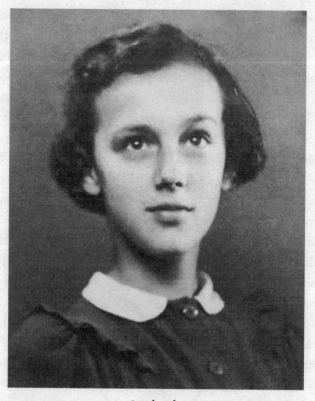

Aged eight

I needed those moments of happiness it gave me as a child because being away from my mother, and being a boarder, made me unhappy. On weekdays, during lessons, I enjoyed learning and working. But the boarding regime was worse than unimaginative. We were a very small group in a school of five hundred girls who came daily to the school and went home to their families in the afternoon. We were left to have an early supper, and all the boarders under ten were made to go to bed at six, even in midsummer. This meant being confined to a curtained cubicle in the long dormitory, while the sun shone outside and we could hear older girls playing and calling to one another. Worse, we were not allowed to read. No reason was given for this, no argument allowed. Reading was my passion, and I devoured books: I was reading the Brontës, rereading my favourite *Black Beauty*, the *Golden Treasury*, *David Copperfield*. My mother's recommendation that I could escape into a book was now blocked. Miss Davies sat in the centre of the long dormitory silently knitting while we lay in our separate cubicles, bored, miserable and, in my case, increasingly desperate. I developed a nervous cough. It annoyed Miss Davies. 'Stop coughing, Claire,' she would call out severely. Then came the torment of trying to suppress the cough. Soon it burst out again and Miss Davies scolded me again. I could not stop coughing and she scolded me more. The problem would have been solved by allowing me to read, but that was not considered.

Another torment came every Saturday morning when our laundry was returned and inspected. Anything that needed mending had to be dealt with there and then. My clothes were in a state of neglect, no doubt because my mother was distracted, and I needed replacements, but did not get any. I can still see myself standing at the table as my shameful pile of clothes was turned over, revealing missing buttons, holes and split seams. Saturdays were spent trying to mend my clothes. Girls were expected to be able to sew, and I was provided with needle, thread and darning mushroom, and left to get on as best I could. I often remained alone in the room where the laundry was handed out until lunchtime, and sometimes had to return after lunch. One Saturday I heard the domestic science teacher murmur that it was not right to put a small child through this. It was something to know that she sympathized, but she was not able to rescue me. I would try to work out the length of the term ahead, how many more Saturdays of misery there were to endure.

My sister had her own problems to deal with. Some of the older girls had heard that our parents were divorcing. Our foreign name was bad enough, and now it appeared that our parents were involved in scandalous goings-on. Divorce was almost unheard of in provincial England at that time: were we corrupted, and possibly corrupting, influences? To me this was remote and incomprehensible, but at twelve Marguerite felt the disapproval of the other girls.

Neither of us understood what was happening between our parents: how our father had set up divorce proceedings, claiming that our mother was insane – this would give him custody of the children – and how she, advised by her lawyer to prove the falsity of his accusation, found herself a job, uncongenial but steady. But I had some inklings of their disagreements, because when my father announced that I needed to have my tonsils removed, and delivered me to the Homoeopathic Hospital in London, I was asked on arrival about my religion and announced firmly, 'Christian Scientist.' The person behind the desk looked startled and put down her pen. I insisted that I meant what I said. I was lining up with my mother.

Émile's next decision was to remove us from Hitchin and send us back to the Lycée, now settled for the duration

In Cumberland with my sister, 1943

of the war in Cumberland, on the banks of Lake Ullswater. In September 1942 I found myself on a train with my father and sister, travelling to Penrith. Again, no one had explained to me what was going on, but I realized my mother was powerless, because when I cried and told her I did not want to be sent away from her, she cried too and said she did not want it either. I learnt that even grown-ups were not always able to control events. Increasingly I took refuge in reading, writing and dreams.

When we arrived at Penrith, Marguerite went off in a bus with the older pupils and I in another direction with the juniors, and after this we saw each other only in the holidays. No matter: the house I was sent to, Hallsteads, was sublimely placed, its gardens reaching the lake, and its windows looking across the water to the fells on the other side. We were left a good deal to our own devices, and I found a tree in the garden I particularly liked to sit beneath. I decided that trees were like mothers, and this one was to be mine. It became a comforting presence to which I could retreat. The beginning of term was difficult, because lice were found in my hair and, without anyone explaining to me what they were doing or why, my hair was cut short and I was sent into class with a beret over my head. It was a humiliating moment, as the other children stared at me, whispered and laughed, but it soon passed. Here no one asked me to mend my underwear, and I slept in an airy bedroom with four other girls who quickly became friends. Lessons were in French, and, although I had no conscious memory of the language – I remember a moment of panic at the first dictation – it quickly came back.

My mother wrote to me regularly every week. She had Arthur Mee's *Children's Newspaper* despatched weekly to entertain me, and sent me parcels of books and chocolate, even once a glorious tin of golden syrup. She never failed me, and she said nothing about the bad times she was going through herself, separated from her piano, her music and most of her friends, working in an office and fighting my father's attempt to divorce her. That Christmas of 1942 he chose to dump us in a house in Buckinghamshire that took in children with nowhere to go – I remember little about it except the chilly face of the woman in charge as we arrived, a few forlorn boys and girls standing about, and the feeling of incredulity that we were to be left there for the holidays. The rest I blanked out.

So returning to Hallsteads was a pleasure. It was now a familiar place, and my French was good enough for me to enjoy the work and read French books. *Sans famille*, the classic nineteenth-century story of a child who loses his family and wanders over France, kept me absorbed for weeks. Our classroom looked on to the garden and the lake, and I liked Madame Bourke, our cheerful grey-haired, Franco-Irish teacher, very much. She was nearly six foot tall and she taught us everything, grammar, composition, arithmetic, history, geography. We were mixed boys and girls, and I soon decided that girls were cleverer than boys, none of whom seemed to care about work, leaving the girls to take our places regularly at the top of the class. In my dormitory, we had debates about religion, since some of the girls were Catholics and the Lycée allowed them to be visited by a priest. I was reading Charlotte Brontë's *Villette* and I took up her anti-Catholic views and proclaimed the superiority of the Protestant faith, with its direct line between each individual and God, and no need for a priestly intermediary – surely a better system? We had fun arguing, and neither side made converts. Since I was not offered church visits – the Lycée being secular – my direct line to God was entirely my own affair. I did not avail myself of it.

Instead I became more of a pantheist. We were taken out to wander on the nearby fells, largely unsupervised, on two afternoons each week, an experience I found deeply interesting and satisfying. We could go where we pleased, and I took delight in being alone with silence or the sound of the wind, the changing weather, the steep green slopes, rocks, streams, the odd mysterious dead and sometimes decomposing sheep. I fell ill during the spring term and the doctor said I should miss classes for a week or two, and that I could go out walking by myself. One day I followed the lake shore, and suddenly found myself faced with a scene I recognized but could hardly believe I was seeing: daffodils in their hundreds, dancing in the breeze beside the lake exactly as Wordsworth had described them. I knew the words of the poem, and here was the real thing laid out to perfection before my eyes.

On 14 July 1943 the Lycée assembled for the annual celebration of Bastille Day. I saw something else I had never seen before: grown men standing to sing '*Allons enfants de la patrie / Le jour de gloire est arrivé*' with tears running down their cheeks. They were our schoolmasters, and also exiles, shamed by what had happened to the French nation.

During that year I learnt many French songs – we sang a great deal at the Lycée, with enjoyment and enthusiasm. I became the French equivalent of a Brownie, a *Petite aile*, with a neat brown uniform, more singing and lessons in tying knots. I knew that we were at war – that the Germans were fighting in Russia and the British in North

Africa, and that America had allied itself with us – but we were given little information about its course. Still, I had my first understanding that history is relative, Napoleon a hero to the French and a villain to the English. I became competitive, wanting to do well in my lessons. I began to read and love French poetry.

As one of my teachers was putting me into the train at Penrith for the summer holidays, she remarked that she would not be seeing me again. Why not? I asked. She looked embarrassed and simply said that I was leaving, without further explanation. I felt a pang at the thought I should not be living beside the lake, going for walks where you exchanged greetings with everyone you passed, arguing cheerfully with my friends, sitting under my tree; but knowing I was to be with my mother again filled me with happiness. The truth was that our father had lost his attempt to divorce her, and that my sister and I were now once more in her custody.

I came away from Ullswater a skinny argumentative ten-year-old, with a passion for reading and writing, a lasting love for the landscape of the fells and lakes, and the French language well enough fixed in my head to stay there and keep me reading the great French writers. But the war meant I had lost all contact with the French half of my family, including my only living grandparent, Grandmaman, who was helping to care for my boy cousins in Normandy. Their father had been taken by the Germans, having been denounced as a communist. No one had news of him, and my aunt – Tante Hélène – and her sons learnt only after the end of the war that he had died in a concentration camp.

The most striking feature of my life had become

discontinuity. It had been divided into small, separate parcels of experience that closed without explanation as I was
shunted on, often with no idea of why or where I was going
next, losing any friends I might have made. Of course
many children of my generation had the same experience
of being shuffled about because of the war, and many had
endured very much worse. For me, being moved about so
much, unable to keep friendships going and obliged to start
afresh repeatedly, encouraged me to live mostly in books:
portable companions, reliable, constant.*

---

* A few years ago I was able to visit Hallsteads and discovered it had
become an outward-bound centre. I was allowed to take a look round,
found my old bedroom and gazed at the lakeside garden admiringly again.
Since then I have found out that it was built in 1815 by a Leeds industrialist,
John Marshall (1765–1848), who made a fortune with his flax mills, became
an MP, helped to establish a Mechanics' Institute and a Literary and Philosophical Society, funded the Leeds Library, and began the campaign to
establish Leeds University. When he retired to Hallsteads, his unmarried
sisters became friends with Dorothy Wordsworth, and visits, which
included William, were made between the two families.

3

Life Lessons

Another existence began for us. Our mother was now living in Welwyn Garden City, a new town built in the 1920s in Hertfordshire. She was occupying the top half of a house belonging to her friend Dorothy Hess, who had moved out of London to be away from the bombs. Dorrie had taken her two magnificent grand pianos with her, and continued to give piano lessons. We called her Auntie Dorrie, although she could almost have been Uncle, with her deep voice, moustache and thick-set frame. She was large of heart too, and she nobly offered to squeeze us in upstairs with our mother.

The three of us would live in two rooms, a bigger one in which we slept, and a small kitchen/living room. To me, it all seemed agreeable, and for the next two years we lived above the pianos, with the sound of Beethoven sonatas filling our ears. Dorrie must have sometimes played and taught work by other composers, but Beethoven came before all others, and she gave me an early education in his piano music that has kept me listening to it ever since. Serious as she was about music, she was also high-spirited and sociable. She liked to organize parties and play jokes, and soon after we moved into her house she gave a nightingale party,

telling her friends there was a nightingale in her back garden, and my sister and I were given the job of keeping her
guests indoors while she slipped out into the garden with a
special nightingale whistle to amaze them. She never made
us feel unwelcome, although it must have been hard not to
have her house to herself. This was the summer of 1943. I
was ten.

Welwyn was a town of leafy streets and green public
spaces, well-designed small houses, a great many churches
of different denominations and, famously, only one public
house. London was within easy reach, twenty miles south,
but there was open country at the top of Dorrie's road, so
that I could be in fields and woods in a few minutes. There
was even a farm where I was allowed to milk a cow. I went
mushrooming with my mother, and we found blackberries
and wild strawberries. I had no sporting skills – French
schools did not go in for sport in those days – so my mother
set out to teach me to ride a bicycle, running beside me
until I could balance. The day it happened, she saw me sail
away downhill into a main road, fortunately empty of
traffic at that point – there was no petrol for private cars
during the war. Bicycling became a passion, and later I
saved up to buy a pale-green Raleigh bike and took to solitary rides into the open countryside. She taught me to
swim too, with regular visits to the chilly outdoor swimming pool until I was safe and happy in the water. I took all
this for granted then and realize now how much hard work
it must have been for her.

At home we cooked, ate and did our homework on one
table. In the bedroom each of us had a window next to our

bed, and I used my window ledge for my books. Over the months the pile grew and gradually blocked out more and more of the window. I read under the bedclothes with a torch when I was supposed to be asleep. Welwyn Department Store had an unusually good book department, and my mother knew the manager, who allowed me to browse for as long as I liked. Through him I first read J. E. Neale's biography of Queen Elizabeth. It taught me that well-told history is in every way more interesting than historical fiction. I read and bought poetry too: Edith Sitwell poems, a complete Keats. I spent my pocket money and my mother often subsidized my book purchases. For my eleventh birthday she gave me the works of Shakespeare in one large volume, which I read with passionate enjoyment, poems and plays alike. Dorrie arranged for a writer friend to give me some lessons in prosody: she had a romantic name, Lady Margaret D'Arcy, and was the kindest of teachers. She taught me not to use 'thee', 'thou' and other archaic words, and to allow myself more freedom in structuring poems. I made the move to writing free verse, which I enjoyed, but after the lessons ended I became obsessed with the sonnet form. Soon I was turning out sonnets by the dozen. The vocabulary was modern but they were still lamentably old-fashioned. What did I have to write about? Imaginary experiences? All I remember is what fun I had constructing them.

We were going to the girls' grammar school in Hitchin again, no longer as miserable boarders but as day girls, by train. I liked being a 'train girl' because it meant I was in charge of myself, responsible for catching the train, free to choose where I sat and how I occupied myself. The twice-daily journey was a beautiful and dramatic one, taking us across a viaduct where you looked down over meadows, houses and a river far below, then plunging into two tunnels, and after that farmland and village stops at Old Welwyn, Knebworth and Stevenage (not yet a new town). Taking the train also made me part of a group of girls of my own age who became my friends – my sister travelled with a different group of older girls. Occasionally we shared the train with American soldiers, gathering in England in their thousands in 1943 in preparation for D-Day in 1944. They were friendly and talkative, but we preferred to find compartments to ourselves – there were still trains with coaches without corridors – where we were unobserved and could read, catch up with homework, do our knitting or practise dance steps, whichever was the current craze, and talk about everything: the war, our parents, books, films, holidays, teachers. At Hitchin a steep walk took us up to the school, set on top of Windmill Hill, with its playing fields, woods and swimming pool. I enjoyed schoolwork and had no difficulty changing languages again. At the end of my first year Miss Chambers sat me down without any explanation to a simple examination. Someone explained to me later that it was the forerunner of the new Eleven-plus and she was making sure of my place at the school.

We were lucky to have several teachers past retiring age who kept going through the war and after. One especially, Miss Hughes – Violet Vera Hughes – was an enthralling presence in the classroom. She was very short and almost spherical, with vivid blue eyes and white hair cropped like a man's, and invariably dressed in a plain coat and skirt, wool in winter, linen in summer. Striking as her appearance was, what mattered most was that she knew how to pass on her enthusiasm for the books we read together. She would come into the classroom already talking: 'Push your desks back against the wall, we are going to act *Macbeth* today,' and we did, she herself making a powerful Macbeth. We read *Julius Caesar* and *As You Like It* with her too, fixing them in our heads for life. We asked to read *Romeo and Juliet* when we heard it was on the syllabus for the School Certificate, but a message came down that the school did not allow it on the grounds that it was unsuitable for girls. Miss Hughes would have brought it to life for us, with full attention to language and drama, had she been allowed to. There were days when she talked to us about her own dramatic experiences, embarking on an account of her years teaching in India, of the poverty and stoicism of the people, describing a child whose toes were cut off as he crossed the road, and who picked them up and ran on before her eyes as though nothing had happened. I remember that she wept on the day Gandhi died – she was still teaching us in January 1948. I was impressed to find that a teacher in a girls' school in England had a heart that beat for newly independent India. I respected her and learnt from her, and wish I had known her for longer, kept in touch, told her how much she had meant to me.

French was taught by Miss Mortimer. To my astonishment, she thanked me one day, privately, for not making her life difficult by mocking her bad accent: it had never occurred to me to do so, since she was a good teacher and

I enjoyed her lessons. She was well read in the French classics, and she had traces of beauty, the word being that her fiancé had been killed in the First World War, which was very possibly true. Miss Finn, who taught physics, was the most old-fashioned of our teachers, insisting to my sister that the atom could not be split, which was what she had been taught when young. Miss Squire, in charge of sport, was energetic and handsome with her Eton-cropped grey hair, and lived with Miss Chambers in a lifelong partnership, which seemed quite natural to us, one in charge of our brains, the other our bodies.

Miss Wells, younger than the others, inspired me to real passion for her subject, history. She was a Quaker and spoke to us as equals, joking about how a teacher had to decide whether to ruin her feet, by standing up to teach, or her behind, by sitting down. She taught us American history, and when we were studying sixteenth-century England, asked us to write an essay giving the thoughts of a monk on being turned out of his monastery. I produced a verse monologue, the style somewhat inspired by T. S. Eliot, which won her praise – I was sent to show it to the headmistress. But I was not always approved of. The maths mistress scolded me for writing poetry in my rough maths book and failing to master theorems. I sometimes rebelled against discipline. Marguerite was a model pupil and rose to become head girl, leaving me the role of the naughty sister.

Marguerite was practical as well as clever. She taught herself how to make her own clothes, and passed on her skills to me. We worked away with paper patterns and our mother's sewing machine, and produced summer dresses.

She joined a youth club, into which I followed her. We listened to music, put on plays and organized debates. I enjoyed debating and took an interest in politics. One of my schoolfriends, Jennifer Hales, newly returned from Canada where she had been sent during the war, and readjusting like me, invited me to tea to meet her family. They lived in the other garden city, Letchworth, where their house was like a country house, big and rambling, with half an acre of garden in which Major Hales grew fruit and vegetables and kept bees. He came of a Norfolk army family and had broken with tradition to become a socialist. He led me down the garden to inspect the bees, and as we stood looking at the hives he said, 'What a lesson for the socialists, the bees . . .' I was not sure whether he meant they were an example or a warning, but I enjoyed hearing him talk about politics and admired him greatly. He made a good father figure, and I became, and remained, a staunch supporter of the Labour Party. He had a sense of humour and offered to canvass for Labour in the safe Tory constituency of Aldershot, driving round with a loud-speaker in his car and preaching socialism: he even stood as the Labour candidate in 1951. Mrs Hales was benevolent with an air of remoteness, possibly to protect herself from politics. Jennifer had some of her mother's apparent vagueness, but beneath it lay her father's brain power and an iron determination to follow her own path. She and I grew to be good friends.

Another girl in my class, Margaret Lander, was a remarkable musician who organized some of us into singing together for pleasure, accompanying us on the piano and teaching us to sing in parts – Purcell, Handel, Mozart. She did it so well and we had such a good time that it encouraged more music-making in the school, and we put on a performance of *The Magic Flute* – in an arrangement for girls' groups – joyously singing the songs of Papageno and Papagena, the three boys and the three ladies. Later I realized that her family must have come from Germany as refugees, but she never spoke of that and I lost touch with her when I left Hitchin. I wish I could thank her for what she taught us with so much skill and energy, and for the enjoyment we had in making music together.

❧

My sister and I were expected to attend the Christian Science Sunday school, but we soon rebelled against the doctrine that sin and sickness were not real but illusions that could be got rid of by right thinking. Even our mother, although she went to church faithfully, sometimes wavered when she thought one of us might need a doctor; yet she never sought medical advice for herself and she was never ill. In the last months of the war, when I was twelve, she was able to buy a small house, and we left Dorrie's upstairs rooms for a home of our own. It felt like perfect happiness: there was a garden with apple trees at the end, we acquired a kitten, and I had my own room and new bookshelves. My mother's piano reappeared, the black Bechstein I had sat beneath so often, and she began to teach in a private school and give music lessons at home. She made music with us too, teaching us to sing Britten's *Ceremony of Carols*, and

Handel and Mozart. She had come through the worst and could feel proud of what she had achieved for us and for herself. She now also agreed to divorce Émile.

I was twelve when peace arrived at last, and realized that half my life had been lived through the war. I could hardly remember the world as it had been before, and I was slightly uneasy when the night ceased to be dark as the street lights came on. At the same time, it was discovered that I suffered from short sight and I was given my first pair of glasses. I detested having to wear them and left them off whenever I could; and I was especially disappointed to find that the stars, which had appeared to me as fuzzy shining shapes, became merely sharp small dots in the sky. I still often take my glasses off during a walk in the country, to see it with a softer aspect, a vagueness I find congenial. Another change brought by peace was the departure of the Italian prisoners from the camp close to Welwyn. We had never been able to think of them as enemies, and felt sorry for them being confined and far from their homes and families. They gave no trouble, and many were allowed out of the camp in their plain brown prisoners' uniforms and became familiar figures round about, smiling and friendly.

In 1946 my mother claimed back her British nationality and it was restored. Now we were all British. We were poor – the divorce settlement gave her very little – but that hardly mattered to us. She took us on exciting holidays, to the Lake District, where we stayed in Youth Hostels, everyone sleeping in dormitories in their own sleeping bags, and helping with the dishes and other chores. I saw Ullswater again, and we made it to the top of Helvellyn.

Our dealings with my father were uncomfortable. Marguerite refused to see him at all once she had reached the age when she could legally decide for herself and display her loyalty to our mother, but I was obliged to. We had awkward meetings in London. I remember an afternoon at the opera with him – Verdi's *Trovatore*, which I found incomprehensible, not least because our seats were half behind a pillar and I was not wearing my glasses. Much worse was being taken to our old flat in Stanhope Gardens, where my new stepmother, Katharine, was now living. She was so nervous of the meeting that she felt ill and retired to bed. Her sister Peg came and played card games with me. I was polite but no more, finding their presence in what had been my mother's home hard to accept. I did not know what to call Katharine, which made conversation difficult – for years I managed to avoid saying her name, even when I became fond of her. After that visit, my father asked me to meet him at his lawyers on another day, giving me instructions as to how to get to them in Holborn. Thinking about it, I decided there was no way he could enforce his will and I could simply choose not to go. Furious messages came and I triumphed in the realization that I had successfully defied him. In any case, he was soon going to New York to work with the newly formed United Nations.

I felt secure and happy in our new house, where I could shut the door of my bedroom, pile up books and read for as long as I liked. I was growing from a skinny child into a skinny adolescent. I went for long solitary bicycle rides, swam, visited the library regularly, read and wrote. Words, poetry, history interested me, and I asked my mother for the two-volume *Shorter Oxford Dictionary* for my thirteenth birthday.

In the garden, 1947

I bought myself Eileen Power's *Medieval English Nunneries*, and Power, a young woman historian, became my heroine. This I reported to my father in a letter. He was sending me stamped self-addressed envelopes to encourage me to write. He and Katharine were now settled in a house on Long

Island. She went to much trouble to make up food parcels for us. They were welcome, since food was still rationed. Then she sent me a present of a white swimming costume. It was probably the most expensive garment in my wardrobe, and I loved it so much that I used to wear it in the back garden on sunny days. The parcels were exciting – they were also of course a lever, telling us that we could expect good things from a father and stepmother in America, encouraging us to think again about our absolute loyalty to our mother. My father wanted me to visit them in America.

Early in 1947 I had to go before a High Court judge in London to explain that I did not wish to visit my father. It was a private meeting at the judge's chambers, with my mother and her lawyer, a stout kindly man known to me as Uncle Rowly, waiting outside the room into which I went alone to talk to the judge. He did not wear a wig, seemed a straightforward person and spoke to me in a friendly voice. 'Most girls would give their right arm to go to America,' he said. 'I don't want to go,' I said in return. Asked to give my reasons, I said I did not like my stepmother. What I really meant was that I hated the situation of having a step-mother. The judge listened, did not press me and accepted that I preferred to stay at home with my mother. When I emerged, Uncle Rowly took me aside and gave me half a crown, which was a week's pocket money. Then he said, 'You ought to see your father.' I knew he was devoted to my mother, so this was unexpected. 'Yes, yes, you really must keep in touch with your father,' he said again.

That year, 1947, was the year of the dancing mania. It began in the summer, when ballroom-dancing lessons were offered at a local hotel, the Cherry Tree. They were not expensive, and a group of us, train girls and other teenage friends, persuaded our mothers to let us go along and learn to dance. We were greeted by Madame Maxine, who seemed quite British in spite of her name. She had sharply cut hair and wore a tailored suit and high heels. She demonstrated the quick step, the foxtrot and the waltz to the music of Victor Silvester and His Ballroom Orchestra on the gramophone, telling us what to do and then holding each of us clamped in her grip in turn as she took us through the steps. We loved it and were determined to master all the dances. No boys turned up at the classes. We decided we would practise our steps during our lunch hour at school, where the hall had a very well-maintained pale polished floor over which we liked to slide.

This set off the dancing mania. Someone brought in a gramophone and a few records. Within a week most of the senior girls at school were circling round the hall after lunch each day. We must have made a fine sight in our navy-blue gym tunics, going slow – slow – quick-quick – slow, waltzing carefully, gliding across the floor as insouciantly as we could in the foxtrot. We took turns to lead or follow: it was unexpectedly enjoyable to lead, to make the decisions, to exact submission. We enjoyed ourselves, joked, laughed, stumbled, swanned about and improved our performances. Junior girls looked in to jeer and stayed to envy. We were all having more fun than we could have imagined.

Then, out of the blue one day, a directive came from the headmistress that the dancing was to stop. It appeared there was something unhealthy about staying indoors, and also – *sotto voce*, from someone who had heard it – about girls embracing each other as they had to for dancing. What rot, we said. It seemed to be as dangerous as reading *Romeo and Juliet*, and there was to be no more of it. We were angry and disappointed.

Despite this setback, the dancing lessons continued at the Cherry Tree. Friends of Madame Maxine looked in to see how things were going, and one was our neighbour, Pat Harland, a glamorous young woman and an excellent dancer. We were friendly with her parents, he a retired captain in the Merchant Navy with a brave war record. He and his wife had sailed the world together before the war, and they had six children, all now grown up and scattered except for Pat. She was always smartly dressed in trousers, and my mother explained that she had lost a leg in an accident and prided herself on living a normal life, and especially on her dancing, as well she might. The Harlands were convivial and she was tough too. They told us their youngest son, Philip, who had spent some of the war years in America and then followed his father into the Merchant Navy, was coming home on leave. They were proud of their young officer – would we come to tea to meet him?

So we went. If I tried to describe Phil, I should fail. Enough to say he was a young man with an agreeable face, an open smile, good manners, a slight American accent and ready to joke like his father. He was twenty-one, and he talked to me as though we were the same age, although I was just fourteen. As I prepared to leave the tea party with my mother, he suggested we might go to the pictures together at the weekend. We could take the bus to St Albans and have tea out. Yes, I'd like that. It was my first date.

Saturday came. I was not going to risk looking plain in my glasses, so I sat through the film with only a dim idea of what was happening on the screen. In any case I had something better to think about, because as soon as it started Phil took my hand in his. He kept hold of it all through the show. Having your hand held may not rate high among erotic experiences today, but it was overpowering to me in 1947.

I suppose Phil was at a loose end. At our next dancing lesson he appeared, introduced himself as Pat's brother to Madame Maxine, and asked if he might dance with me. Like his sister, he danced very well. I felt I was being taken into another state of being.

I had lived passionately in books and words, but I never formulated what I felt with Phil because it seemed impossible to find words for it. 'O for a Life of Sensations rather than of Thoughts!' Keats wrote, and this seemed to be it, the Life of Sensations. I don't remember having conversations with Phil, learning what his interests were or even making an estimate of his character. He didn't ask me about my ideas or work either – I didn't expect him to want to hear about my American history classes or the stories of Kipling, or Keats's poems and letters. We were both there together, and that was enough.

But he was there for only a few weeks before going to sea again. He suggested we might meet at night, slip out of our houses and rendezvous at the far ends of our gardens, where there was a wild area with trees and shrubs. We managed it once and embraced and kissed in the soft summer darkness.

A day or two later Pat appeared as I was going out of our front door and spoke to me angrily, saying something about my getting her brother into trouble. I was too startled to reply. The next time Phil and I tried our midnight escapade my mother heard me opening the back door, called out, took me in her arms and told me I must not go out. She was surprisingly gentle and did not ask me what I was doing. So Phil waited in vain. A few nights later he managed to climb in through a landing window – quite a feat – and arrived in my small bedroom. He was wearing very little and he took off most of his clothes. We lay down in the narrow bed with our arms tightly round each other. We hardly spoke, we kissed and kissed, and held each other. Nothing more. We said goodbye because he was about to leave.

I never saw him again. I went to school, he went to sea. I said nothing to anyone – what would I have said? In the autumn I started on my School Certificate year syllabus, which I loved: nineteenth-century European history, revolutions, the unification of Italy, social and political turmoil; Shakespeare's *As You Like It* and modern poetry – Auden, Eliot, Yeats, D. H. Lawrence; biology, French; even maths began to mean something to me. My sister went up to Oxford to read French. There was still rationing of bread, eggs, meat and sweets. I lost interest in food; my mother said it was because there was nothing good to be had.

In the new year the Harlands had a romantic story to tell us: Philip's ship had met another in the Pacific, with some New Zealand nurses aboard. The two ships had spent three days exchanging visits, during which Phil and a beautiful nurse had fallen in love. They asked to be married at sea.

And so they were. He was going to settle in New Zealand. Everyone was touched and pleased by this turn of events, and I was glad for him – our idyll had ended when he left.

I have thought of him over the years, his sweetness and tenderness, the revelation he gave me of the power of sensation, and his care in not taking things too far. I have never met another dancer to match him, and I can still just about remember the delight of being in his arms and guided by him. We had nothing to talk about, but we were drawn to one another by a force we could not resist. Whatever we did together pleased us both as long as it lasted. I like to think he made a happy marriage and enjoyed a good life in New Zealand with a beautiful wife and many children. I would send him a loving message if I could.

❁

A new friend appeared in my life, and a whole family, the Kaufmanns, who had just moved to Welwyn. I was asked by an acquaintance of my mother to take their daughter Auriol under my wing, as she would be going to school in Hitchin. So I met this gentle, grey-eyed, intelligent girl, and we became friends on the instant. She was a reader like me, and we started talking and found we could hardly stop, both so eager to discuss books, poetry, history, plays, films, politics, the state of the world. We exchanged opinions and ambitions. I told her I aimed to become the first woman prime minister. I wish I could hear some of our conversations now to laugh at my absurdities. I showed off, and Auriol was too good-natured to make fun of me.

Each of us had a long walk in the afternoon from the station to our homes, in different directions, but our talk was so interesting to both of us that we often walked together all the way to one house, then to the other, scarcely noticing, until finally one of us had to turn back again alone. Auriol came in for tea with my mother, who approved, and soon I was invited for my first encounter with the Kaufmann family. Their house was ordinary enough outside, but once through the door it was like stepping on to a stage on which everything was brighter, funnier and more entertaining. Where our house was quiet, clean and tidy, with defined areas for music and books and no other papers in sight, the Kaufmanns' sitting room was a fine chaos of cushioned sofas, magazines and newspapers, empty coffee cups and glasses, a box of mah-jong tiles, scattered opened envelopes, letters and photographs, packs of cards, dropped scarves and unfamiliar small books. They were Mills & Boon romances, I discovered, something I had never seen before.

I was welcomed like an extra daughter – their eldest had become an actress, was now on the stage in London and had apparently stopped coming home, and the second, Charmian, had left school and was still at home. She and Auriol called their mother by her first name, 'Joyce' – I had never heard anyone do that before – and Joyce expected Charmian to make and bring in the tea to her when she came in. This was a different sort of mother. She had been shopping and she sank into a sofa, her parcels around her, and kicked off her shoes. She was not young but her hair was arranged in a girlish wave; she was powdered and lipsticked and smelt delicious. She gave me a charming welcome and said how lovely it was for Auriol to have a friend, and how she hoped I would make myself at home with them. Hilary – Auriol's father – would be back from London quite soon and he would be especially pleased to meet me.

Mr Kaufmann was in the Colonial Office, now working in London, and took the train each day. He had met his wife in Kandy, in Ceylon, when he was posted there. Her father had been a tea planter. It was a marvellous life, she said, in the good days before the war: tennis, horse-riding, dancing, and servants – she had never lifted a finger. And she had danced with the Prince of Wales – before she was married – when one of his tours took him to Kandy. He was a good dancer.

Mr Kaufmann – Hilary – was not a dancer. He had greying hair, wore glasses, carried a briefcase and was altogether unremarkable in appearance; and he was a very nice man, well read, well informed, gentle and sweet-natured. He showed great interest in Auriol's and my studies, and encouraged our friendship. It was he who suggested I should stay for supper, and he often invited me to lunch on Sunday, even though rationing made food short. Much of the preparation of meals was done by him. The kitchen was the one dark room in the house and what you could see of it badly needed cleaning. A smell of burnt frying pan sometimes came from it, mixing oddly with the smell of Elizabeth Arden bath essence.

One evening when I was expected at the house, I found it empty downstairs, laughter coming from above. I went up and found the girls and their mother in the bathroom, fooling about, doing things to their hair and faces in front of the mirror, with Mr Kaufmann in the bath, concealed only by bubble-bath foam. They were all joking and giggling. Mr Kaufmann began to fart under the water, and everyone fell about with laughter. I who had never seen my own father undressed or heard him fart experienced a moment of astonishment. Then I saw that this was the most innocent of family parties, enjoyed by everyone. The unheated houses of the 1940s made bathrooms the perfect place to gather, damp paradises, warmed by hot water and steam.

The Kaufmanns enjoyed themselves being light-hearted and silly, I saw. I fell in love with the whole family. They made me aware of how quiet and serious my home was: my mother kept a single lipstick and box of powder in a drawer, read no magazines and took the *Sunday Times* only for its music criticism. While we had no alcohol in our house – Christian Scientists are teetotal – the Kaufmanns had drinks in the evening – gin, whisky, sherry, rum – and insisted on pouring unnamed concoctions for me. Mrs Kaufmann went out for pub crawls at night, collected by young men who arrived in sports cars and zoomed off with her. One Saturday, Mr Kaufmann escorted Auriol and me to London on the train and Underground to Piccadilly Circus for an amazing treat: my first Chinese meal.

Close as Auriol and I were, she did not explain much about her family to me. One day I ventured to ask her if Kaufmann was originally a foreign name, as my name, Delavenay, for which I was often mocked, was: no, she said, she thought not. She never mentioned that she had been born in Ceylon – something I found out only after her death. Another day I arrived at her house to find a tall, dark, good-looking young man standing in front of the fire, looking cheerful, and the centre of attention. This was Maurice, I gathered. He was being teased by Joyce about where he had been and with whom – girlfriends, she insisted, and he did not deny it. No one explained to me what his connection with the family was, but it was clear that everyone adored him and he was quite at home. He was about to start at RADA in London, training to be an actor, and for the present was living in the house. There were plenty of beds in the various bedrooms, as I knew because I sometimes stayed overnight after chatting late with Auriol. She took Maurice entirely for granted and expected me to do the same. Only when I heard by chance that his second name was Kaufmann did I guess that he might be a cousin. The following week, a small, cowed-looking woman appeared and sat down for lunch with us. No one took much notice of her, but she was addressed as 'Auntie'. I had no idea who she was, and it took me weeks to ask myself: could she be Maurice's mother? He did not call her mother or speak to her as though she could be his mother – she was 'Auntie' to him too, and he scarcely spoke to her at all. It was hard to connect someone as bedraggled and apologetic as she was with someone as smart and confident as Maurice. No good asking Auriol, and I never had the nerve to ask anyone else about Auntie. Or why her eldest sister never came home to see them. How mysterious other families could be.

No matter, Auriol was my Best Friend – something I had never had before – and she seemed as close as an ideal sister: my real sister was now away at St Hilda's in Oxford. Auriol spent a holiday with me and my mother in Dorset, and I was always in and out of the Kaufmanns' house. Suddenly, with no warning, there was a crisis. Auriol broke down in hysterical tears one afternoon, saying her parents preferred me to her and she was useless, wished she had never been born . . . I was appalled and told her it was nonsense, all in her imagination: her parents adored her. No doubt her father did his best to cheer her, and comforted her with assurances of his love. I don't know how Joyce reacted. Then, as fast as the crisis had blown up, it passed. Our friendship was restored and was as warm as ever. But I was left wondering where her anguish came from. And it was a warning.

❦

All that year I thought about my father's invitation to America, and in the spring of 1948 I agreed to fly to New York. My mother was badly upset. She wept and told me she would put her head in the gas oven and kill herself if I went. I thought about this too, and decided she would not carry out her threat. But it was difficult, because I loved her and felt entirely loyal to her. My father was in correspondence with the new headmistress at Hitchin, and she gave the American trip her blessing. I was seen to be supremely lucky to be going.

My mother stopped threatening suicide and accompanied me to the airport. The plane had to land twice to refuel, at Shannon and Gander, and I was sick each time it went down, which made a miserable journey, but once there I was overwhelmed by America – so glossy and luxurious, the unrationed food, the clothes, the cars, the ice creams, the advertisements in the *New Yorker*, my father's friends, all employees of the United Nations. I also saw for the first time in my life beggars in rags, asking for money in the streets of Manhattan. I had led such a sheltered life that I thought beggars were strictly historical figures and had disappeared from the world in the twentieth century.

I soon put them out of my mind. I was offered and gingerly tasted my first avocado pear. I was taken to the top of the Empire State Building, and photographed looking suitably impressed. Kath took me to Lord & Taylor on Fifth Avenue to choose some clothes for myself. Christian Dior's New Look had just arrived, and I went home dressed in a soft-shouldered, wasp-waisted jacket and full skirt. People turned round in the street in England at early appearances of the New Look, and I enjoyed being stared at and showed off shamelessly. Most important, I found I liked my stepmother, and could now talk to my father on reasonably equal terms.

In this way my father became the victor in the fight against my mother for their children. He had the money; he could offer travel and excitement; he had an excellent wife who was ready to support him by making friends with us. Once I had been to America, my sister changed her mind and agreed to go too. It was not that we loved our mother any less, but we could not resist what he had to give us. The world was enlarging around us, offering new excitements. It was now possible to be in touch with our French grandmother – Grandmaman – Tante Hélène, who came to see Marguerite and me in London, her sons Jean-Pierre and Michel, and other cousins; and, although some were shocked by Papa's divorce and

In America, 1948

remarriage, they had no choice but to accept it. We were encouraged to accept his offers by all but a very few of our mother's friends. For her, it was a cruel blow to see us divide our loyalties after she had worked so hard to make a home for us. We remained loving daughters, but we were being carried on an irresistible wave. I went to New York again in the summer of 1949, and left Welwyn eighteen months later for a different sort of life, going to boarding school at Dartington Hall in Devon.

4

My Last School: Dartington Hall

Just as my mother had feared, I was unsettled by the visits to my father, and by the knowledge that there was an alternative way of life open to me. In the autumn of 1949, hardly thinking what I was doing, I wrote to him suggesting I might leave school and live with him for a while. It was a piece of sixteen-year-old rebellion against the constraints of school and what I saw as my mother's old-fashioned ideas, which seemed more oppressive now that I was facing them without my sister's support. I dashed off my letter on a bad day, and hardly expected a response. To my surprise, he took it seriously – and saw it as a justification for taking a greater part in arrangements for me. He was about to leave his job with the United Nations and return to Europe, where he would be living in Paris and running a department at UNESCO. In the midst of this upheaval he decided the best thing would be for me to go to boarding school in England. Knowing little about schools, he consulted with his friend David Astor, who advised sending me to Dartington Hall School in Devon.* Astor sent his

* David Astor (1912–2001) became editor of the *Observer* in 1946. It was owned by his family – his father was second Viscount Astor and his

own children there later and he strongly approved of its progressive ethos. My father accepted this advice, quite why I don't know, since progressive education was not something I had ever heard mentioned by him – and I knew nothing about it at all. But it was lucky for me. He was coming to Europe to make preliminary arrangements for his return from New York, and he arranged to meet me in London and travel on a night train to Torquay, and from there we would take a taxi to Totnes, close to Dartington. The headmaster, William Burnley Curry, would join us for breakfast in a hotel in Totnes, to discuss the possibility of my becoming a pupil at the school.

I was astonished by my first sight of Curry, because he looked nothing like a headmaster to me. I had expected a man of formal appearance and manner, wearing polished shoes and probably a dark suit, and instead a very small man with a very large head, wearing a well-worn mackintosh, hurried into the hotel dining room. His manner was informal, and he began by explaining to us that really there was no room for me at the school, and that in any case he did not like taking older pupils who had not had the benefit of Dartington's educational methods from their early years. This was a bit of a blow. But he was friendly, and, having delivered his warning, he turned to me and began to ask me about myself and my interests. We got on at once, started

---

American mother Nancy the first woman MP – and he made it into an outstandingly well-written and progressive paper. My father knew him through a committee, Political and Economic Planning, on which both sat during the war.

talking about life, books and history and went on to music, poetry and politics. He talked with me as one human being to another, not like a headteacher assessing a candidate.

The conversation had to end, and at this point he said he was prepared to squeeze me into the senior school at Dartington. There was no time to visit now, and he explained that I would have to sleep in a linen cupboard for my first term. If that was acceptable, he thought things might work out well. He would be in touch with my father about the details, and would expect me in January, at the start of the new term.

So it was arranged. It was an adventure for me. I knew nothing about Dartington, but I was intrigued and not at all nervous. Curry's reason for taking me, I understood in due course, was that he thought I would get into a university in a few years' time, and that would be good for the reputation of the school – progressive schools did not have much of a record for preparing pupils for higher education. The danger, from his point of view, was that I might run amok with all the freedom allowed at Dartington.

Curry need not have worried. At Dartington Hall I settled into a calm and generally cheerful life. The senior pupils lived and worked in a white two-storey modern building set around a large rectangular courtyard. It was called Foxhole. Our simple bedrooms and bathrooms – and my still smaller linen cupboard – looked out on to the courtyard on one side, and on the other over the woods and meadows surrounding us. The hall, dining room and kitchens were at one end, near the road, and through the other end of the courtyard you went out into the woods and down the path to the swimming pool. There were classrooms, a library and a gym. Also rooms for housemothers and housefathers – some of them single teachers, some with domestic responsibilities.

The headmaster's house, High Cross, a bold Modernist building, was just up the road, and we were often invited there by Curry. Further up the hill stood the medieval Hall itself, restored from ruin to stately grandeur, with its grey stone outbuildings around it. There lived Dorothy and Leonard Elmhirst, the rich idealists who had bought the estate in the 1920s and established a well-organized community, setting up workshops, farms and small industries as well as the school. Dorothy Elmhirst had supervised the creation of the great gardens. Terraced and planted with trees, they were a mixture of wide grassy steps, statues, shrubs, flower borders, bulbs and areas of wilderness, with a vast central area of lawn that could be used as a stage. Its open spaces, tall trees and long views make it a serene and magnificent place, and we were allowed to walk there whenever we chose.

My fellow pupils were for the most part the sons and daughters of middle-class British parents with progressive ideas, some from local families, many from London. There were children of artists, notably the triplet children of Barbara Hepworth and Ben Nicholson, Rachel, Sarah and Simon. Others had come from abroad in the aftermath of the war. I made friends with Jasia Ceglowska, who had survived the war in Poland against the odds, emerging imaginative, warm-hearted and brilliant. Anne Hogben, a talented and lively English girl, became another good friend. Miriam May, younger than me, was the gifted and beautiful child of German Jewish parents and had spent her early years in Jerusalem. Niall O'Casey was the son of the Irish playwright Sean O'Casey, settled in Devon. There were a few Americans – one was the nephew of the dancer Katherine Dunham. Another of the older boys was Lebanese, his first language French. Max Fordham, an English boy of my age who had spent the war years in the West Indies, helped me to understand the conventions of life at Foxhole and was always ready to give up his time to listen and offer brotherly advice. What impressed me was how tolerant all the children were of each other's behaviour and eccentricities, mine included. Max might laugh gently at my attempts to show off, but he was unfailingly kind.

I took my Latin lessons alongside Ralph Leavis, son of the two contentious Cambridge critics F. R. and Queenie. Ralph was very much better at Latin than I was, and I admired him for that, but found communication with him almost impossible as he remained entirely silent outside class. We were taught by the learned and gentle Mr Rosenberg, who accepted being called Rosy with good humour and often gave way to our request to have our lesson outside on the grass. History was taught by Ted Fitch, young and handsome, and I soon had a crush on him. And, although history was the subject I most wanted to study, Curry insisted that I should concentrate on English instead. There was a reason for this: the school's English teacher, Raymond O'Malley, had already successfully coached several pupils for Cambridge. He was an exceptional teacher.

I wrote essays for him, memorized chunks of poetry and prose, and walked with him in the afternoons and evenings through the gardens of the Hall, talking about Jane Austen, Keats and Shakespeare. His manner was mild, and I was allowed to address him simply as 'Malley', but he was severe in his literary tastes – he would not study Dickens and was shocked to learn that I enjoyed the novels of Dorothy Sayers. I wrote to my mother boasting that I was studying 'the philosophies of Wordsworth and Keats, not to mention Aristotle, or the history of the United States, or Sir Thomas Browne on *Urn Burial'*. Malley kept me working, and made a habit of leaving clippings of advertisements in my room in order to educate me in the low tricks of copy writers. He was a loyal pupil of Leavis, but kept this from me in case it might jeopardize my chances of getting a place at Cambridge. Malley was as good a teacher as anyone could hope to have.

Practical education was on offer too, and I seized the chance to be taught pottery. I still have a few of the pots I made on the wheel. I did some woodwork too, producing simple boxes, and was taught how to replace a broken window pane. Then there was music. Imogen Holst was in charge of the Music School, and we joined the chorus for a performance of Handel's *Messiah*, an ecstatic experience. A group of us was taken to hear Britten's new work *The Little Sweep*, written to introduce children to opera. We were invited to join in the choruses during the second half, and sang out loudly and enthusiastically.

As for sport, we played hockey against the Dartmouth boys, I on the left wing, and, although we were naturally beaten hollow by those tough naval cadets, it was good fun. In the summer term we all swam in the pool. The tradition of the school was that no one wore swimming costumes. No problem for skinny teenagers. Some of the teachers swam with us, and our history master Ted appeared as a godlike figure to me as he prepared to dive. Rather than encouraging sexual curiosity, it settled it down. We did go in for kissing and hugging, but for the most part we were more like brothers and sisters – the way we lived, sharing bathrooms as families do, helped to make us feel like family.

I have a dim memory of being involved in a play we improvised, in which I was required to put on quantities of make-up and speak with a supposedly sexy French accent. I was never any good as an actress, and that was my last effort. I also recall keeping a diary in which I wrote about my inner struggles – how I longed to have a baby but also wanted to go to university, and how university must take precedence. This may have been prompted by my sister's pregnancy, which put an end to her studies at Oxford. I travelled from Dartington to Oxford to be her bridesmaid when she was married to her romance philologist, who was a Roman Catholic. Marguerite, in thrall to him, converted. The Catholic chaplain gave a bold modern sermon, starting with the assertion that the young couple had been drawn together by nothing but strong sexual attraction – at which point my mother, sitting beside me, shuddered visibly. He went on to say they had moved on to something purer, but I had seen how upset our mother was, and made a private vow that I would on no account put her through such an episode again. My sister was happy and her life was not ruined – she awaited her baby eagerly – but our mother saw it as shame. That baby, my niece, whom Marguerite called Claire, only seventeen years younger than me, became a close friend to me later.

At school we had occasional debates: jazz versus classical music, Labour versus Conservative, whether it's better to seek riches or become a poor artist, the usual topics. I knew very little but I liked speaking, arguing fiercely and show-ing off. Curry called me in once to scold me for talking arrogantly and putting down one of my schoolmates too fiercely. I was taken aback but had to accept that he was right to take me to task. Another time he told me I was behaving like a tragic opera heroine over some mishap. He had become a respected father figure to me, so I tried hard to behave better.

On Sunday mornings, senior pupils were invited to his house for philosophical conversation – a few Christian pupils went to the local church, but I thought talking about moral questions with Curry was not to be missed. He would sit by the fire, always engaged in the curious ritual of tapping and filling his pipe as he led us through discus-sions. He had written two books in favour of European union, and I found him entirely persuasive on the subject, as a child with a French father was likely to. And he also told me before I left that, although he was in charge of a school in which the pupils were meant to make the most important decisions about how it was run, he had come to believe that the best way to run a school was as a benevo-lent despotism.

Curry and the school have been strongly criticized over the years, and I want to defend them both. For me, Dartington was a place where I was taught extremely well by remarkable teachers, where I was encouraged to think about moral and social issues, and where my adolescent turmoil was peacefully sorted out. My education was broadened and I was happy. As the ideas that inspired it were increasingly taken over in mainstream education, it lost some of its importance, and it had ceased to lead the way or even develop by the time it closed in the 1980s. But that was forty years after I was there. The place still has something paradisal for me: those serious, dedicated and gifted teachers, the fine buildings, and the soft Devon air and green landscapes.

It was decided that I should take a trial run at the English papers for entrance to Newnham College, Cambridge, at the end of 1950. I sat alone in the dining room at High Cross to do the four papers on two consecutive days. Curry looked at my efforts and told me he did not think I had written a good essay. I was summoned to Newnham for an interview. Before I set off for Cambridge, Curry said, 'You won't wear lipstick for your interview, will you?' Of course not – he need not have asked. Plainly dressed and pale-faced, I travelled by train to a freezing Cambridge. No matter: I fell in love with Newnham and expected to be turned down, looking at all the sophisticated girls from Cheltenham and Roedean who were my rivals. The interviews went well and Miss Enid Welsford, head of English at Newnham, told me I had written a particularly good essay – so much for Curry's disapproval, I thought.

I was to spend Christmas with my mother, and while I was with her a telegram was put into my hand offering me a place to read English at Newnham. No one forgets that moment. As we rejoiced, I saw ahead three years of rewarding intellectual effort. Then, back at school in January, Malley told me he wanted me to stay on for another year, take the entrance exam again and win a scholarship. I was happy with the idea, but Curry thought otherwise. 'The school is not a country club,' he declared. He ruled that I should leave school and spend the next nine months with my father in Paris.

So I was dismissed from paradise after one year. I left behind half-formed friendships. I never took my Higher Certificate exams. Curry came to see me in Cambridge once, took me out to lunch and embarrassed me by kissing me on the mouth when he said goodbye. I was more innocent than he realized. For many years I did not return to Dartington. Curry retired in 1957 and died in 1962: I am sorry I did not see him again. After he left, the school gradually lost its way.

Decades later, when a literary festival began to be held at Dartington in the summer, I went back. At each visit I spent as much time as possible in the gardens, finding it almost unbelievable that I had taken English lessons from Malley in such perfect surroundings. When the National Trust acquired High Cross, I revisited the rooms in which I had talked philosophy with Curry and sat my exams for Cambridge. And I usually walked over to Foxhole, a little apprehensively. For a while it housed the Devonshire Social Services Department, which discouraged visitors. The Social Services did not stay for long, and at my latest visit I found the Foxhole buildings fenced off. It was a distressing

The Courtyard of Foxhole

sight. I managed to clamber through the fencing to find that they were empty, abandoned and becoming derelict. Soon, I thought, the woods might grow over the site and no trace would be left of what had been there.

5

Higher Education

For the next nine months I lived with my father and step-mother Kath in Ville-d'Avray, a village between Paris and Versailles, set among woods and ponds; they had rented a large and slightly ridiculous house, nineteenth-century Gothic Revival, with turrets at each corner. On most weekdays I took the train into Paris, going to the Sorbonne to attend lectures on French literature and history. They were given by young French academics who knew their subjects and how to deliver, and they gave us plenty to take in and think about. Otherwise, I explored Paris, its streets, gardens and open spaces, the banks of the Seine, markets and churches. I had no friends and did it alone.

I went by myself to museums: the Louvre, the old Musée de l'Art Moderne, the Musée Carnavalet, the Musée de Cluny with its tapestries, and my favourite, the Jeu de Paume, where the Impressionists were shown in those days in concentrated glory. I spent hours in front of Monets, Sisleys, Pissarros, Degas, Renoirs: meadow paths, river banks, tree-lined lanes, small gardens, skies full of clouds, dancers, Paris streets and bridges, melting snow, winter sun, moonlight – the very essence of France, they seemed to me. On other days I worked in the elegant library of the British Council – long since closed – installed at a table, reading my way through the long book list sent to me by Newnham.

Sometimes Kath took me out in Paris, once to see my first Marx Brothers film, another time for a performance of *Le Cid* played by Gérard Philipe – a young actor of incomparable gifts who was to die in 1959, aged only thirty-six. At home, she let me play her Charles Trenet records, kept with an old wind-up gramophone in an attic room, and I listened until I knew all the lyrics and tunes by heart, from 'Boum!' to 'Le soleil et la lune'. One day she took me to her smart Paris hairdresser, and I so hated what he did to my hair that I walked out into the pouring rain hatless to wash away his work. I was forgiven for that bad behaviour. Sitting waiting for her in the car near the Galeries Lafayette, I couldn't help noticing something I had never seen before: the prostitutes standing in the street, picking up clients. What struck me most was their speed: they were sometimes back in the same place within ten minutes. Kath laughed sardonically when I described this to her. Another sight that puzzled me was the array of ancient ladies seated in the expensive cafés, dressed in high fashion and with their wrinkled faces thickly and elaborately painted. Did they think they were keeping up appearances? Making up for the war years when they had not been able to display themselves in cafés? They made a spectacle as macabre as a dance of death.

That spring I had my first experience of Wagner in the opera house when a friend of my parents took me to *Valkyrie*. Richard Fort was a Conservative MP, and I naturally expected him to be a villain and was amazed to find him open-minded, interesting and delightful. Neither my father nor Kath was interested in opera and Richard invited me to go with him. I accepted and we travelled into Paris by train, talking all the way. He listened patiently to my naive and strongly expressed opinions about social justice. His views seemed closer to mine than I expected and he spoke to me without condescension. I was greatly impressed by him, and charmed. *Valkyrie* was an overwhelming experience, through the amazing richness of its music and its themes: illicit love, death, gods in argument, a quarrel between an all-powerful father and his daughter who is disobedient but right. I was lucky in my first experience of Wagner and it set me on course to hear more.*

My parents encouraged me to invite my friend Auriol to stay, and to my joy she arrived in May. We all made much of her and took her out to see Paris sights and eat Paris meals. She and I spent hours gossiping, discussing our ambitions and listening to records. She was due to stay for a week, but on the fourth day, to my astonishment and dismay, she burst into tears and said she wanted to leave immediately. No explanation. She seemed distraught, as though darkness had descended on her, and kept saying she must go home. My father rang her parents and they talked to her but she would listen to no one and we had to put her on a train for London. Perhaps it was just acute homesickness, I thought, baffled; then I remembered the earlier episode when she had become hysterical, saying her parents

---

* Tragically, Richard Fort was killed in a car crash in 1959. He left four sons and a daughter; his widow, Jean, became headmistress of Roedean.

did not love her. When we met again in England nothing was said and we were friends as before, but it remained disquieting.

I was eager to learn Italian and took lessons with a black-clad lady living in a flat in the Sixième. Presently her teaching was supplemented by an Italian who picked me up in the Luxembourg Gardens. He was called Alfio – 'like Alph, the sacred river in "Kubla Khan",' he explained. He was years older than me, very handsome, told me he had been a Partisan, and did his best to seduce me. I liked him, but when I agreed to visit his flat things got out of hand and he kept shouting, 'Take off your knickers.' His English was excellent but I was not going to obey his orders and I made my escape. My progress in Italian stalled. There were a lot of misunderstandings like this for girls of my generation: we aimed to be free and seemed to be free spirits to the men we met, but we were not as free as they thought.

In June, my father drove us south. It was my first experience of that heady journey in which the air grows warmer hour by hour. One evening, as we began our descent from a high pass, I was puzzled by the sight of an enormous pale-pink ball floating in the sky. It took me several minutes to understand that this was the moon as I had never seen her before, in her southern attire. Fields full of sunflowers and olive trees came into view. Our destination was Vence in the Alpes-Maritimes, where Kath's English aunt, Hetty, had lived for most of her life, looking after her weak lungs. Kath loved Vence and aimed to live there herself one day, as indeed she did, persuading my father to build a house on a hillside nearby. I understood why she felt as she did as

I got to know Vence, a small walled town going back to Roman times and still busy, full of ordinary citizens working, set between mountains and Mediterranean, with an ideal climate, airy and sunlit, where orange and olive trees flourished and roses bloomed through most of the year. At that time Matisse still lived there. He had built and decorated the town's Rosary Chapel; no longer painting, and devoting himself entirely to his paper 'cutouts' and drawings, he was frail and rarely seen, but he was a presence. The most striking waitress in the café we favoured on the Grande Place had been one of his models. He died in 1954.

We were within easy reach of the coast and swam regularly in the Mediterranean, walked on coastal paths and drove up into the mountains for more demanding walks and visits to perched villages. On a very clear day you might catch a glimpse of Corsica across the blue sea below. There was so much to see, to learn, to enjoy. And I was looking forward to Cambridge in the autumn. I arrived back in England for the last day of the Festival of Britain, went round it with my mother, surprised, amused and entertained, but not entirely sure what the point of it was after my year in France; and then it was on to Cambridge with my trunk, to start my studies as an undergraduate.

From the first I loved Newnham. Basil Champneys's redbrick buildings, set squarely and lightly round three sides of the gardens, have windows so big that small birds have been known to fly in. The gardens, part formal, part

Peile Hall and Gardens

unmown grassy spaces with trees, offer places where you may stroll and talk, or settle with a book when the sun allows, or just enjoy green thoughts in the green shade. The East Anglian air fills your lungs. When rain falls, you are never far from shelter. I felt privileged to have a room overlooking the gardens, and adored having my private territory, in which I could arrange my few possessions as I liked and live as I chose. It was in Peile Hall, reached by a ten-minute walk along what seemed like a mile of corridors from the main entrance. Men in Cambridge lived on stone stairs set round courts – or often enough in lodgings outside their colleges – while we girls lived on our long wooden corridors, and never had to go into lodgings. All the colleges were single sex then and there were only two colleges for women. Girton was more than a mile out of town. We were much better placed, close to the centre and the river, and to the best urban view in England, of the Backs – the Backs being the name given to the stretch of grassland between the river Cam and the backs of several college buildings including Queens', King's and its Chapel, Clare and Trinity Hall.

Beautiful as Cambridge is, it is also bitterly cold for most of the year. The only heat in our rooms came from coal fires. The grates were emptied and the rooms cleaned by German girls. I found this embarrassing, as though they were the vanquished sent to serve us, the victors, six years after the war, and I felt they regarded us as spoilt creatures, which in a sense we were. The German girls were not given to smiling and I failed to make friends with any of them as I should have done. That was a bad start.

We were of course privileged, but our lives were not luxurious. We couldn't keep our fires going all the time, so we shivered a lot and wore thick sweaters. I found the best way to keep warm was to sit on the floor with my nose as close as possible to the heat, and I did a lot of work in front of the flames. We were asked to have only two baths a week, a request not all of us obeyed. One bathroom served our corridor; there were no washing machines; and we washed out our underwear and dried it on the bathroom pipes. Sometimes it disappeared. The food was terrible. I remember especially the depressing smell of hot dogs chopped into dry rice. Food was still rationed and we were not allowed to sign out of college meals, so we had to force them down as best we could. In any case few of us could afford to eat out. Presently a group of us made a formal protest about the bad quality of the meals. We were summoned by the principal and scolded for having reduced the domestic bursar to tears. Feeble, I thought, as a response. Kind Kath sent me an occasional slab of butter from unrationed France, and the day eggs came off the ration in my second year – February 1953 – I went out, bought a dozen and a half and gave a scrambled-egg party.

Newnham was an agnostic foundation with no chapel or chaplain, the only such college in Cambridge. A group of enthusiastic Christian girls got permission to use a room near the Porters' Lodge in the evening to lie in wait for anyone coming in along the corridor. Like the Sirens, they tried to lure us into their room with offers of cocoa and Christian instruction. I laughed at them, but had to admire their persistence.

Our principal, Dame Myra Curtis, was a retired civil servant in her sixties, and an imposing presence. When she invited all the new Eng. Lit. students to sherry, the obligatory Cambridge drink, she told us that, while English was sometimes regarded as a soft option, more girls applied to read it than any other subject, so we had done very well to be offered places. There were twelve of us, scattered into different parts of the college, and with different interests, many eager to join theatre groups. Juliet, a beautiful and sophisticated-seeming London girl, was a Catholic and would never eat or drink on Saturday evenings because of Mass in the morning, but in spite of this she and I formed a bond of friendship. I was to do supervisions with Anthea Hume, the most intelligent of us all. I remember shy Jennifer and resolutely silent Dudi, clever and destined to play star parts in all the Cambridge productions of our years. Jane Llewellyn became a theatre director and went to New York, Wendy a successful actress, Jane Ayre switched from English to Economics, and the others have fled my memory.

The closest friend I made was Sylvia, reading History and with a room next to mine in Peile Hall. She was already engaged to be married, to an older childhood friend now running his own business. She was seductively beautiful, and many heads were turned by her in Cambridge. A Persian admirer sent her a dozen red roses every week for a year, and she was wooed by cricket blues. She did not entirely discourage them, fitting a few discreet romances around her fiancé's occasional visits, and married him when she went down. She was gentle, thoughtful and sensible. We talked about everything freely together; and we agreed that, good friends as we were, we gave our first loyalties to men. It sounds shocking today – it was shocking – but it was so in 1951, and we both took it for granted.

❧

Our tutors were all women, scholars and lovers of literature, serious, formidable and thoughtful. The first assignment we were set was to write an essay on the poems of John Donne, the most magnificent of the English poets: witty, difficult, complicated in his thinking and wording. You have to work hard to untangle his imagery, as we were expected to do. There are mourning poems in which he calls himself a dead thing, made of 'absence, darkness, death', and joking poems like the one about the flea who mixes his blood with his girl's. But on the subject of sexual love Donne comes straight to the point. He chides the sun for sending his morning rays into the bed where he and his beloved are lying late. He insists that bodies must join as well as souls, 'else a great Prince in prison lies'. He tells us that love has one right true end, and if you don't go for it, it's like a man going to sea 'for nothing but to make him sick'. And he offers some of the most erotic lines in English poetry:

> Licence my roving hands, and let them go,
> Before, behind, between, above, below.
> O my America! my new-found land,
> My kingdom, safeliest when with one man manned.

Donne set down what young men feel and want. Perhaps our unmarried tutors thought we should know about this as we entered a social world in which there were ten young men to each one of us – that is how it was in Cambridge in 1951. We read with fascination and took note. If it made a somewhat surprising start to our studies, it was a glorious one. The young men were reading Donne too, and could and did quote him to us. None of us forgot Donne's poetry. Then on to Chaucer, *Troilus and Criseyde*, a verse novel of love and betrayal written in the fourteenth century and set several centuries before Christ, with characters whose dilemmas, ambiguous feelings and fear of having their private lives exposed are timeless. And on again to Marlowe and Shakespeare.

How happy I was with this. But not everything was good. I went to Cambridge expecting to be mentally stirred and surprised, to find some new and tremendous intellectual stimulus – an awakening, an opening of doors, fresh ways of looking at writing. And, although I liked nothing better than reading and discussing what I read, this awakening did not happen. Perhaps it was too much to expect. The lectures I attended in my first weeks were a severe disappointment. One series on Shakespeare in particular began with the male lecturer telling us to acquire editions of the plays with blank pages between the pages of text so that we could take down everything he told us: it would be invaluable during our future careers as schoolteachers, he told us. Possibly, but I believed we had come to university to be encouraged to think for ourselves, not to be told what to think. I gave up going to the lectures. I observed that other lecturers had already published books on their subjects, which I could read and think about at my leisure, and I spent more time in libraries than in lecture halls. Now I regret not having explored further afield by going to lectures on other subjects, history, anthropology, archaeology, geography – I could have learnt a great deal.

I did not even go to hear Dr Leavis. He was probably the most popular lecturer among English students then, admired with almost religious fervour, and he could not be disregarded: you had to be with him or against him. I read my way through his critical works with considerable respect for his detailed approach, but I also saw that he wasn't always to be taken seriously. His praise of D. H. Lawrence convinced, but his remarks on Dickens were absurd. His view was that Dickens was a mere entertainer who had written only one novel worth reading, *Hard Times*. I disagreed and wrote an essay setting out my reasons for admiring Dickens as a great novelist. I was forced to think hard and it did me no harm with my supervisor, Joan Bennett, who was no Leavisite. Eighteen years later, in 1970, when all Leavis's obedient students had gone forth spreading the word that Dickens was no good, and saving themselves the trouble of reading or teaching him, Leavis and his wife Queenie published a book on Dickens's novels in which they retracted their earlier opinion, suddenly describing him as one of the greatest of creative writers, and presenting warm and brilliant analyses of individual novels. This was an extraordinary volte-face, made without explanation or apology for the earlier dismissal of Dickens. It was also one of the strangest of literary recantations, closer to a spiritual conversion than a critical reappraisal.

One of Leavis's star pupils at Downing was Karl Miller. He and I went up in the same year, and he stood out among the middle-class English students through his intelligence and force of character. He was a fierce, eloquent, arresting, witty Scot. We were both outsiders, and we formed a tentative friendship which grew in time to be a close one. He quickly established himself as one of the most brilliant of our generation, and a serious scholar. We talked, sparred, joked, flirted. With all our joking, we were both intense. I admired him – there was no one else like him.

❧

With so many young men and so few women in Cambridge, we had to chart our way carefully. The imbalance had some absurd effects. Early in my first term a message came from a boy I had known very slightly before Cambridge, asking if I would lunch with him in a restaurant in the town. His name was Guy and he explained that he wanted nothing more than to be seen with me once, because his college friends refused to believe he knew me – so rare a thing was it to know a girl student in Cambridge. Of course I agreed, met him, exchanged polite words, ate modestly, thanked him for the lunch and was thanked for being there. I did not notice anyone watching us. Guy and I parted in a friendly manner and never saw one another again.

A more conventional invitation came early in my first term from Nora David, a childhood friend of my stepmother, now married with children and living near Newnham. 'Come to tea on Wednesday at 4.30,' she wrote, 'and bring a friend.' I invited Juliet, and we put on – what? – neat skirts and twin sets probably. We found Nora serving cake and tea to two young men from King's College, a tall one named Anthony Barnes and a smaller one, Tony Mitchell. They were both also in their first year, but two years older than us because they had been through their military service. Although this took place in the mid-twentieth century, the tea party was one Jane Austen might have approved, as our hostess made formal introductions between the son of one family she had known for years and the daughter of another, plus a chosen friend for each.

It was like this: Anthony was the son of Nora's friend Anne Barnes, Tony the son of another of Anne's friends who had been at Newnham with her in the 1920s. Nora had also been at Newnham, and she had married a fellow student, Dick David, at Corpus, who now worked for Cambridge

University Press. I was being introduced into a tightly knit group of highly educated and successful people. Anthony's father, George Barnes, had read History at King's and gone on to become director of talks at the BBC and set up the Third Programme (the forerunner of Radio 3); and he had recently been appointed director of television. Nora herself, as soon as her four children were old enough, became a Cambridge councillor and then a Labour-appointed baroness, a strong presence in the House of Lords into her nineties. Other members of the group taught at King's: the historian Noel Annan, and George Rylands – known as Dadie – who changed the face of English theatre through his productions of Shakespeare, crucially influencing John Barton, Peter Hall and Trevor Nunn.

I knew nothing of this formidable group of adults then, but I liked Anthony from the start. He had emerged from Eton with strongly held socialist views and insisted on doing his military service in the navy on the lower deck as a naval airman, seeing off pressure to take up the responsibilities of his class and become an officer. He and Tony took me into King's and introduced me to their friends. It became my second college, and the walks between Newnham and King's – across the Backs or over the Silver Street Bridge and round the side of Queens' – became so familiar that I might still be able to do them with my eyes shut. Neal Ascherson arrived at King's the following year, back from fighting in Malaya: I have a vivid memory of being taken to meet him for the first time, and of the admiration he commanded from all his friends. Robert Erskine was an art historian, knowledgeable and entertaining: when someone spilt red wine over my white dress, he knew the right treatment was white wine and poured it liberally over me. It worked: the stain disappeared. Ronald Bryden from the West Indies was writing a thesis on Carlyle – he was older, enthusiastic and warm-hearted. Stephen Haskell, reading English at Magdalene, was another of Anthony's friends with whom I formed a close bond, talking about poetry and nineteenth-century novels. They were like a band of brothers to me.

When Anthony's parents came to Cambridge, he invited me to meet them. From the first they were more than kind to me. George Barnes was a dazzler. He was used to being in charge of situations and people, effortlessly authoritative, tall, handsome and full of jokes. He teased and flattered me, delighted by my French name, Delavenay. He believed the French were more cultivated than the philistine English, and he made me feel I might become part of his tribe too. I did not even think of resisting his charm. Anne also talked to me kindly, her eyes intelligent and amused, and with a sweet smile, touched with wryness when George was being preposterous. George was the star, obviously.

They seemed quite old to me. In fact they were in their forties. I did not ask myself why they were so friendly because they behaved as though it were the most natural thing. They made it plain that they were pleased by my friendship with their son – they called him Ant, as I learnt to. Somebody joked to me that they were worried about his becoming a homosexual, a fate I was meant to save him from, although there was never the slightest doubt of his liking for women. It was not that they disapproved of homosexuality, since many of their friends were openly so, but they presumably wanted him to marry and have children. Ant said they took to me because of my French blood: they were devoted Francophiles and knew a great deal more about France than I did. It did not seem to matter to them that my feelings for Ant were strictly sisterly, and that he was keen on a great many different girls. In spite of this, Anne saw me as a daughterly companion, and both she and George set out to educate me, rather in the way a young woman in a Henry James story is taken up by cultivated and sophisticated mentors. I was invited to stay with them in their modest country house, Prawls.

So it came about that my years at Cambridge were also the epoch of my great friendship with the Barnes family, and I spent many weeks of the vacations at Prawls. It was a small eighteenth-century house, standing on an old cliff edge at the sea end of the Isle of Oxney, on the Kent–Sussex border: brick built, with sash windows and floors of brick and wood, cellars below and a loft above. When I was there, heat was provided by log fires, and chopping and stacking wood was a regular job for the men. Outside, an orchard and a vegetable garden, tremendous views across the marsh to the sea – you could see ships, and to George, a naval historian who had at one time hoped to become a naval officer, this was a constant source of interest and delight. He kept binoculars handy and took them up frequently to inspect passing vessels.

They had lived in a large London house until the war, when they acquired Prawls. George kept a flat in town, and Anne moved in before there was piped water or electricity, and at a time when civilian visitors were not allowed, since the coast was so near. German aircraft flew over unchallenged and invasion seemed likely. An unbeliever, she told me she had nevertheless gone into the village church to pray at the time of Dunkirk. She was alone at the house a great deal. George came for weekends when he could and Ant for holidays, first from his prep school, which he detested, as so many boys of his generation did, then from Eton, then Cambridge.

You reached the house down a rough lane and entered most easily by the back door – to get to the front you had to walk right round the house. I always slept in the guest room above the kitchen, which kept it warmer than the other rooms. Ant slept in the other back room – the coldest, he told me, reached up a narrow staircase – and next to the bathroom and lavatory. Anne's bedroom was at the front, as was George's, across the landing, which had elegant banisters. The front staircase was steep and straight, with a rope to help you up and down. Downstairs was a dining room with a great beamed fireplace: at the time of the flying bombs Anne and Ant had slept in that space for protection. On the other side of the entrance hall was the study or library, with bookshelves and an upright piano on which George played. Steve Haskell, put in there to sleep for the night, said it was so bitterly cold that he did not shut his eyes at all.

Prawls had been rented by George's half-sister Mary Hutchinson, from whom they took over the lease in 1939, later buying the freehold. She was a flamboyant figure, cousin of Lytton Strachey, married to lawyer St John Hutchinson (and mother of another splendid lawyer,

Jeremy Hutchinson). She lived as she chose and carried on an open affair with Clive Bell for many years, which her husband took calmly. Virginia Woolf disliked her; she was a friend of T. S. Eliot and Aldous Huxley, and a patron of the arts. This was the Bloomsbury connection. She came over for tea one day when I was there – at that time I had no idea who she was, and she was not explained to me.

I don't remember George making any comment on her or Lytton Strachey, but he was proud of his Barnes uncle Kenneth, director of RADA for many decades, and his aunts, the actresses Violet and Irene Vanbrugh. He owned a large, loose cashmere pullover that had once belonged to Irene, and which he sometimes allowed me to wear as a treat. He was a collector: of books, of pictures – John Piper watercolours of the Romney marsh, oil paintings of eighteenth-century ships – and of Wedgwood, for which he had a passion. Anne collected Victorian picture plates and gave me a liking for them. Country life had not come naturally to Anne. Her father had been master of Trinity Hall and she had been brought up comfortably in the Lodge and married straight from college. She told me that through the first twelve years of her marriage, until 1939, she had not known how to boil an egg or make a cup of tea. She and George had a cook and a maid in their London house. At Prawls she had taught herself to cook first with an oil stove and then an ESSE that burnt anthracite – and learnt to live as a countrywoman, supplied with rabbits by the farm labourers and persuading an ancient gardener to produce potatoes and lettuce. Piped water arrived during the war, and electricity soon after. A small refrigerator came next, which she distrusted – I noticed she preferred to keep food cool in the larder with a damp cover, or in the cellar. She gave us solid conventional meals, roasts and vegetables, salads, cheese and fruit, and was amused by my efforts to make summer puddings and other such frivolities. She always had a gin and tonic on the go as she cooked lunch and dinner, and took it to the table.

My father's house outside Paris was far more comfortable and convenient, and full of books too – but I was very happy to abandon it and spend vacations at Prawls whenever I was invited. Why? Because it laid a spell on me. It was partly the beauty of the landscape – sky, field and marsh, viewed at different seasons and times of day. It was also that living at close quarters with people so highly educated and privileged, who were also careless of appearances, of comfort and of the outward signs of status, was more interesting than anything I had known. It was not all plain living and high thinking at Prawls, because they enjoyed wine and opera at Glyndebourne, but, like my mother, they believed that education mattered more than money, and friendship more than fame. George went to church on Sunday, while Anne, like George Eliot, believed in duty without believing in God or immortality. She won my love and admiration by her goodness and good sense. George fascinated; she reassured.

He lived a compartmentalized life, whose boundaries were respected by Anne, who rarely went to London, and they seemed always to have kept a distance in their activities, often holidaying apart. Quite soon she took me as her companion for a trip to France, by train to Auxerre and on to Vézelay to see the great striped Romanesque church on its hilltop, where we met Ant, who was taking architectural photographs.

During the summer of 1952 I worked on the farm of neighbours, Clissold and Diana Tuely, to earn some pocket money while I stayed at Prawls. I helped with the harvest, and made friends with Fred Shingles, a farm labourer of few words and some charm who kept his family of six fed mostly on the rabbits he shot. He could have stepped from the pages of Thomas Hardy, whom I was beginning to read and love. At Prawls I cooked with Anne, and we went shopping together for cheese, Bath Olivers and other groceries, taking the bus to Rye, where her first stop was always the pub for a strengthening gin. We had to carry our bags of groceries to the bus and from the bus stop down the long lane to Prawls. There was still plenty of time to read, to go for walks, to sit and talk. Once, tired from walking in the fresh air, I fell asleep in an armchair and woke to find George in the room: 'How lucky to be young and fall asleep without looking terrible,' he said to me. I found his face, with its regular features and smooth skin, beautiful, and could not imagine him looking terrible; but I was pleased with his compliments. Ant's friends came down: Tony Mitchell expounded on the local churches and the Royal Military Canal, dug to keep Napoleon out; with Stephen Haskell we talked poetry and novels; Neal Ascherson inspired us with his knowledge and enthusiasm for history and politics. I talked about George Eliot and Thackeray. We played croquet, pushed a wheelbarrow about helpfully and took over the washing-up. Kath sent us parcels of French cheese for the dinner table.

At Prawls, in the garden, 1952

The Barneses knew a good deal about wine, and there were maps on the walls of the lavatory showing the names of French vineyards, and French wines in the cellar. George refused to believe that I, being half French, could be ignorant of wine, and persisted absurdly in asking my opinion of what we were drinking. All I knew was that claret was Bordeaux and came in a bottle with shoulders, to distinguish it from Burgundy, in smooth bottles. I decided I had better learn what I could from the maps. I studied and memorized the beautiful names, Margaux, Pouilly Fuissé,

Aloxe-Corton, Vosne-Romanée, Aligoté, Saint-Émilion, Bourgueil, Sancerre. The names chimed like bells and were easy to remember, but I still could not always be sure whether I was drinking claret or Burgundy. I was relieved when George gave up on my supposed expertise and brought out the red wine from Cyprus.

John Betjeman made one of his visits when I was there in the summer of 1953. He was an old friend of the family, and I enjoyed and admired his poetry and found him charming and funny in person. He talked and laughed, teased George, calling him 'The Commander' in tribute to his naval days at Dartmouth. He kept us all entertained, insisting on his dislike of abroad – the first time the Barneses took him to France he had fled. Knowing how much he enjoyed good food, Anne had acquired for this visit a pot of caviar, which she left in a bowl of ice in the centre of the dinner table while we had drinks outside in the evening sunshine. When she went in to check that everything was in order with the dinner, a cry came from the dining room, where she had discovered the pot of caviar, now empty, with a spoon beside it. John confessed at once: 'I couldn't resist! It was so tempting . . . when I saw it I simply had to eat it all.' Anne forgave him with one 'How could you, John!' He was as remorseful as a naughty boy caught out, played the part to perfection and got us all to laugh.

Another evening, when I was alone at Prawls with Anne and George, she went to bed early. George summoned me to sit at a table in front of a mirror and set down her jewel box. 'I've borrowed Anne's jewels and I'm going to put them on you,' he said, and proceeded to do so. Slowly he brought out necklaces and earrings, bracelets, pins, pearls, topazes, rubies, diamonds – I'd never seen her wearing any of them – and arranged them around my neck, my head, my wrists, considering the different effects as he did so, adjusting, taking away and adding the gleaming silver and gold, the starry or glittering stones. I could not speak, fascinated at seeing myself as a different person altogether, transformed into a girl I might read about in a novel, getting ready for a ball perhaps, preparing to dance, to meet her partners. So we sat for a while. Then it was time to put Anne's jewels back into their box. I had no idea what went on in George's head while he played this strange game.

There was a different day when George chose to talk to me in a consciously schoolmasterly way about sex. He explained to me that it was just like going to the lavatory – those were his exact words – simply a matter of getting rid of something. I didn't know enough to argue, or even to ask whether he meant getting rid of a feeling or of sperm, in which case his account presumably did not apply to women. In any case it seemed a bleak view to me. I knew so little about it, and I heard him out silently and did not tell him that I imagined sex more as an intense form of bodily and emotional communion.

Years later, when I was taking refuge with Anne during a bad moment in my first marriage, she gave me some advice about getting on with men by not showing too much feeling. 'Men don't like women to cry,' she said. 'It's better not to let them see you cry.' Again, it suggested to me a bleak view of human relations, and I felt Anne must have been put through a hard school; or it may have been standard English middle-class wisdom, to avoid intensity. She certainly saw her role, I believe, as looking after others – husband, son, friends – for which she maintained a calm and undemanding presence. She had wanted to write, made an attempt, been told by Dadie Rylands, who was devoted to her, that she did not have the gift and given up for good. The strengthening gin she drank and joked about may have been consolation against disappointments and sadnesses she would never talk about.

George talked well about books. He collected first editions of the great Victorian novelists – Dickens, Thackeray, George Eliot, all intensely interesting to me – and was enthusiastic about Henry James, whose work I was discovering. A copy of *The Europeans* arrived in the post at Newnham for me after a visit to Prawls, from George. He also urged me to read Melville's *Moby-Dick*, and I bought myself a small edition of that very long book, dating it January 1953 – I'd been at Prawls just before Christmas. I tried and failed to get on with it, but kept my copy for six decades and, when I finally read it in 2015, I found that George was right: it is a great and noble book, presenting many men of different faiths who live tolerantly together, different topics, chunks of history, distant seas, complex feelings and sensations. I thought of him as I read it and renewed my gratitude to him for his recommendation.

He was a music lover too, and he and Anne took me for my first visit to Glyndebourne, when Verdi's *Macbeth* was being televised in Carl Ebert's arresting production. I did not know the opera and was startled by the chorus of witches, but as it continued Verdi's music made the tears

pour down my face, as I told my father in a letter. Glyndebourne, with its lake, lawn and gardens set in the South
Downs, cast another lasting spell over me.

One day, when I was due to leave Prawls, George offered
me a lift to London. He drove me through Blackheath and
Greenwich for a quick lesson in architecture, to show me
the Observatory and the Naval College, and from there
into London and his flat in Marylebone. There he sat me
down, made me tea, served in a Wedgwood cup, and wan-
dered about the room with his cup in his hand. Then he put
it down and came slowly across to stand in front of me. He
leant towards me from above, and I saw his face getting
closer and closer to mine. I suddenly thought, 'It's an old
man's face –' and without saying anything I edged sideways, got to my feet and moved away from him. He said
nothing; I said nothing. I thanked him for the lift politely,
took my bag and left, finding my way to a bus stop. He had
done me no harm and I had learnt something about myself.
After that I was no longer dazzled by him.

A few years later, when I had left Cambridge and was
engaged to Nicholas Tomalin, he and I were invited to
Prawls for a weekend. George spent the two days humiliating Nick. He was working for the gossip column of the
Daily Express – it was his first job – so it was easy to sneer at
him. At every meal George put him down. He asked him
to get up on to the roof to dislodge a bird's nest blocking a
gutter, and Nick, who was unwisely wearing his good suit
for the weekend, did not enjoy having to scramble
across damp unstable ledges under his host's instructions. I
watched and saw what George was doing. Nick was young

and brash and had got the girl, and he was being punished for it. If I had stood for Isabel Archer, Nick was Caspar Goodwood or Gilbert Osmond, and George was making it clear that he saw I was making a mistake. Anne was cheerful and kind as ever throughout the visit.

I never saw George again. He did not find being in charge of television congenial and he left the BBC in 1956 to become principal of University College of North Staffordshire (Keele University). Anne moved to Staffordshire with him. They both missed Prawls, but he enlivened the life of the university, encouraging more music, and brought in artists, writers, scholars and politicians to talk to the students. I believe he hoped to move on in due course to Cambridge, as head of a college, where he and Anne would both be among friends. Fate ruled differently. He became ill while still at Keele and died in 1960, aged only fifty-six: a loss to the cultural life of the country. Anne remained a loved and tranquil presence in many lives, mine among them, and my friendship with Ant is now in its sixth decade. His parents gave me lessons in living and helped me to grow up, and I have always felt indebted to them, and grateful for what they showed me and gave me.

✿

I enjoyed my work at Cambridge, and when in the middle of my first year my tutor told me she expected me to get a First in my Prelims, the end-of-year examination, I was amazed and encouraged, and succeeded. 'I have a First like a penny in my pocket,' I told my father, and 'I am frightfully keen to get on to the Elizabethans and the Romantics and the Victorians.' I also told him, 'I don't want to be a woman don, they never write any interesting books' – rather harsh. I kept writing poetry and some of my poems were published in student magazines. They were wordy and inchoate. I did no sport, had no ambition to act and was altogether unenterprising. The Union, the debating society, was not open to women. At some point I joined the English Society. With my friends I talked a lot, walked and bicycled. I spent a good part of each vacation with my mother and the rest in Paris, where Cambridge friends came to see me and to stay. We moved from the large Gothic house in Ville-d'Avray to a smaller one romantically set on an island in the Seine at Bougival, and reputedly where La Dame aux camélias, Marguerite Gautier, had lived.

In Cambridge I was pursued briefly by the most glamorous, witty and sophisticated boy at King's, Mark Boxer, editor of the student magazine *Granta*. He told me that various dons at King's had advised him to have all the sex he could while he was young. Possibly they were hoping to interest him themselves, but Mark preferred girls. I found him charming and entertaining and admired his style and skill as an artist, but I resisted his determined pursuit and our flirtation ended. I wanted to make my own choices. After this I found a third-year boy at King's with curly golden hair and a seductive voice, whom I liked: James. He was reading classics and not famous or glamorous. We fell in love, and that year I spent too much of my time lovemaking when I should have been reading *Sir Gawain and the Green Knight*. I knew I was neglecting my studies, and I got only a 2.1 in my second year. But it was a sweet journey of discovery for both of us.* Years later, when he was married and a happy father, he told me he believed he would have been gay had he not met me. I have no idea if this could be true, but our inclinations are presumably set by early experiences that put us on one path and block others. He had been at Eton and had little experience of girls before we met, so perhaps I appeared at a moment when he was uncertain which way he was going. I broke off my love-affair with him, but we were friends till the end of his life.

In 1952 Mark Boxer was rusticated – a formal punishment banishing him from Cambridge for a period – for printing an allegedly blasphemous poem in *Granta*. We students rose up indignantly, and, after a dramatic mock-funeral for which we all gathered in the centre of town, he handed over editorial responsibilities to two second-year students reading English: one Karl Miller, already my friend, the other Nicholas Tomalin, then unknown to me. In 1953 they became co-editors. Karl and I were seeing a good deal of one another. There were times when he could be mysteriously playful, and one day when I was with him in his room at Downing he asked if I would let him put on my coat and scarf. Yes, I said uncertainly, and watched him dressing up as me, with my pale-blue silk headscarf tightly tied to conceal his hair. I can still see him as he did it. He went out and knocked at the door of his neighbour's room, using a funny voice to see if he could fool him that he was a

* I took charge of birth control, persuading a slightly surprised Dr Bevan, our college doctor, to prescribe a Dutch cap for me.

woman looking for Karl Miller's room. The trick worked, it seemed, and he came back laughing triumphantly. I laughed with him but I was baffled, with no idea why he had done it. Role-playing hardly fitted with what I saw in him.

During the vacation he wrote me a letter telling me that when we met again 'I will kiss your lips until they are black.' Donne could not have written so well, I thought. I wrote to my father about Karl: 'He is brilliant, attractive, classless, intolerably difficult and moody, Scottish, defensive, fair and bony. I was uncontrollably in love with him and he with me for a few days, now my native caution has reasserted itself, and he is jealous and possessive and secretive. I think we should drive each other mad . . . I should like children by Karl and I think he would like to marry me. At bottom I think we're all too young to be married and too old not to be.' This was true: we were certainly too young to commit ourselves. I was also frightened by the strength of my feelings for Karl. I thought he would overwhelm me. Things went wrong; a letter went astray. We both took up with others. Still, our loving friendship endured, and my admiration for him as editor, teacher, writer and father was always strong. We teased one another, we met and talked regularly throughout the decades, and some of our last conversations, sixty years later, were about poetry: Charlotte Mew, and Burns.

In my third year I made up my mind to devote myself to hard work. I met Nick that October as I was walking back to Newnham from the English faculty library, along the lane that takes you past Trinity Hall and King's College Chapel. A dark head appeared at one of the windows of Trinity Hall and a voice spoke my name to attract my attention and asked if I had any poems he might print in *Granta*. Then he told me his name, Nicholas Tomalin. I was too short-sighted to see him clearly, but I said I might have something for him to consider. Back at Newnham, I asked friends if they knew anything about him, and was told he was in the Union and the Labour Club, and that he was very good-looking.

When he called on me the next day at Newnham to collect a poem, I saw a tall young man with dark hair and a slight cast in one eye which gave an edge to his good looks. He was an original. He did not have the confidence of a conventional public schoolboy, but his hesitations and defensive jokes made him interesting, and he knew something about art and music. He had done his military service playing oboe and cymbals in an Air Force band that had taken him round the world.

We talked, filling in about our schools and families, and found we both had divorced parents. His mother, Beth, was Canadian and had taken him to Canada during the war to live with his grandfather, a professor of French at the University of Winnipeg. His father, Miles, had fought against Franco in the Spanish Civil War and was still a communist. Nick told me he had intended to become a doctor but failed in the practical, and his school, Bryanston, swiftly got him to switch to reading English and apply to Trinity Hall, where Miles had been. I knew about Bryanston and

Dancing with Nick

he knew about Dartington. Our families were artistic, academic, unconventional, left wing.

Would I like to go to a classical concert for which he happened to have tickets? Yes, I said. I had made up my mind to avoid love entanglements and stick to plain living and hard work in my last year, and Nick seemed quite safe. In January 1954 I told my father I was writing about T. S. Eliot, Dickens and Coleridge – adding firmly, 'I am still in love with <u>nobody</u>.'

I thought Nick could be my light-hearted friend. He didn't see it like that. We were young and carefree and somehow I allowed him into my bed one afternoon. I half pretended to myself it wasn't happening. Another letter to my father: 'I <u>like</u> Karl about as much as is possible . . . and we have the same values, and no pretences at all between us. But we both want other lovers.' And, again, 'Nick is very fetching but I think I've been fonder of the men I'm not in love with than anyone – Steve, and then Karl most of all.'

I was working hard, enjoying reading and writing essays for my demanding new tutor, Dorothea Krook,* and that was the foreground of my life. My serious friends did not approve of Nick, but flirting and occasionally making love with him did not seem dangerous. When he became president of the Union, I was pleased for him, and because he was a Labour president, but not interested beyond that. Then his parents came to Cambridge to hear a debate and he invited me to meet them. Both visibly adored Nick: Miles the stalwart communist son of a successful businessman, Beth still dashing in her forties. Each had a younger child by a current partner: Miles lived in Primrose Hill and wrote poetry and children's books; Beth was a psychiatric social worker and shared my liking for Henry James. They smiled on our friendship. So did my mother, enchanted by Nick from their first meeting. My father and Kath were also instantly charmed when they met him.

Nick was funny, quick, affectionate, generous, original, ambitious – and hard to resist. His tutor Graham Storey approved of me and encouraged our relationship. The day

---

* Dorothea – Doris – Krook (1920–89) was a philosopher, critic and teacher; born in Latvia, educated in South Africa, she arrived at Cambridge in 1946; moved to Israel in 1960. Sylvia Plath became her pupil at Newnham after me.

before the Tripos – our final exams – began, Graham drove us both out into the country to his parents' house. He told us work was forbidden, gave us lunch, took us for a walk and filled my arms with branches of white lilac from his parents' garden to take back to my rooms. It was a sort of blessing, and a generous one, since he was certainly fonder of Nick than of me.

I got a First. Noel Annan rang me with the news, and Nick sent me a jokey telegram he had devised with Miles:

> May age and distance be the worst
> Of differences that shall ensue
> Between a first class twenty-first
> And a mere two-two twenty-two.

No one at Newnham suggested I might go on to research, or made any suggestion about what I might do. I had thought about applying for the civil service and decided against, and the same with teaching. My father simply booked me into a secretarial training college in London. He had a fixed, old-fashioned view: a First was all very well, he said, but women needed shorthand and typing. I see now that I had become dull and without any particular ambition. I had imagined my future as a poet, but as I reached the end of university I realized that I did not have an original poetic voice and stopped writing: very sensibly, given that Sylvia Plath was about to arrive in Cambridge. But my decision left me with an emptiness in my life which has never quite been filled.

At the secretarial college in the Cromwell Road where I learnt shorthand and typing we were told we were being prepared to work for Conservative MPs – 'What about Labour MPs?' I enquired, raising a laugh but getting no answer. I learnt Pitman's and then scarcely needed it, but touch typing I've been grateful for all my life.

I found lodgings in Shepherd's Bush with the painter Roger Hilton and his violinist wife Ruth, who gave me a basement room hung with Roger's powerful abstract paintings, with a tiny cupboard in which I could cook. I paid a low rent and did some babysitting for their two small children, Rose and Matthew. I helped to organize a birthday party for Rose, which became a riotous success when Nick arrived through the basement window and narrowly avoided putting his shoes down in the carefully prepared jellies: clearly he impressed her enough to stay in her memory for half a century. I was happy there. Ruth told me about the Czech composer Janáček, whose opera *Jenůfa* she was rehearsing at the BBC – although it was written around 1900, it was not performed in England until the 1950s, and I could hear from what she played for me how sharp, dramatic, spellbinding his music was.

Nick decided to leave his parents' home in St John's Wood and find a place of his own – he was earning a princely £10 a week from the *Daily Express*. We heard that another artist, Patrick Heron, whose parents were friends of my mother, had a room to let round the corner from my lodgings, in Addison Avenue. Nick rang their bell. Patrick gave me his recollection of Nick: 'He blew into the room – to ask if we'd got a room to let – and within half a minute I said, "I know your voice . . .

you were on the radio a fortnight ago . . . you were the – president of the Cambridge Union!" "Yes! That was me!" he said, tapping himself on the chest, with a grin!' He moved in. Living so close, we were in and out of one another's rooms, and he sometimes drove me on the back of his two-stroke motorbike to Mrs Hoster's, my secretarial college, and collected me, causing a stir among the other girls as we flew off together.

I applied for a job at the BBC and was rejected. They informed me that they did not take women as general trainees, adding that they doubted I would be accepted even as a secretary. I took my father's advice and went for an interview in the publishing house of Heinemann, where he knew one of the directors. This was 1955. As I walked through an outer office to the room where Roland Gant, who would be my boss, was sitting, I passed another man. After fifteen minutes' talk with Roland, this man – he was James Michie, a poet – came silently in and put down a folded piece of paper on Roland's desk. I thought nothing of it, but later, when we were all friends, they told me that they had agreed that James would give me marks out of ten for my looks. I got seven, just enough to be offered the job as secretary/editorial assistant, at £5.10 a week.

I dealt with the piles of submissions that came in, some handwritten, sent them out to readers and was allowed to report on some myself. The most distinguished of the readers, Moira Lynd, came into the office with her handwritten reports – she had refused to learn typing – and I typed them out. After a while I was allotted some editorial tasks, but I was not a good copy editor and I worked mostly as another reader.

My relationship with Nick continued. We had fun together and I let myself be welcomed by his family, and saw that mine were happy with the situation. They made everything easy for us. In our post-war generation early marriages were the norm, and, although we thought we were making our own decisions, we were swimming with a powerful tide. Nick was lovable, a charming wooer, full of ideas and plans: I let myself be carried along, although I knew there was something missing. In the summer we set off together across the Channel on his two-stroke motorbike, along the old roads edged with poppies, through Abbeville and Amiens, then a night with my parents at Bougival on the Seine outside Paris, on through Sens and Auxerre, and still on south to Grenoble and the route Napoléon, ending in Antibes, where he had found us a cheap room in the house of an artist.

It was my first grown-up holiday. We were so innocent we worried that French landladies might be shocked at our sharing a room. I washed out my knickers at night and held them up to dry in the breeze as we drove off in the morning. We thought of ourselves as a Lawrentian couple, experimenting with love. D. H. Lawrence, so much admired by our generation at Cambridge, told us that sex was important and serious, not wrong or frivolous. We could have done with more practical advice. We must have had rows, but mostly we laughed, made love ineptly, sunbathed, swam, talked. At our ages – he was twenty-three to my twenty-one – there was always something new to talk about.

By then we were engaged. Our Cambridge friends were scattered. We were in no hurry to marry, but one day my landlord, Roger Hilton, looked through my basement window and saw that the gas fire had been left on by Nick, who had been there after I set off to my secretarial college. Roger was angry at the gas being wasted, said Nick had done it before, and gave me notice. Why don't we get married? asked Nick. At once his father helped him to find a small flat to rent near Primrose Hill.

I believed I was in love with him and he must have felt something similar. There were days when I felt that I was making a wrong choice: I remember thinking about it as I sat alone in a train. But I did nothing, said nothing. I should have had more courage. If he also had doubts, he made no sign either. We were such good friends, and we had good times together. Surely this was love? Soon it was impossible to stop the wedding – the dress, the cake, the invitations – to get rid of the flat we were moving into, reimagine the future, reject the affectionate support of our parents. At our wedding my director of studies, Enid Welsford, remarked that Nick was the handsomest bridegroom she had ever seen. But my most vivid memory of the reception is of Miles in his grey morning suit standing beside us and saying, 'You will be good to her, Nick, won't you?' with an unmistakable note of doubt in his voice.

6

Becoming a Tomalin

Nick and I had no money beyond our earnings, but we were able to furnish our rented flat with furniture, dinner plates and paintings that came from his late Tomalin grandfather, who had been a rich man, chairman of the Jaeger company founded by *his* father. The family history seemed to me as intriguing as the *Forsyte Saga* and the present generation strikingly glamorous and cosmopolitan. Jaeger was now headed by Nick's Uncle Humphrey, a charming businessman with left-leaning political views, a patron of the arts and a writer of plays in his spare time; his wife Bözsi was from Budapest and he had mastered Hungarian – no small task – in order to woo her. Humphrey and Bözsi made me welcome, often took us to the theatre and invited us to their country house in the Sussex Downs. Uncle Roger was an architect who had studied in Germany, spent the war in the navy braving the Atlantic, and married a serious Bostonian wife, Janet: we babysat for them, and Roger sometimes took me to hear Wagner. Nick's father, Miles, was the middle brother, a romantic, a poet and writer of children's books. He was in the process of separating from his second wife, Suaja, a fine fabric designer and a refugee from Germany with a personality so strong you had either to agree with her views or flee. Miles had a penchant for forceful women and a stubborn belief in the virtues of the Communist Party that made him oblivious to their crimes.

Last came Aunt Elizabeth – Liz – the odd one out in this handsome family. She was a remarkable woman, and she became my good and trusted friend. When I met her, she was newly returned from Switzerland, where she had lived most of her adult life. Nick described her to me as 'an old family retainer', apparently forgetting that she and his mother, Beth, had been friends since their boarding-school days – it was through her that his parents, Beth and Miles, met. Liz's story was this: she had been born in 1906 with a harelip and cleft palate and endured a childhood of painful plastic surgery, not yet well developed, and only partially successful. Sent to a finishing school in Switzerland, she attached herself to the woman principal, Madame Gorska, a musician, and refused to return to her family in England. Only on the death of Madame Gorska in 1950 did she leave Lausanne, and she was now settled in a thatched cottage in a Suffolk village, Great Waldingfield, near Long Melford. There she cultivated her garden next to the church – this is the country of magnificent churches built in the fifteenth century on the proceeds of the wool trade. She joined the Liberal Party, took in stray cats, played her piano and established herself as a pillar of village society and someone to be reckoned with. She loved Nick, whom she had known as a small child, and extended her affection to me. She lent us her cottage for our honeymoon and as soon as we had children she interested herself in them, becoming an

Elizabeth Tomalin – Aunt Eliza

honorary grandmother. Great Waldingfield became a second home for all of us.

❦

Sooner than planned, our first daughter, Josephine, was born, on her father's twenty-fifth birthday, 30 October 1956. Childbirth came absurdly easily to me and Nick was at my side, with an old schoolmate in charge of the delivery at University College Hospital. Her birth coincided with the Suez Crisis: on 31 October, Britain attacked the Egyptians to prevent them from taking control of the Suez Canal. At the same time, the Hungarians rose up against communist rule. I was in hospital during these terrific events – you were kept in for ten days then. Karl Miller came to visit me with his wife Jane, who told me she was pregnant with their first child, and I rejoiced with her. They were on their way to a protest in Trafalgar Square and I longed to go with them. There were furious debates between those in favour and those of us who thought Britain was in the wrong. The sister in charge of my ward stood at the end of my bed and gave her view: 'I know the Gippos,' she said, 'they won't fight.' But they did, and within days Britain, under pressure from the Americans and the United Nations, was forced to agree to a ceasefire. The Hungarian rebellion was put down by Soviet tanks after a heroic resistance in which thousands died and 200,000 fled to the West. While many British communists broke with the party, my father-in-law did not, asserting his belief in the justice of the Soviet response. The prime minister, Eden, resigned within months ('Hurrah!' I wrote in my diary) and Macmillan succeeded him.

Learning to look after a baby brought the usual problems, not only sleepless nights but the realization that the total dependence of a small creature means you are no longer free to go where you please or do as you like. My diary notes some low spirits. In spite of this, I was so enchanted with Josephine that I decided I must give her a companion as soon as possible. When I was pregnant

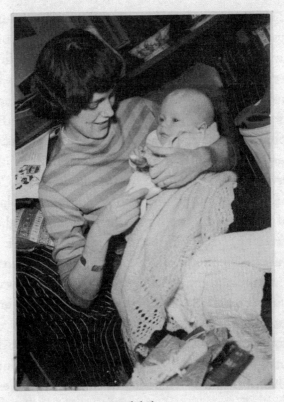

With baby Jo

again, we started looking for a house. We saw an adver-
tisement in the *Observer* for a four-storey one next to
Greenwich Park, on Croom's Hill. Nick rang the sellers
and was asked to call at 11. He expected other would-be
buyers to be there, so he arrived at 10.30, pretending to
have noted the time down wrongly. He confessed to the
vendors that he would need a week or two to raise the
£5,000 they were asking, and at the same time charmed
them so conclusively that they simply turned down the

poet Cecil Day Lewis and his wife Jill Balcon, who arrived at 11 to be told the house was already sold. Fortunately there was an even larger house on Croom's Hill for sale, which the Day Lewises bought. We managed to scrape together the money with loans from our families, and I put in my meagre earnings for translating a book by the French sociologist Maurice Halbwachs, *Esquisse d'une psychologie des classes sociales*, published in 1938 in France.*

Greenwich was unknown to me, cut off from Central London by mile on mile of shabby streets, and when we arrived we knew no one living there. Weather and house were freezing, but we had a small garden, with a peach tree and a sand pit for children. We also had two bath-rooms, a large nursery, a dining room and our first washing machine – top loaded – kindly left by our predecessors. On our first morning the milkman rang the bell and we saw he had brought his milk down Croom's Hill on a cart drawn by a small horse. I told Josephine we would take a lump of sugar out for the horse the next day. But when we went out with it, we found there was no horse – the milkman had switched to an electric van. We had caught the end of an era by a single day.

The Royal Naval College was at the bottom of the hill, and the Queen's House and the River Thames; and at the top stood the Observatory. Our bedroom looked out over Greenwich Park across the road. We found lodgers for our two top floors: Ronald Bryden, our Cambridge friend and

* Maurice Halbwachs (1877–1945) was a French sociologist who died in Buchenwald Concentration Camp in February 1945.

best man at our wedding, and the critic Nick Furbank. Ron went to work for the *Spectator* and presently brought me children's books to review: my first literary journalism. We found welcoming neighbours, as the middle classes moved into one after another of the large and neglected houses near the park, having discovered, like us, that they could buy for much less than they would have to pay in Central London. Soon we made friends among them: actors, stockbrokers, painters, doctors, Foreign Office families and advertising executives. Most of us had small children and were planning to have more. Years later Nick told me that when an invitation to dinner came from Anne Broadbent at Number 14 Croom's Hill, he decided, seeing her beautiful handwriting, that she would be the first of our neighbours he would have an affair with. It was not a good choice since she was a pious Roman Catholic, and a formidable person. He gave up his plan, we became close friends with her and her husband, and she teased Nick, putting him in his place by telling him his name 'Nicholas Tomalin' made him sound like the hero of a romantic novel for women.

Our second baby was due at the end of April. I made my plans to give birth at home, not wanting to leave Josephine and confident that it would be easy. Nick had been promoted to reporting and was often abroad. In early April he was in Paris covering the crisis over Algeria that preceded De Gaulle's return to power. While he was away, I had a haemorrhage and had to be moved speedily to the nearest hospital. I hated leaving Josephine but there was no choice, and Aunt Eliza immediately volunteered to come to Greenwich to look after her.

I found myself in St Alfege's, the old workhouse hospital. There I was told I had a *placenta praevia* – it means the placenta is blocking the birth canal – and a caesarean would almost certainly be necessary. I had to stay in hospital and in bed, because the new baby was small and needed time to grow larger. I was anxious about Josephine, who had never been separated from me before, and miserable without her. When I asked for her to be brought to visit me, a brisk woman doctor dismissed my worries – 'You shouldn't read John Bowlby,' she admonished me – and said Jo would not be allowed to visit me at all. Nick arrived back in England and tried to have me moved to a more humane hospital but failed.*

I was put into the longest ward I had ever seen. It was full from end to end with what seemed like very young local girls having babies, and ruled over by a Sister of military ferocity who refused to allow more than one visitor per bed during the very limited visiting times, 'or we'd have a football scrum in here'. Luckily for me she decided to take me under her wing and even allowed me to have a bath in the single bathroom serving the ward. I found she had assigned me to a bed next to a young woman strikingly different from any of the others. My neighbour was a beauty, cool, glamorous and silent, who spent her time polishing her nails, attending to her face and hair, and reading *Vogue* and other fashion magazines. She had no visitors and talked very little to anyone, but kindly offered to let me look at her magazines. We did not exchange any

---

* John Bowlby's ideas about the bad effects of separating small children from their accustomed carers were beginning to be published.

confidences. She showed no sign of being pregnant or having had a baby. After a few days she left, without a goodbye and alone. The Sister told me her story in a few words: she had given birth to a baby boy who was to be offered for adoption. St Alfege's, only a few miles from Central London, was so remote from the world to which the young mother belonged that she must have been confident nobody who mattered would know where she was or what was happening to her. It must have taken desperation and a steely will to do what she did. Whether she was tough, indifferent or masking her feelings, I pitied her deeply. I still think of her – the girl with *Vogue* and no baby.

After a week in the ward, doing my best to be calm while missing Josephine, I felt the onset of labour and told Sister. I was informed that I was to have a caesarian delivery, taken into an operating room and put on a narrow table, more like an ironing board than a bed. That was fine, but I knew the labour was advancing and told the junior doctor that I could feel my baby was going to be born very soon. 'We are waiting for the consultant,' he said; 'she'll be here soon.' She did not arrive and my new daughter slipped out without any trouble. She was very small and I saw that she had eyes as blue as periwinkles. I had hoped for, and expected, a second daughter and we named her Susanna, after the Susanna of Beaumarchais and Mozart, a name that carried our love and hopes for her.

Before I could even hold her, they carried her away to an incubator. I was taken back to the ward and given a blood transfusion. The effect was rather like having a large brandy. That was pleasant, but the rest was not, because for

With Jo and Susanna

two days the doctors would neither bring me Susanna nor let me go to see her. I became distressed. When I finally got to her, I found her strong and healthy, but weighing only five pounds, and needing me to feed her, which I did. I wanted to take her home; permission was refused. No reason was given. My GP, a sensible woman, came to see me in the hospital and said, 'Just tell them you are going home with her.' So I did. I was scolded for my irresponsibility and made to sign a document saying I was acting against the hospital doctors' orders. But Nick fetched me, we went home happily, and our two little daughters met. They were seventeen months apart in age and were always dear to one another.

This was the spring of 1958. Within weeks Nick heard that Lord Beaverbrook wanted him to take over a column in the *Express* called 'This is America'. It was promotion, and thrilling, and meant living in New York and travelling around America. Nick said yes, adding that he had a family to be sent out with him. Lord Beaverbrook said it would be much better for him to go alone, without encumbrances. Nick dug in his heels. He agreed to be flown out but said he would pay to bring wife and children on the cheapest crossing available. Off he went, we found tenants for our house, and I prepared to travel with the two little ones. We crossed on the *Flandre*, a French liner. Getting about a ship was difficult with a toddler and a baby-in-arms, but we managed for the six-day crossing and Nick was there to meet us in New York. We went first to an apartment on Long Island and then settled in a furnished one on the Upper West Side.

He had to be away a lot, travelling all over the US, and I knew no one in Manhattan and could not yet drive. Just occasionally we found a babysitter and got out to hear some jazz. I remember we were invited to a dinner where I first encountered transatlantic drinking habits: several dry Martinis of killing strength pressed hospitably on you by your kind hosts before the meal, then no wine with the meal. I realized it was a different civilization. The woman paediatrician I went to could not believe I wanted to breastfeed my baby and tried to persuade me to change her to 'formula' and bottles. I searched for another doctor and found an elderly German who was surprised and pleased to find a breastfeeding mother. Another cultural clash came at Jones Beach in the hot weather, when a cop came up and threatened me with arrest for letting Jo, not yet two years old, appear without a bathing suit. 'You may do that sort of thing in Europe – over here we don't allow it,' he said. On most days I took the children in a pram to Riverside Park, where I made one American friend, walking with her two small boys, and we kept each other company. As the days grew colder, very few other mothers appeared. Once, as I was walking alone with my girls, an American policeman stopped me and asked suspiciously what I was doing out in such cold weather. What could I say? I'm a British mother, I told him; we take our children out for walks in winter.

Another memory: in our twelfth-floor apartment, as I was alone with the children, the doorbell rang. I was not expecting anyone but I opened the door. An immensely tall and dignified black man was standing there and announced, 'I'm the exterminator.' Slightly at a loss, I replied, 'No, thank you', which was the wrong answer because he had come to deal with cockroaches, and we had plenty of them.

I had no work and should have been lonely, but I found my children such good company that it was a time of happiness, playing with them in our apartment, seeing their love for each other, telling them stories, reading to them and hearing Jo start to pick out letters. '*J* for Josephine, *E* for England,' she called out as we passed a sign in the street reading JESUS SAVES. Nick made a success of his column and we went for dinner with Lord Beaverbrook. To me, he was a Mephistophelean figure, but he was so pleased with Nick that he sent us all back to England first class on the *Queen Mary*, in incongruous luxury.

Leaving New York, 1959

Our house in Greenwich was waiting for us. We had saved so much money during our months in America that we decided to install oil-fired central heating. The firm that put it in had until then worked only on public buildings and they used great pipes, setting them snaking through our early-eighteenth-century walls that had never known such heat. We were back with friends, mostly from Cambridge and Oxford, many engaged in journalism, publishing and the arts: young graduates found jobs easily and salaries were rising. I was offered work as a reader for

Dinner on the *Queen Mary*

several English publishers. I remember recommending *To Kill a Mockingbird* – it was easy to see it would be popular – and, to Fredric Warburg, André Schwarz-Bart's *Le dernier des Justes*, a novel about the persecution of the Jews through history, culminating in the transportation of Jewish children from France to Auschwitz. Mr Warburg sighed as we discussed it, not I think over the story so much as its poor sale prospects, but he published the English translation, and it made its mark. Nick was appointed 'William Hickey', the *Express*'s gossip columnist, which he found uncongenial. I thought he deserved better. It felt as though there was a pause in our lives – what was coming next? The Sixties.

7

The Sixties

The Sixties: a memory comes to me of my father, then in his sixties himself, visiting us from France, standing beside me on a London pavement on the first day of his stay, stock-still but for his head, which was turning slowly as he saw with incredulous eyes girls walking past wearing skirts so short they only just skimmed their knickers. He was astonished, shocked at first, and then delighted.

I, his respectable married daughter, was shortening my skirts too, and buying white boots, and dancing the Twist. I was also working, of course, and busy as a mother with a house to run. There were a great many strands to my life in the Sixties: two more children born, one bringing sorrow, the other joy; a house move; schools for our daughters; new jobs for Nick and me; many new friends; holidays in France. There were parties and dances, visits to Glyndebourne, the Coliseum and Covent Garden, because opera had cast its spell over me and I had made up my mind that I was going to hear all I could. And our marriage was in trouble. We were parents, but in many respects we were hardly grown up ourselves.

After Susanna's birth I had planned to wait for several years before having any more children, but soon after we returned from America I found myself pregnant again. The unplanned baby arrived in March 1960, a boy, Daniel. He was born with problems, not foreseen and never explained to me. The doctors who came to my hospital room were unhappy but unable to account for what had happened. My baby was brought to me as a small bundle in white wrappings, with only his head visible, his dark eyes and dark hair. I wanted him to fight for his life. I breastfed him, spoke to him and sang to him. Nick brought Jo and Susanna to visit me and they saw the little bundle. On the fourth or fifth day a nurse decided, against doctors' orders, to unwrap him and show me how badly his body was misshapen. I knew she was right to do this – she was a brave Australian girl who understood that I had to see my baby for myself. His body was covered in growths or swellings that made it unlikely he could live a normal life. Now I had seen for myself, and still nobody was able to suggest what might have gone wrong. After two weeks I was encouraged to go home to my girls, and Danny was moved to the children's ward, where I came each day to visit him. I thought he was putting on weight but it was only swelling, a bad sign. I kept expressing milk for him and taking it in to the hospital, and we took the girls to see him several more times, over the Easter weekend. After that he was put in an oxygen tent, and on 21 April he died. Jo told me later she and Su had not understood what was happening at all: not surprisingly, since they were only three and two years old.

I was given his body to hold, and it seemed the coldest thing I had ever felt. I dressed him in a white embroidered christening gown and we buried him in Suffolk, in the graveyard of the church next to Aunt Elizabeth's cottage. She remained constant in her support. We put up a headstone and planted spring flowers, and for months I grieved. I am sure Nick did too. As a family we were in shock. Doctors told us there was no reason to think the tragedy would be repeated. I decided I must have another baby at once if I were not to lose my nerve. I said to myself, it's like falling off a horse: you must not let it defeat you but get back up there and ride on. Very soon I was pregnant again.

In August, Nick moved to edit the 'Londoner's Diary' on the *Evening Standard* – the editor, Charles Wintour, had asked Beaverbrook to allow this transfer from its sister paper, the *Express*.* Charles was a severe intellectual who, against the odds, made a success of editing a popular paper, and he became a friend, respected by both of us. I found him intimidating and admired him. The Diary put Nick in charge of a group of smart young men and women, aspiring journalists, who knew how to charm, how to have fun and how to be ruthless. Nick, still in his twenties and destined to go far, made himself part of the team, and they all set out to enjoy themselves, at work and at play. Nick was handsome, entertaining and greatly liked by his colleagues, and he found himself surrounded by attractive young women. A wife and family became an encumbrance. He set off on new adventures.

---

* Charles Wintour (1917–99) was a formidable newspaper editor who ran his papers with military discipline – he had fought in the war – while discovering and encouraging many adventurous and gifted young writers. Two of his children, Anna and Patrick, followed him into journalism, she to edit American *Vogue*, he to write for the *Guardian* in England.

The contrast between office life in Fleet Street and domestic life in Greenwich was sharp. What was I doing? Learning to drive. Preparing for my fourth baby in five years. Reading typescripts for Secker & Warburg, Weidenfeld, Heinemann. Entertaining visitors – Anne Barnes, now widowed, came to stay, and my old schoolfriend Auriol. I gardened, entered into the world of children's tea parties, and had dinners with neighbours. A group of us found an excellent nursery school not far away and took it in turns to deliver and fetch our four-year-olds. We took them on the bus, and one day as I chatted with the driver before getting them all off, he said, 'You're a social worker, aren't you?' 'What makes you think that?' 'Well, because you talk to the children,' he answered.

I saw *Billy Liar*, *La Dolce Vita* and Pinter's *The Caretaker*, and in the last month of my pregnancy I heard Klemperer conduct *Fidelio*, my first experience of Beethoven's account of guilt, suffering and the arrival of hope. My third daughter, Emily, was born on 21 March 1961, a year to the day after Daniel. She was a perfect baby, energetic and adventurous from the start. There was another wonder at home when I realized that our three-year-old, Susanna, had learnt to read unaided – she had simply picked it up as her elder sister mastered the skill.

When I went for my post-natal, my doctor, having pronounced me fit, took up a packet from his desk, leant forward, smiled and said, 'You might like to try this new form of contraception – it's a pill you take. Very easy to use.' Yes, I said without a moment of hesitation, yes, thank you, how wonderful. No more messing about with Dutch caps, no more worries. A new era had arrived, a liberation for women. We all saw very quickly that this would not only take away anxiety and allow spontaneity; it would also change the balance of power between the sexes.

But the new era was not what I expected. Suddenly I found myself living through the most banal of stories, as the neglected wife of a faithless husband. Nick had fallen in love with one of his office beauties. He told me later that she could look across a table adoringly like no one else. My role now was as the boring suburban wife with too many children who held him back. The diaries I kept then tell me how I reacted. One day I advised myself, 'Don't be jealous, don't be frightened, don't disapprove.' After a party I wrote, 'I think he likes projecting an image of himself as the bold, sexy, philandering journalist, which other people take at face value and I find appalling.' When he was at home he could be 'N furious, black', as one diary entry noted. His love-affair did not go as he hoped: for him it was serious, but she wanted only a light romance, and had a queue of admirers. As he fought to keep her, his moods swung from joy to jealousy. He disappeared for weekends with the car, and often stayed out all night. He had many London friends to console him and entertain him. Our life together was disintegrating. I struggled not to fall into depression.

It seemed sensible to look for a real job and be ready to earn my own living. Cecil Day Lewis, our Greenwich neighbour, offered me work at Chatto, which I would have liked to accept, but at the same time another publisher, Hutchinson, proposed twice the money for half the work. I felt I had to go for that. While I was making up my mind, Nick asked

me to meet him in a bar in London, where he announced
formally that he was going to leave me. 'I don't think he
will,' I wrote in my diary, adding, 'I feel peculiar & unstable
but better – things could be worse – must fight . . .' I took
the Hutchinson job, which meant a day a week in their London office and the rest of my work at home, an ideal
arrangement for a mother of small children. At this point
Nick did leave home, saying it was for good. I had no idea
where he had gone, but was told by his friend and fellow
journalist Ron Hall that he was in Venice with yet another
girl. I had a letter from Nick as he left for this trip saying he
was short of money, asking me to economize and saying he
was planning to sell our house. This threat alarmed me. I
realized I should begin to consider divorce, and wrote in my
diary, 'I shall never never live with Nick again, never.' It
might have been sensible to have stuck to that plan.

The collapse of our marriage was not all his fault: we
were too young to marry, and I was not the right wife for
him. I was too serious, too critical. I was charmed by him
but I did not adore him, and he fell in love with girls who
either did adore him or knew how to convey adoration. He
was generous, adventurous, witty, brave, good at making
friends and giving parties, and he was admired and greatly
liked, even loved, by his fellow journalists. I had been
shaken by the death of our baby son, I was absorbed in our
children, I saw him changing into an almost unrecogniz-
able person and had no idea how to respond.

A friend with a flat standing empty in Duke Street
offered it to me for a week, saying it would give me a
chance to get away from my problems. He added, 'You

must promise me not to commit suicide in my flat.' I assured him I had no intention of doing so. I took the children to stay with ever welcoming Aunt Eliza in the country for the week, I rested, went to galleries and was asked out to dinner by old boyfriends. With this regime my spirits revived. When my Cambridge tutor Doris Krook arrived in London, she insisted that Nick's behaviour was so banal that he could not be taken seriously. I began to think I could manage on my own and even to enjoy myself. I fetched my daughters home and prepared for a different future.

At this point Nick began to woo me again. The children rejoiced to see Daddy, although he did not yet move in with us. But I believed in the importance of the family, and remembered how both Nick and I, children of broken homes, had wanted six children. Banal as he might be, he was a charmer, and I let myself be charmed. My diary notes dancing at the Establishment, Peter Cook's newly opened club for satire and music in Greek Street. Nick was an energetic dancer – so was I – and the Twist had just arrived. We danced the Charleston too – we both loved dancing and danced half the night. Things got better between us. We saw *Jules et Jim* together, and *Beyond the Fringe*. He escorted me to a party given by Mary Quant. I wrote in my diary, 'I think Nick will destroy me,' but I also went with him to inspect a house for sale near Regent's Park. I was eager to move after all the unhappiness at Greenwich. He fell ill with flu and I agreed that he had to come home to be nursed. Recovering, he booked a trip for us both to France without asking me, so that we could visit my father to show off our restored harmony. Later he let me read the letter my father had sent him, in which he told Nick that he had not been able to live with my mother and was not surprised that Nick could not live with me. Just as well I did not see it at the time. I needed confidence to establish life with Nick again.

⚜

He left the *Standard* and went to edit *Town*, a magazine owned by Michael Heseltine and Clive Labovitch. It was a glamorous job, making what had been a men's tailoring magazine into a glossy guide to smart London living. Nick did it well. He had a feeling for style and made it stylish. He got Gerald Scarfe and Michael Heath to do cartoons, and photographers Don McCullin, Terence Donovan and David Bailey contributed striking pictures. They all worked hard, but the financial situation was precarious, the books so tight that Nick told me he was regularly instructed to delay sending cheques to contributors – 'Unfortunate hold-up, coming next month,' he had to say. He learnt about editing and had a good time too, flying off to Le Touquet for a day photographing models, and getting his suits made by the best Savile Row tailors. The magazine looked good, and it wasn't all about clothes and girls: one issue had a picture of Harold Macmillan on the cover, with an article by Heseltine inside.

Michael Heseltine himself came to dine with us in Greenwich one evening, arriving with his large Alsatian dog. He said the dog should be kept out of the dining room during dinner – why not put him upstairs in the nursery to amuse the children? So we did. At the end of the evening we found children and dog asleep and Michael departed peacefully with his well-behaved pet. The next morning he arrived at work white-faced: the dog had gone mad, he told Nick, and he had been obliged to have him put down at once. Either it had been a narrow escape for our daughters or they had cast a spell on the dog, we said, making a joke of it. I liked Michael and believe he would have made a good prime minister.

World politics were in a dangerous phase, and in October 1962 came the Cuban Missile Crisis. We held our breaths as Khrushchev and Kennedy appeared to be ready to consider nuclear attacks. Nick told me to put food and water in our cellars in Greenwich. I refused. I knew I would rather die with the children on the surface than slowly underground. And I did not think nuclear bombs were going to be dropped on us. The crisis passed.

⁂

In December 1962 we started looking for a London house. As well as escaping the unhappiness of the Greenwich time, I was eager to move because I knew I would not always be able to work at home, and realized we would see little of our children if we were commuting. We favoured NW1, where we had started our marriage. Nick had ambitions to live in Park Village West, but, after being generously entertained there by Woodrow Wyatt, who explained that it was cheaper to eat off gold plate than china, we realized it was beyond our means. Gloucester Crescent round the corner was more affordable, and we were told that Number 57 was for sale. I first noticed the house on a cold day in January 1963. I had walked past it earlier often enough, when I lived in Regent's Park Road, seeing it simply as part of a terrace, and dismissed the whole Crescent as a dull and gloomy street. Almost all the houses had been in multiple occupancy, with several families crammed into each. Since then a smart businessman had acquired the leases and got rid of most of the tenants, and now they were on the market, solid mid-Victorian terraced houses on five floors, with narrow walled gardens at the back, and trees in many of the front yards.

Nick's father, Miles, lived nearby and he urged us to look at them quickly, because they were selling fast. Number 57 looked pretty grim, almost derelict, with Yale locks on most of the inside doors and a warren of small dark rooms in the basement. Then a friend, Juliet Roeber, newly installed a few doors along, invited us to tea and showed us how attractive she had made her house, which encouraged us to think we might be able to do something with 57. We met the artist David Gentleman, who also lived in the Crescent with his wife Rosalind and daughter Fenella, and we heard that Jonathan and Rachel Miller were about to move into 63: I had known him since Cambridge, and they had been neighbours in Regent's Park Road. Ursula Vaughan Williams, the composer's widow, was another resident, and also several good architects. It seemed that an interesting community was establishing itself.

We discovered that no two houses were quite the same, having in common only the London characteristic of narrowness and height – birdcages, the French called them.

57 Gloucester Crescent from a watercolour by David Gentleman

You had to be prepared to spend your life running up and down flights of stairs, from the kitchen in the basement to the drawing room above, to best bedrooms, up again to children's bedrooms, up yet again to the airy attic. I thought about what the houses must have been like in the 1840s, when Gloucester Crescent and Regent's Park Terrace alongside it were built: then servants inhabited the basements and attics, and toiled up and down the stairs from morning to night with water, clean and dirty, coal and ashes, food and waste, for their middle-class masters and mistresses living on the three main floors. And I appreciated how well the houses adapted to our entirely different style of living.

We made up our minds to buy, put our house in

Greenwich on the market and sold it for £15,000, enough
to pay for the Gloucester Crescent house – £8,500 – and all
the work we wanted done on it. We invited a couple of
young architects, man and wife, Henry and Catherine
Matthews, to work for us. 'Do you hang much game?' was
Henry's first question to me when planning the kitchen,
which rather threw me, as I had to confess I had never hung
any, and wondered if I ever would. In April we laid a cere-
monial brick as work started. Our worst mistake was that
we went along with Henry's suggestion that he should
hire direct labour rather than a building firm. It was
cheaper in theory, but unreliable in practice: directly hired
men just walked away from the work when they felt like it,
and this happened dismayingly often. Despite this draw-
back, Henry and Catherine made marvels, transforming
the muddle of dark little rooms in the basement into one
great space with windows across each end, a glass door into
the garden, a tiled floor and new wooden staircase up to
the landing. We had a lot of stainless steel, and fashionable
white Formica on our worktops. I put an upright piano
against a wall and bookshelves in the recesses – some for
cookery books, more for others and especially my 1911
Encyclopedia Britannica – one of my eccentricities is that I
like to be able to consult it at mealtimes, with or without the children. At the garden end we set a sofa under
the window, next to a wooden sill wide enough for the
children to pile on to and around. The room was to be
kitchen, dining room and a place for family life and friends.
There was a larder with a dark space behind it for wine – it
was the old coal store. And we chose some terrible orange

hanging lights which we had to take out again after a few weeks.

We made mistakes, but we enjoyed ourselves turning a sad, neglected building into a cheerful and comfortable house. New boilers, new bathrooms, wooden floors sanded and polished, almost all walls white, except the drawing room, which was hung with amber-coloured silk – that was Nick's idea. Mine was to have the staircase papered from top to bottom with William Morris's leafy green wall-paper, then sold cheaply: it was my attempt to bring the country into our urban house. The morning sun came into our bedroom, the evening at the back and on the stairs, through the tall sash windows. The children had the second floor to themselves. From the back windows you looked straight out at a gigantic plane tree just beyond our garden wall: tree men we saw working on it told us they could see all Central London from its summit.

We went over regularly from Greenwich to oversee progress. Forgetting our key once, we dropped our stalwart and adventurous little Emily through the coal hole and she ran round and upstairs confidently to let us in. The lime trees in our front garden put out their fresh leaves; the garden at the back, which was a simple slope down to the house, with brick walls on each side, contained nothing but rough grass, runner beans and oyster shells which must have piled up over many decades, legacies of the previous inhabitants. I made plans to terrace it in three levels. By July things were looking good enough for us to believe we might soon move in. One day, as we were arriving, a well-dressed and cheerful woman came out of the house next door to greet us, saying, 'We're not the sort of people who live in Camden – we're really Kensington people – but here we are, do come and have a drink with us . . .' This was Tessa, an American computer programmer married to an English company lawyer, with children of an age with ours, and we became very good friends. On the other side was Barrie, an old-time resident, equally welcoming, with no one but a tottering ancient mother upstairs. His garden was an unused wilderness and he invited our children to make use of it, an offer they took up enthusiastically. Soon they were playing with other neighbours' children, running along the walls between the gardens and helping us to get to know everyone. Jo reminds me that they took to sleeping in the garden when the weather was hot.

Nick had been offered a job on the *Sunday Times*, writing the 'Atticus' column, and was to start in September. He was making his name as a columnist and broadcaster. I was talking to Tom Maschler about working at the publishers Jonathan Cape as a reader, after Nick had introduced me to him on the roof of the Festival Hall during a concert interval. Josephine and Susanna were starting at South Hampstead School. I had taken Susanna from Greenwich to be interviewed there when she was still so small that I held her hand for safety on the journey by train and Underground. She was perfectly self-possessed as she was led away into another room by an unknown teacher, and they both looked pleased when they reappeared. The school wrote offering her a place, saying she was ready for second-year schooling but they had a policy of keeping children in their own age group and would therefore start her in the first year. Jo went into the third year.

We found that there was a group of girls going from the Crescent and the Terrace, and we could join the car pool.

We packed up our Greenwich house and on 15 August 1963 we moved. Number 57 Gloucester Crescent, London NW1, became my address for the next forty years. The day after we moved in I saw Tom Maschler at Cape in Bedford Square, and on the 19th I started work there, three days a week as a reader.

⚜

As soon as we started living in Gloucester Crescent, I saw that it was border country. In one direction we were ten minutes from Regent's Park, with its green expanses, trees, lake and flowers, presided over by elegant Nash terraces. The Zoo, the Canal and Primrose Hill were all close, with sights of giraffes, boats, bicycles on the towing path and slopes where the children could enjoy rolling on the grass and sledging when snow came. My plan to bring primroses back to the hill never materialized, but I still hope it will be done one day. There were days when we were woken early in the morning by the rhythmical clattering of hooves, as the Royal Horse Guards exercised from their base in the nearby Albany Street barracks. I never failed to jump out of bed to gaze at this fine anachronistic sight.

On the other side of the border, down Inverness Street, you were quickly in what I called Dostoevsky land, with Camden Town Underground Station at its heart. During my first weeks I saw two men fighting with knives on the pavement outside the station. The crowds were rough, the streets and the air were dirty, the traffic was dense and difficult to negotiate – in 1961 Tottenham Court Road was made one-way heading north and the traffic thundered faster. A block away from the Crescent loomed a large building, Arlington House, the last and largest of the London houses for homeless men, built by Lord Rowton and opened in 1905. Since then it had been a refuge chiefly for Irish labouring men who had lost the will or the means to return to their homes in Ireland. Some of them were no doubt our direct labourers on the house. Most of them were drinkers. They were a permanent part of our landscape, standing about in the street, in and out of the pubs. They looked after one another, and they did no harm to anyone else; and one morning, when I was hurrying too fast so that I tripped and fell on the pavement, several of them came quickly to help me with the greatest kindness. They picked me up and made sure I was all right. I saw them with different eyes after that, and became interested in Arlington House, where, I learnt, the poet Patrick Kavanagh had stayed in the 1930s, and later Brendan Behan.

There were some hopeless shops – the sad old Co-op at the corner was one – but good ones too, a Greek – or was it Turkish? – grocer, also a reliable Irish one for bacon, a lovely family-run Italian restaurant, the Lucca, run by Mamma and Papa and their two sons; and a fine bookshop with an Austrian-born manager. There was a pet shop, from which the children brought home a very small ginger kitten taken from its mother too young: Jo fed him devotedly with milk from a dropper, and soon he flourished. The fruit and vegetable market in Inverness Street was picturesque and handy.

Another stall, standing apart on the corner of the Crescent, belonged to Reg, who dealt in small goods from house clearances. We tried to get there early in the day to find treasures, and sometimes did, a Wedgwood teapot, Victorian dishes, a shining well-shaped glass.

In those days we parked our car outside the house and Nick rarely bothered to lock it. One morning, both of us late for appointments, we hurried out of the house and into the front seats, and as Nick started the engine a terrifying figure rose up behind us and I gave a small scream, answered with the words, 'God bless you, sir, God bless you, madam, God bless you both – I was – er – I was just taking a nap in your car,' as he scrambled to open the back door and get out, and Nick put his foot on the brake. Poor old man, unable to afford even Arlington House. Another came begging to the door and I made him a good beef sandwich, which plainly disappointed him.

We told our friends George and Diana Melly about another house for sale beyond Tessa's, and they moved in soon after us. George was an adorable man of many gifts – as a musician, as a connoisseur, as a writer – and he and Diana were good neighbours and enlivened the street with their joie de vivre. In the middle of their ground-floor front window, facing outwards to cheer the passers-by, he hung his Magritte painting, one of the series showing a much larger than life penis with a face and hair. Occasionally you saw a startled response from a pedestrian, but the neighbours took it in their stride. One evening, quite late, as I was going to bed and Nick was out, George rang the bell and asked if he could bring a party of friends in to our downstairs room, where we had our upright piano. Yes, I said, of course, and at once a crowd materialized, in high spirits and carrying bottles. They filled the room quickly. There was music and dancing, and George put on his famous act of impersonation, 'Man, Woman, Bull-dog', which involved going out into the back garden, removing all his clothes and reappearing three times in different poses, the final one backwards on all fours with a good view of his testicles. There was an innocence to George's outrageousness: it gave him great pleasure and entertained his friends. Soon after this Nick arrived home, expecting to tiptoe in without waking me, to find the house shaking with music, laughter and thumping feet.

One of the good things about the Crescent was that you could walk into Central London across the park, or back from the theatre in the evening if you were feeling energetic. Many actors had lived here in the nineteenth century for this reason, and when I researched the lives of actresses later, I noticed that they expected to walk home, often long distances, after their shows. The most famous past inhabitant was Catherine Dickens, who moved into Number 70, the pretty house on the corner, after her separation from her errant husband Charles in 1858, and remained there until her death in 1879. With the coming of the railways – Euston, King's Cross, St Pancras – the air of Camden grew foul and the district declined steadily as the middle classes moved out to the suburbs. Family homes turned into cheap lodging houses. Victor Pritchett, who moved into a house in Regent's Park Terrace in 1956, assured us that there were two brothels there at that time. If he was right, things changed fast, and when we arrived there was a celebrated philosopher, Freddie Ayer, with his clever and glamorous

American wife, Dee Wells, at Number 10, Regent's Park Terrace, and presently another brilliant couple, Claus and Mary Moser, arrived at Number 3.

Our new life arranged itself well. I found my work as a reader at Cape entertaining, my children made friends among the neighbours and at South Hampstead School, Emily started at a nursery school across the road. Nick started at the *Sunday Times* in September and set his own mark on the 'Atticus' column. Living in Central London pleased us all and our circle of friends was enlarged. Among our neighbours, Colin and Anna Haycraft were great publishers and party-givers, filling their house with philosophers, historians, poets and novelists. David Gentleman became a dear and admired friend. Beryl Bainbridge arrived, and a few years later Alan Bennett.

❦

The Sixties brought beautiful clothes, some inspired by Courrèges, many designed by Mary Quant. I smartened myself up: I find in my diary 'Bought boots!' and 'Had my fringe straightened.' My friend Daphne Michie introduced me to a Hungarian dressmaker who made me exactly the clothes I wanted. I chose the materials, we conferred, and she made them up into skimpy cotton jackets in clear colours, short skirts, sleeveless shifts, white dresses and summer suits that I loved wearing. I still have and wear some of them fifty years later.

In 1963 came the Profumo Affair, when sexual scandal filled the newspapers for months. The public followed the coverage with more amused interest than disapproval, especially when grandees were made to look silly and Mandy Rice-Davies made her famous response to being told in court that Lord Astor denied sleeping with her: 'Well, he would, wouldn't he?' The moral climate was changing fast. People were readier to accept that truth was not the prerogative of the rich and powerful. A married woman friend of great respectability was heard to say, 'I rather envy Christine Keeler.' The swimming party at Cliveden did seem the sort of thing we might all enjoy.

My behaviour changed too. I could say that Nick's carryings on over the past few years had had their effect, but it may be that I simply moved with the times. What happened was that I was wooed by a clever and likeable journalist, and when I saw my thirtieth birthday approaching, I decided almost on the spur of the moment that, as *une femme de trente ans*, I might lunch with an admirer and embark on an affair. I was not in love and had no intention of going any further than a few afternoon assignations. He was charming and we both enjoyed having a secret. I refused his pressing invitations to go away for a weekend. No one would know, no harm would be done to the children. But if you are a gossip columnist people bring you stories. Someone must have heard something and carried word to Nick. I was standing alone in the kitchen one evening when he came in and advanced angrily with clenched fists raised to punch me in the face. I ducked. His blow broke the wooden bar that held the roller towel on the larder door, where I was standing – I have kept it ever since as a reminder.

I thought at once, goodness, *The Marriage of Figaro* gets it exactly right: it's fine for the Count to have affairs and tell lies,

1960s

but he will not allow the Countess any equivalent freedom. The next thing that happened was that Nick tried to run over my discreet lover, luckily without success. Because my heart was not involved, I got through this easily enough and even gained in confidence. My lover forgave me for refusing to commit myself to him, quickly consoled himself with someone else, and a good friendship remained between us. After this I had to expect violence from Nick when he was angry.

Yet those early days in Gloucester Crescent were full of sunshine and convivial occasions as I look back. One memorable party was given for a book of essays published in October 1963: it was about the 1940s and called *The Age of Austerity*. The essays, edited by Michael Sissons and Philip French, were by some of the cleverest young journalists then writing, among them John Gross, Godfrey Hodgson, Michael Frayn, Anthony Howard, David Leitch, David Watt, David Hughes, Peter Jenkins. I knew and admired most of them. An older political journalist, Henry Fairlie, was invited to the launch party and in a characteristically extravagant gesture he insisted on taking a group of us on to dinner at the Ritz. Fairlie was a man known for his charm, wit and brilliance, inventor of the term 'the Establishment' – meaning those who wield power socially as well as politically – and we were all in thrall to his conversation. He was also an alcoholic, up to his eyes in debt, with a chaotic life. After I got home, in the small hours, the telephone rang: it was Fairlie, with an impassioned declaration of love. I believe this was something he went in for often, and it was at once absurd, meaningless and beautifully done, like a golden shower from a minor god. No response was necessary and I never met him again – he moved to America.

When I started work as an in-house reader at Cape, William Plomer had just retired. I felt it an honour to follow him, and hoped I could keep up his standards.* I was given a fine

---

* William Plomer (1903–73), poet and novelist, editor of *Kilvert's Diary* and librettist of Britten's *Gloriana*, followed Edward Garnett as chief reader for Jonathan Cape.

light and airy office next to my boss, Maschler, with a hatch
between us for quick consultations. Tom was a dashing figure who took over an old-fashioned firm, fired by ambition
to make his mark in publishing. He succeeded triumphantly.
He had a good, if not infallible, eye for a bestseller, and a
flair for promoting his books that few other publishers
could match. He and I got on well together and I found him
easy to work with, but some aspects of his view of life baffled me: he told me, for instance, that he had decided he
would sleep with a hundred women before he got married.
I decided he must be less at ease in personal relations than
working ones. The reps, who went round selling the books
we published, were not entirely convinced by Tom at first:
he organized sales conferences like theatrical events, making sure everyone was seated in the board room before he
made his entrance, sweeping in as a powerful and glamorous figure who commanded full attention. I remember him
telling the reps that he had a book that was guaranteed to
outsell all the others, producing a small volume called *In His
Own Write* – this was early in 1964 and it was by John
Lennon. The reps were not impressed. Of course it became
the most desired book of the year, and after that Tom could
do no wrong with his reps.

Cape was a busy place under Tom and his fellow director, Graham Greene, the novelist's nephew. They were
not afraid to publish unusual books and encouraged journalists to take on the challenge of full-length works. They
commissioned a study of Harold Wilson, the new leader of
the Labour Party following the death of Hugh Gaitskell,
from Tony Howard, political correspondent of the *New*

Statesman, and Richard – Dick – West, who had just left the *Guardian*. It was to be called *The Making of the Prime Minister* and published as soon as possible after the election of October 1964, which Labour won with a majority of only four seats. We had the final manuscript in November, full of fly-on-the-wall observations and acute insights, and highly entertaining; and it appeared in January. Dick West had already written another good small book attacking the growing power of public relations people. It was called *P.R. The Fifth Estate*, and narrated the founding in 1961 of 'the Society for the Discouragement of Public Relations' by Michael Frayn (described as looking like 'a good-natured eagle'), with the support of Robert Robinson, Nicholas Tomalin, Cyril Ray, Malcolm Muggeridge, Marghanita Laski and others. I naturally knew about this, admired their stance and was encouraged by Nick to attend one of their lunches. I worked with Dick on other books, including *The White Tribes of Africa*, an original study, and we became good friends.

Other books I admired in typescript included Edna O'Brien's *August is a Wicked Month*, a novel that traced the sexual adventures and humiliations of a young mother with a failing marriage. What a writer she is, never afraid to give the bad news. Paul Bailey's wonderful first book, *At the Jerusalem*, arrived on my desk in 1966; my enthusiasm for it was shared by everyone at Cape, and its success was great and deserved. Tom gave me some curious editorial jobs: one was to cut the very long manuscript of John Fowles's novel *The Magus* by something like a quarter. I was to be silent about it, as Tom would tell Fowles he had made the cuts himself. I thought the book pretentious and approved of Tom's wish to shorten it, so I worked away, slashing out chunks. Then it became a top bestseller and Fowles insisted on having all the cuts restored in a later edition: a triumph of popular judgement over editorial interference.

I enjoyed working with Jim Ballard, then embarking on his powerful visions of drowning and drought-stricken worlds – science fiction but in its own special category. He was an original, a charmer with a streak of melancholy and a magnificently weird imagination, his visions all his own. He told me about his childhood in a Japanese prison camp after the fall of Shanghai, and I urged him to write about it, but he had more volumes of science fiction to deliver before he would take on that task. And in 1964 he came into the office after his summer holidays and told me, simply, even abruptly, that his wife had died of pneumonia in Spain. I could hardly believe the fact or his contained response to such a sudden tragedy. He was left with three children – the eldest eight years old – whom he brought up beautifully; I remember how impressed I was when he brought them over to lunch with me at home. *The Crystal World* came out in 1966, and we went on working together. He had old-fashioned manners – he once presented me with an orchid – and I always enjoyed our meetings. But as the years went by both of us left Cape and we lost touch. I was amazed and very happy when in 1984 he finally published *The Empire of the Sun*, read it with admiration, delighted in its success and saw him again to tell him how pleased I was. It is a slightly fictionalized memoir, told with pinpoint clarity so that the slightest details imprint themselves on your imagination as you read. It won prizes, as it deserved to, and was filmed. His writing career continued, always surprising, disconcerting, effective, sometimes shocking, and, although I could not follow him into the psychosexuality of car crashes or technologically mediated masochism, I always liked him.

⁂

As to my inner life: it was calm in spite of all the parties of those years of the mid-Sixties. I had a steady and pleasant job that did not make great intellectual demands. Nick's career flourished as he made a notable success of 'Atticus' and his increasingly frequent television appearances; and in 1965 he moved to reporting and was often away in Europe, Africa and further afield. Our family life was good, better than our life as a couple. I lived without any plan for the future beyond the bringing up of our daughters, whose education and happiness mattered more to me than anything else. I was proud of them and they were good companions as they grew, each with a different temperament and different interests. We drove with them through France most summers, to visit my father and Kath in Vence, and they became brilliant swimmers, with pool morning and evening and often beach and sea in the daytime: a sandy and luxurious beach at Antibes, where the ghost of Scott Fitzgerald haunted, pebbly and popular at Cagnes. Sometimes we got up before dawn to climb the Baou – the mountain above Vence – and see the sun rise, with the Mediterranean stretched out as far as the eye could see below, shining as the sun came up.

We spent other holidays in rural Suffolk with Aunt Eliza, and in 1966 we bought a small house on the Essex–Suffolk border and threw ourselves into weekend country life. I loved the landscape, the hares in the fields, the silence and darkness at night; I grew vegetables and fruit. At home the girls had troops of friends among the children of the Crescent and the Terrace. One of Josephine's was Fenella, daughter of David Gentleman, and through this friendship, and my admiration of David's work, I had the idea of commissioning him to do some illustrated children's books for Cape. Four beautiful small volumes were published in 1967 and have become collectors' pieces: *Fenella in Greece, Fenella in Ireland, Fenella in the South of France* and *Fenella in Spain*. David fitted his own text around luminous watercolours. They convey the period as well as the places, and looking at them now you see scenes that have disappeared since he brought them so freshly to the page. The friendship I formed with David then has lasted ever since, and his later marriage to Susan Evans brought me another good friend and neighbour.

I gardened in London too, terracing the slope and trying out many more plants than could possibly flourish there. I took piano lessons. I visited my mother, and she came to stay with us regularly, and made music, sometimes with Nick. I made clothes for my daughters. I was often at the London Library. I caught mumps and our doctor said I must stay in bed for a week for fear of encephalitis – bliss, because I felt quite well and read extracts from Pepys's diaries for the first time, wondering at this extraordinarily frank and funny man's record of his life in the seventeenth century. I did some research on folk music for the film of

Hardy's *Far from the Madding Crowd*. And in 1966 I began
reviewing novels for Terence Kilmartin, literary editor of
the *Observer*: first shorter notices, then longer pieces. I was
so pleased to have this work that I kept at it even when on
holiday in France in the summer. Kath told me she was
impressed by such dedication, but the truth was that I was
grasping at the chance. Journalism was tougher and more
exciting than publishing. I wanted to do more.

※

Nick very sensibly acquired a scooter for getting around London. It had many uses, taking him to work and back, and also
allowing him to fetch draught beer from our local pub, the
Good Mixer. He brought the beer back in a saucepan held
between his feet. The pan lived in a compartment with the
spare helmet for a passenger, and Jo remembers that the helmet always smelt of beer when she put it on. He liked carrying
passengers, and would take his daughters and their friends out
on it, one in front and one behind. This was not strictly legal,
and one day he was stopped by the police carrying Jo and
Fenella on their way to the Hampstead ponds. He contrived to
get away with nothing worse than a warning. He was a risk-
taker with enough confidence and charm to get away with it.

His curiosity about the world made him the excellent
journalist he was. He began to be interested in canals and
used his scooter to explore them, driving it along towing
paths. I got a call from him one hot day when I was at home,
asking me to fetch him with the car. He had misjudged the
bank of a towing path and fallen into the canal on his scooter.

Luckily he had been able to scramble out of the water and get to a telephone box. I drove into Buckinghamshire and found him soaking wet but cheerful. The scooter was pulled out the next day. After this he took us all for a trip in a canal boat. I cooked in the galley as we inched our way along, finding the relationship between time and space puzzling – it must be the slowest form of travel, and there is something enchanting about that leisurely pace. Also about the business of the locks. As he dealt with one lock, his glasses fell off into the water. He dived in to try to find them and amazingly came up with them in his hand. Continuing his love-affair with water, he acquired a dinghy and became an enthusiastic sailor.

He made the children laugh by doing ridiculous things like taking them out in the car and waltzing it from side to side, to my consternation and their delight. Another of his habits was to drive them to school in his pyjamas, which seemed fine until the day the car broke down and he had to get out to deal with the situation. When he drove faster than the speed limit and I chided him, he told me that speed limits were meant for people who didn't drive as well as he did.

I was the careful one and found myself increasingly dealing with practical matters. Nick put off paying bills on principle, and one day the bailiffs arrived, finding the children with me downstairs. I had no idea what a bailiff was, and they were embarrassed to tell me in front of my daughters that they were going to stay until a particular bill was settled. I managed to speak to Nick on the telephone, settled the bill and made a joke of it. He told me that he always had an overdraft as a way of keeping himself from overspending. I worried about it occasionally but it seemed to work for him, and since we kept separate bank accounts I accepted that it was none of my business.

I earned steadily, if little, from my part-time jobs in publishing and then in journalism, and I kept writing more reviews, for *The Times Literary Supplement*, where Ian Hamilton commissioned me, for Terry at the *Observer*, for *Punch* and for other papers. Terry taught me with his light touch and good judgement and became my most admired and best-loved mentor. Ian was good to work for too, laid back and acute. Reviewing is an education in itself. You learn from the books, and you have to order and condense your thoughts and capture the reader's attention. I did a bit of television, a literary guessing game called *Take It or Leave It*, set up by my Cambridge friend Julian Jebb, in which we had to do our best to identify extracts from books, either classics or those recently published. Lord David Cecil, Mary McCarthy, Cyril Connolly and other such titans led the teams, and comfortingly they did not always come up with the correct answer. We juniors were expected to get some right. I can't think now how I had the nerve to do it. When it was filmed in Manchester, we travelled up together on the train and breakfasted as a group. Once I had the honour of sitting next to David Cecil, who talked with such charm throughout the meal, and such spluttering enthusiasm, that towards the end of the journey I found myself coated with flying toast crumbs like an escalope, and had to retreat into the lavatory to brush myself down. I knew how lucky I was to be meeting such grandees, and was well aware that I had written nothing longer than a review myself. Philip Roth, whom I first met at this time, remarked that I *looked* like a literary person: this was not a compliment, I understood, but we had several lunches together in the course of which he dazzled and slightly intimidated me. He told me recently that I had seemed 'the very embodiment of Englishness to a boy from New Jersey' – but he was not a boy to me. I knew he was the real thing, a grown-up writer, and I learnt that he worked every day, including Christmas. My admiration for him grew over the years, and with his novel *American Pastoral* he established himself among the great novelists, an American Balzac.

Nick rarely stayed for long in one job. In 1965 he took up foreign reporting for the *Sunday Times*, first in Europe, then all over the world. Very quickly he became an outstanding reporter. In 1966 he went to Vietnam twice to cover the war there. I was proud of him, and anxious for his safety. On his second visit he sent back a deadpan description of flying with an American general from Texas in his helicopter over villages, dropping napalm, shooting and taking prisoner a wounded man running out of a farmyard. The piece appeared as 'The General Goes Zapping Charlie Cong' and was thought so damaging to the American cause that no US paper printed it. At the end of the year he won the Granada Reporter of the Year Award, presented to him by the prime minister, Harold Wilson. Nick could cover pretty well any story he chose after that. He was also becoming well known on television, with a natural gift for contributing to talk programmes such as *Three after Six*. He had many fans.

At this point he made a move no one understood, I least of all. He let himself be persuaded to leave the *Sunday Times* and take on a job utterly unsuited to him. Paul Johnson, editor of the *New Statesman*, invited him to become his literary editor. Nick was always restless, and perhaps memories of Cambridge made him want to step into the shoes of Karl Miller, our friend, who had made a notable success editing the books and arts pages at the *Statesman*, only to fall out with Paul Johnson. Paul thought Karl's pages were too highbrow. Karl resigned and his loyal reviewers declared they would not work with Nick. Paul believed Nick would make the pages more accessible, even popular. Once Nick had accepted the job, I went with him, at his request, to look at the Literary Department, where piles of books and unopened parcels with more books inside were laid out on the tables. It seemed like heaven to me, but I saw Nick quail.

Kingsley Martin, retired editor of the *Statesman* who had made it essential reading for intellectuals, asked to meet Nick and we drove to Sussex for lunch with him in his house on the Downs. He and his partner Dorothy Woodman seemed old and frail, and my chief memory of the occasion was how intently they watched the bird tables outside the window as we ate our lunch. I watched the birds too, with pleasure, and took little part in the talk. Afterwards we went on to tea with Leonard Woolf at Monk's House in Rodmell. He was older than Kingsley Martin, but vigorous and responsive. I had read the first four volumes of his autobiographical books as they appeared, and was eagerly awaiting the next, due to be published in the summer. Consequently he was a revered figure to me; and a visit to the house where he and Virginia

Woolf had lived together felt like an extraordinary privilege. I spoke shyly of the pleasure his books were giving me,
and we walked round the garden together. I admired the
flowers and mentioned that I knew Sissinghurst and wondered whether Vita Sackville-West had made any suggestions
about the planting of this garden. This brought a hard look
from my host. I had no thought of offending him – I was an
attentive reader of Sackville-West's gardening columns, and
her friendship with Virginia Woolf was well known. He did
not answer my question but turned the talk to something
else and we walked on through the garden. So I did not do
very well, but still I came away grateful to have met a man I
admired so much, and who had lived at the heart of the culture of his time.

The *Statesman* did not suit Nick and he stayed with it for
only a year. During that year he fell in love again, this time
with a beautiful and well-connected young girl who was
eager to marry him, and whose family made him welcome.
For two years our lives were chaotic as he left home,
returned, left again, returned again. He was helpless in the
grip of love and could not turn his back on the girl who
adored him and the happiness this gave him. I tried to
understand him, to remain calm and wait for the storm to
pass. I did not always succeed. He was not a light-hearted
bolter but a romantic: when he fell in love his whole life
had to be transformed. He announced to his parents and
mine, to friends, colleagues, lawyers, that he had now

discovered love at last and wanted to start again. I have a vivid memory of his father explaining to me that Nick had found true love. I told Nick I accepted what was happening and only hoped it would not last for too long. I was the guardian of the family, deeply committed to him and attached to him by our children, by the habits of our lives, by the years we had been together, the houses we had shared, the sorrows we had faced. But he was now in another world.

Looking back, I see that she gave him the adoration that I failed to give. I gave love and friendship but was also critical of him, not always faithful, intent on making a career for myself. For all that, finding our family life destroyed was a nightmare. He was going through a nightmare too, of course, because he was divided between the thrilling new love that had come to him and his guilt feelings. I understand now the power of that helpless falling in love he experienced, and why he could not make up his mind what to do, and so behaved badly to everyone. In his distress he became more violent towards me. On one occasion he hit me so hard across the face with the back of his hand – we were in the car – that I needed stitches in my lip for the cut made by his heavy wedding ring. I lied to the family, saying we had been in a small crash. Emily began to have asthma so badly that she was in and out of hospital.

Once again I decided I must look for a change of job – I had been a publishers' reader for long enough. I aspired to work on a paper or magazine, or for the BBC. I got nowhere with the BBC or the *Observer* – David Astor told me I should stay at home and look after the children. But Terry

Kilmartin remained a stalwart freelance employer, and Katharine Whitehorn was also helpful to me. I asked Charles Wintour for advice and he suggested that Magnus Linklater, the current editor of the *Evening Standard* 'Diary', might try me out. So, as though in a curious round dance, I joined the 'Diary'. I had to learn fast how to use a telephone in a great noisy room where everyone else was shouting on their lines, how to scribble and dictate a story from a telephone box, how to get a quote from a politician. It was terrifying at first, but I just about managed, and met with nothing but kindness and encouragement from my colleagues.

While I was there, Nick left the *Statesman* and returned to the *Sunday Times*. In November he announced that he wanted to come back to Gloucester Crescent. We both made an effort to get on, but his heart was not in it. His girl put on pressure. There were rows that made both of us miserable. In February the new literary editor of the *Statesman*, Anthony Thwaite, asked me to become his deputy: the dance continued. Charles Wintour advised me against taking the *Statesman* job, but I leapt at it. I knew enough about it to feel confident I could do it and enjoy it, and it was for three days a week, ideal for me. I was to start on 8 April 1968. Five days before that Nick left home yet again. This time he delivered a beagle puppy to the house, a gesture so inappropriate to the situation that I didn't know whether to laugh or rage. Then he set off by car for Greece with his lovely girl and we heard not a word from him for four months. The children and I walked the dog and attempted to train her without success; otherwise our lives continued much as before. I made a flat in the house and found a lodger.

In June I had a message from Nick's lawyers asking me to find a legal representative for myself and set up divorce proceedings. I obliged, spent several hours with a kindly solicitor and went away with a migraine, the only time in my life I have suffered from one. I was helped by a counsellor of great goodness and sense, Eva Seligman. Nick's mother, Beth, had advised both Nick and me to seek counselling through the Tavistock Clinic and I was lucky enough to be sent to her – Nick took against the man he saw. Mrs Seligman had come to England as a child from Berlin and trained here. She was a poet as well as a counsellor and she understood how families work and how people can be trapped in unhappy patterns of behaviour. She lived in a part of North London I did not know well, and for my first visit I went on the Underground, emerging into unfamiliar streets where I could not find my way. I called her from a telephone box and burst into tears of humiliation and childlike misery. I remember her opening her front door to me and a feeling of calm reaching me. She saw me once a week and we talked. It was not psychoanalysis but conversation. We found we spoke the same language and she gave me help just as I needed it most. She was a remarkable person. She told me I did not need to repeat my mother's experience, gave me good advice about the children and encouraged me in the direction of real independence. And she helped me to reject the role of victim so effectively that, when I met Nick again, he commented on the change in me. I found myself able to see when he was going to be violent and remove myself to safety, which was better for both of us.

But we did not see Nick for a long time. The children and I agreed that the dog he had brought us would be happier in the country and a home was found for her with a beagle-loving family by Aunt Eliza. We spent many weekends and whole weeks with her in Suffolk, bicycling and making picnics. At home I took them to the swimming pool and to the Zoo, to Brownies, to fly a kite in Parliament Hill Fields, to Shakespeare in the Open Air Theatre in the park, on a day trip to Sissinghurst. Our house was full of *The Sound of Music* and *My Fair Lady*, two records they played almost continuously – or so I remember it – over several years. I found something comforting about hearing the same music over and over again, and they are good shows. I listened to my classical music records when I was alone at night, chamber music mostly, Schubert, Mozart, Beethoven, Haydn. I took myself to the opera and my passion for it grew. My mother came for weekends and I drove out regularly to see her. Ronald Bryden, now theatre critic for the *Observer*, often invited me to join him to see new plays. I had many friends and made new ones.

Looking through my diaries, I see a busy life laid out. That year my friend Charlotte Jenkins, wife of Peter, was ill with the cancer that finally killed her, and I visited her as often as I could. I worked Tuesday to Thursday at the *Statesman*. On Friday I crammed in everything else: a typical Friday in May 1968 shows:

9 a.m. visit to Mrs Seligman
write piece [probably for the *Observer* and of course
   on a typewriter]

10.15 piano tuner [I was taking piano lessons]
arrange car servicing
1.00 Chez Victor for lunch with John Hale [the historian, a new and delightful friend]
6.00 take Su and Em to Brownies
8.00 dinner James R. [old Cambridge boyfriend]

Weekends were for family.

A colleague who knew I had a room to let asked me to take in his cousin, a young American woman who turned out to be schizophrenic. It was an eerie experience. As I arrived home from the office one day, my new lodger ran to me and said, 'I have raped your daughter.' An alarming moment, even though it was her fantasy – I had young daughters and did not want anyone fantasizing about them. The unfortunate lodger became still more disturbed and a few days later had to be taken away in an ambulance. I lived pretty levelly most of the time but occasionally wished I had someone to advise or reassure me. Driving home alone late after a dinner party on a frosty night, my car went into a spectacular skid as I speeded past the Zoo. It turned right round on itself and I ended up facing in the other direction. By great good fortune there were no other cars on the road. I was shaken and arrived home wanting to tell someone what had happened – Nick came into my mind, ridiculously. At least I had learnt not to speed.

❧

Later in the summer I had my own taste of helpless love. A colleague, brilliant and witty, invited me for a drink after work. As we sat in a bar he said something totally unexpected: 'I'm in love with you.' I didn't know how to respond but something stirred inside me. I smiled; he talked; I listened. I talked; he listened. I had no husband to think about; his wife was away, he said. We talked about ourselves, we laughed, suddenly we couldn't keep our eyes off one another. What could we do? I suppose I was desperate for the reassurance such an offer of love gave me. It was like a balm healing my sore heart, soothing my bruised confidence. I explained to him that I was going to the opera that evening, but we could meet afterwards, late. It was a hot summer night. We met, went to my house, fell into each other's arms. The children were sleeping upstairs. Two days later I was due to drive them to Aunt Eliza in Suffolk and then I would be on my own in London for a week.

After that I would be taking my children for a farm holiday in Devon. His wife would be returning home. We were both in a state of passionate excitement and we had only a very short time to explore what this meant. We were stirred, shaken, in thrall. How could we ever bear to part? We knew we mustn't lose each other; we also knew we must and would part, whatever we said. Or could we turn everything over? And then? Each night we seized everything we could take hold of, our bodies, hopes and desires, and set aside fears and impossibilities. The world seemed to be spinning around me when I was at work. Living with incompatibilities is exhausting.

And then our brief time was up. I drove off with my children, a happy mother who had so carefully planned a holiday at a farmhouse in Devon, and we found it all we had hoped:

peaceful, comfortable and quiet. We ate the lavish breakfasts made by the farmer's wife, and were warned by the jovial farmer to keep clear of the ram in the field full of gentle sheep because he might attack us with his horns. We went to the beach, fished for mackerel at Lyme Regis, saw Lulworth Cove and Forde Abbey, walked over Tarr Steps on the River Barle, wondering at the beauty of the falling woods, happy to be all together. I arranged riding lessons for them and took them to see my old school at Dartington.

One night, as a great shining moon spread its light through the sky outside the farmhouse, my lover rang me and we spoke words of longing, knowing they were impossible.

And one day, when the children and I had the beach to ourselves, our beach ball bobbed away on the waves and I said I'd bring it back. I swam after it, and swam; it bobbed further; I swam on. So it went on until I realized I would never catch it. I turned round and saw three small figures standing on the beach a very long way away across the water. A moment of panic – I had swum too far and the current might be against me. I am a steady swimmer but even so – I swam and swam, sometimes on my back, sometimes my front, then on my back again. After what seemed a very long time I saw that the shore was not so far away, and knew that I could do it. The children held out towels and I did my best not to show how chilled I was and how frightened I had been. We went back to the car and drove to a pub. I took the children in with me and asked for a whisky for myself and orange juice for them. The pub let them stay with me. They were safe, my infinitely precious children.

Back in London, I found my friend Charlotte was now in hospital, as brave as ever but not getting better. I met my lover, and even as we told each other we wanted to be together we knew it was not going to happen. A few desperate conversations brought things to an end. I agonized, hurled myself into work and flirtations, determined to show how tough I could be, revealing nothing to the world and denying my real feelings to myself. It was not easy. Much later we were able to be good friends. Neither of us ever spoke again of what had happened between us.

Nick was in England again and asked to take the children away for a week with his girl: fine, although he brought them home early, as the holiday did not go well. I immersed myself in the Autumn Books number, literary lunches, the children's activities. In September Nick sent me flowers. I did not want him back. I did not trust him, his gestures, his letters, his declarations of love. I had friends I found more congenial, more trustworthy, better company. I did not lack admirers. The more I went my own way and kept him at bay, the more he knew he wanted to return to the family.

The children and I spent Christmas in Suffolk with Aunt Eliza and my mother. My father invited me to join him for a week in February in Chamonix, where we skated and walked in the snow, and I went through the proofs of his book on D. H. Lawrence with him – long planned, now realized. It was the only week we ever spent on our own together. I gave his work close attention and praise, making clear that I understood what he was doing, which pleased him; and he was able to show me a little of his native land of Savoy for the first time. He was not a man

Jo

who opened his heart in conversation, but we were both the better for our shared winter week.

Nick grew more pressing. My daughter Jo was now twelve and I decided I should consult with her. I told her he was eager to come back and said I thought he would never change and that we could make a better life without him, and maybe I could marry a steadier partner one day. She listened, and then said in a very small clear voice, 'I want Daddy.' And I answered, in a voice I made cheery, 'All right – we'll have Daddy.' I could have said nothing else to her. So Nick returned to Gloucester Crescent, abandoning his poor girl, whom he still loved – he loved us both, he said. On that basis our family life had to be put together again.

8

A Birth and Two Books

Nineteen seventy restored our family life. Nick took up his oboe again and began to play with a wind group, and from now on we had musical evenings at home from time to time, always a treat. Our daughters amazed us by their cheerfulness and success at school, their lives filled with friends, music lessons, parties, pet hamsters, school plays, concerts. We went *en famille* to galleries and museums and an occasional opera – I remember *The Magic Flute* and *Hansel and Gretel*. We swam regularly. We cooked together, and they helped me with the annual marmalade. I read aloud to them: *Mansfield Park*, *Middlemarch* and *Vanity Fair*, while they made themselves dresses or baked cakes. Jo reminds me how Nick insisted on reading us the Waterloo chapter from *Vanity Fair* that ends with George Osborne lying face down in the field with a bullet through his heart.

I had my three days a week at the *New Statesman*, book reviewing for other papers and occasional broadcasting. Now Nick uncovered a story about a lone sailor, Donald Crowhurst, who disappeared during a round-the-world race. The *Sunday Times* sent him to investigate Crowhurst's abandoned boat in the West Indies, a thrilling and disquieting sight, and he decided to make a book with his colleague

Ron Hall out of what they were able to establish. They researched closely and worked together at a great pace, producing a tragic marine adventure that was also a subtle character study. *The Strange Voyage of Donald Crowhurst* had a deserved success, has gone on finding readers and is now (in 2017) a film. Nick was justifiably proud of it, and he began to think that writing books could be as exciting and rewarding as journalism.

I decided to have another baby. Why? I thought of our old wish to have six children, and told myself I was honouring that wish with a fifth. A baby would be good for us all and fun for the girls. I was only thirty-six. Now, looking back as dispassionately as I can, I think I wanted another child for myself, as a treat, because I loved having children, and to bring us happiness. I was greedy for more children. The trouble was that we had not recovered from the chaos and misery of the Sixties. Nick and I were both chastened. We were doing our best to put together the broken pieces of our marriage. At times it seemed to work, but I no longer really knew my husband, and could not be sure what he might do next. Or what I might do.

In the spring my friend Charlotte Jenkins died. She had been ill for nearly four years. I loved her for her grace and spirit, and can still see the turn of her head as she spoke, and hear her soft Bloomsbury voice. We talked together about our lives and she told me how she had married for the first time at seventeen, to find her husband's male lover waiting to join them in Paris on the honeymoon, having filled their hotel room with flowers. She fled from these complications to a happy second marriage to Peter Jenkins, with whom she had her daughter, and then became ill with a slowly advancing and painful form of cancer. She bore it with the utmost courage and patience. Her many friends surrounded her with love, but illness is isolating, and she told me that only the doctor who looked after her understood exactly how it affected her. Her funeral was in May, and as I mourned I decided I would call my baby Charlotte should she be a girl.

June brought an exasperating election. The polls steadily predicted that Harold Wilson would get in again, but they were wrong, and the Conservatives came back, under Edward Heath. At the same time there was turmoil at the *New Statesman*, where Paul Johnson suddenly gave up the editorship and Richard Crossman, fresh from being secretary of state for health and social services under Wilson, took over. He also left Parliament, where he had been a leading figure among the group of public school educated and idealistic socialists: he had been told at Winchester that he might become prime minister one day.

I had to see Crossman almost as soon as he arrived at the *Statesman* to explain that I needed maternity leave, to which he reacted generously, saying I should come back when I was ready, and write pieces for the paper while I was off work; James Fenton would fill in for me as deputy literary editor. My last press day was in July; we celebrated the English publication of Nick and Ron's book on Crowhurst a few days later and left with the children for our

French holiday. The day after our return in August, Nick flew to New York for the American publication. The baby was due in September. I saw my doctor, who pummelled me fiercely, explaining when he'd finished that the baby had been the wrong way up and needed pushing into a good position, head down, which he had just managed to do. Now I was all set for the birth.

Susanna went to Ireland with friends and Emily to Aunt Eliza in Suffolk. Josephine was at home, and on 21 August I took her and my mother to the Garrick Theatre to see Michael Frayn's first play, *The Two of Us*. I laughed so much that something budged inside me. Back at home, I went to bed but within a few hours knew I ought to ring Guy's Hospital and talk to a nurse. They said I should come in to the hospital, and at 3.30 a.m. on the Saturday morning I woke my mother to explain and ordered a taxi. Then, realizing it was still evening in New York, I dialled Nick's hotel. I failed to reflect that I was wrecking his publicity tour. He, bless him, said without hesitation that he would fly back to England on the next plane.

The doctors at Guy's knew me, and I was allowed to keep walking about as I liked while labour progressed, easily as it always did for me. My own consultant was on holiday but his colleague Mr Morris was there. Nick arrived from Heathrow at lunchtime. My mother and Josephine came in to see me. We were all joyfully excited. Nick was in the delivery room with me as the baby was born: not a little Charlotte but a boy. I said to Nick, 'Now you have a son, he can go to football matches with you.' He was to be Thomas – Tom. He was small, but then he was three weeks early. 'Little baby,' said the midwife, 'why are you being born early?' And she carried him out of the room. I thought they must be washing him, although I wondered why they had not put him into my arms to hold. For quite a long time nobody seemed to be doing anything, then I was tidied up and taken back to my room, and Nick went with me. It was teatime now, about four o'clock. He brought out a bottle of champagne and began to open it, and we prepared to telephone grandparents and daughters. As Nick poured the first glass of champagne, Mr Morris came into the room and said, 'Stop that – you mustn't do that.' We couldn't understand what he meant. He paused, helplessly, then said again, 'Don't do that. I have to tell you, your baby has a condition called spina bifida. It's bad news, I'm afraid.' Words to that effect.

I had no idea what he meant. I had never heard of spina bifida. I think Nick had, but only vaguely. A lot had to be explained to us. Spina bifida means that the spine has not developed properly during the pregnancy, and part of the spinal cord is exposed and unprotected. It is possible to operate to protect the exposed spinal cord, although it is not likely to do much good. The almost certain outcome will be paralysis, incontinence and other problems. Nick and I were asked to decide at once whether we wanted our son to be operated on that evening. We had to make a choice, we were told, between leaving him as he was and having the operation performed. I asked, 'Supposing we decide against the operation, what happens?' I was told that his condition might become much worse without an operation, making his life still more difficult. I said, 'So there is really no choice, is there? If not having an operation means he will be worse off?'

That is what we were told. The truth is that without an operation a baby with spina bifida will almost certainly die within a few months. On the advice we had, we accepted that Tom should be operated on, and it was done at midnight, with a further operation ten days later. Another bad possibility was hydrocephalus, the head swelling with the pressure of spinal fluid, producing brain damage. We were warned that he might even go blind. Ronald MacKeith, the paediatrician who had helped us when my son Daniel was born, and with Emily's asthma, came back from his holiday to see us in the hospital. It was an act of extraordinary kindness. He was already a friend and now he became an immensely comforting presence, even though he explained at some point that spina bifida affected almost every part of the body in one way or another, as we were to find out. As to the cause, no one knew what it was.

The first closing operation was done, Tom was laid on a supporting backing, and I was able to hold him and to start breastfeeding him the next day. He was very beautiful, he was my son, and I fell in love with him. It's hard to describe the intensity of the bond formed between mother and new-born child, but it is as fierce and romantic as any love-affair. When the situation is uncertain, precarious, threatening, the love grows fiercer. Each day I delighted in seeing his eyelashes growing longer. Josephine came to see us on most days – she was also doing a holiday job – Emily was brought up from the country, Susanna came as soon as she was back from Ireland. Friends visited, and family. Nick took me

Holding Tom

out for a rapid dinner. At home he was installing a small fountain in the garden. He gave me a necklace of moonstones to mark the birth of his son. The sun shone in the hospital yard. In the evenings Dr MacKeith often sat late with me, talking. I saw occasional movements in Tom's legs and dared to hope he might not be badly paralysed. I thought, who will love him if he is severely disabled? And answered myself: if no one else, I will, and I will make sure he has the best possible life. Nick did not have my consolations and he suffered more.

One day he said, 'I've given you a bad baby.' How could I comfort him? We had some grim conversations when we were warned about other possible complications, and asked ourselves whether Tom could possibly have a life worth living. His head was growing larger than it should. We had to see a neurosurgeon for advice about whether they should put a shunt into his head to drain off the fluid. The danger was brain damage. For some time it was touch and go. The neurosurgeon was a sweet and dedicated man who told me how he envied our having a child, since he longed for one and had none. Josephine pointed out that her head was larger than the average, and this had not damaged her mental powers. But Tom had to be seen regularly by the neurosurgeon for many months, and each time the question was raised of whether a shunt was necessary. Finally it was decided that the hydrocephalus had settled down and he did not need one. But his legs did not work. Tom never walked and was never able to stand.

He had the second operation on his back on 1 September. He began to put on weight: '5 lbs, 8½ ozs', I noted in my diary. When he was two weeks old, still in hospital, Nick, Josephine, Susanna and Emily were each able to hold him. This was at Ronnie's insistence, ensuring that all the family bonded with the new baby. We gave Tom his father's name and Ronnie's: Thomas Nicholas Ronald. On Friday, 11 September, we took him home. A new life was beginning for him, and a new sort of life for all of us.

When you have a child with a serious disability, you move into a different category of existence. You are classified differently by other people, even the kind and helpful. We were told that spina bifida was rare in middle-class families, I recall – but really very little was known then about its prevalence or causes. A harelip in an earlier generation was often found – and of course, Nick's Aunt Eliza, so dear to us all, had been born with one in 1906. Lack of folic acid was another contributory cause: had I failed to eat properly? How could I know? A health visitor called, and I asked, 'What do people do when they have a child with spina bifida?' She replied – I have never forgotten her words – 'They move into a crummy bungalow in the suburbs.'

At Great Ormond Street Hospital, I said something to a Sister about wanting to know the worst: she gave me a look and said, 'The worst? You certainly don't want to know and can't begin to imagine the worst.' Her life was spent dealing with intolerable situations patiently and compassionately, and she was shocked by my facile phrase. I saw many forms of disability at Great Ormond Street, and met mothers who told me they could not have faced having a child who would never walk. Could I face such a thing? Of course I could.

Dick Crossman, when I spoke to him about postponing my return to work, was full of sympathy. He told me that when he was minister of health he had visited hospital wards full of severely disabled children, and noticed particularly ones with hydrocephalus, left to languish. Whatever you do, he said to me with great insistence, don't put your son into an institution. I had no thought of doing that. When Nick's father suggested to me that I should think of it, I found it hard to understand or forgive him.

I watched Tom for signs of progress, and had an anxious wait for him to smile. At six weeks there was no sign of a smile and I started to worry. I had a friend whose baby had never smiled or responded and had finally been sent away to just the sort of hospital Crossman described. Anxiety grew in me and turned to agony. I made an appointment to see one of our GPs, Dr Modell. He listened to me, then asked me to put Tom down on a couch on one side of the room and sit myself a little way away. For several minutes the doctor observed us without speaking. Then he said, 'I think I can see something between him and you – I can't say exactly what, but there is something there –' He reminded me that Tom had been born prematurely, and said with a smile of his own that he expected Tom would smile soon. The doctor's calm calmed me. Within a week, at the beginning of November, Tom was indeed smiling. By December he could roll over. His hair grew golden, giving him an angelic air. He laughed and splashed in his bath. Since all babies are incontinent and unable to walk, there was nothing to mark him as different, so I showed him off cheerfully. But we had hospital visits every week – at Guy's, at the Maudesley, at Great Ormond Street. I got used to driving across London with Tom in his carrycot in the back. There were no seat belts then.

Nick returned to New York, and was away for a month. He spent part of the time testing a cure for smoking. It meant going on a cruise on which he was treated by a hypnotist. It worked for him, and he came back cured, to my considerable delight, as I worried about the effect of cigar smoke on the children. But after a few weeks he said he could not write without smoking, and the cigars appeared again. He agreed, when I asked, not to smoke in the car when the children were with him, and only in his study at home.

At six months Tom was speaking simple words and could sit at table in his high chair. Then he learnt to crawl by pulling on his arms, getting along so fast that he managed to fall down half a flight of stairs while I was running his bath, and the doctor took a grave view of my negligence.

Living as we did in a London terrace house, five storeys high, we ran up and down the stairs all day; even our garden was on a slope which I had terraced, with steps. There were steps up to the front door, steps down to the kitchen door. Steps are everywhere in the world, loved by architects, unnoticed by everyone except those who can't use them. We could hope to carry Tom until he was three or four, but after that he would have to use a wheelchair. How could he possibly manage our steps?

Nick started looking for another house, one flatter or at least easier to manage or adapt. We visited several, in Highgate, in the Camden Road, on the Canal. We tried to imagine ourselves in them, consulted an architect friend about how they might be made to work. None of us was keen to move. Could we build out at the back of our present house? I was thinking of something else: how about a lift? I thought we might squeeze one in at the side of the basement kitchen, giving access to three floors. And that's what we did. The lift was just big enough to take a wheelchair, and the grinding noise it made as it went up and down became part of the life of the house. Neighbours' children came to play in it, and I had to explain that it was not a toy. We built a ramp that ran down from the road to the basement kitchen door, allowing Tom as he grew to wheel himself into the house, and then take the lift to the sitting room and to his bedroom and the bathroom above. To pay for all this we sold our cottage in the country. Money is the thing you need most if you have a child with a disability.

※

In March 1971 the *Sunday Times* sent Nick to Vietnam again – he had been there twice in 1966 – and he went on to Bangkok. He was away for a month, and during that time I managed to write a full-page article for the *Statesman* (and rejoice over Tom's first tooth). It was about Mary Wollstonecraft, the eighteenth-century feminist who wrote a book that became famous in its day – the 1790s – and took herself to Paris to see the Revolution in action. The piece was published in May and I had a totally unexpected response: letters from publishers suggesting I should write a biography of her, the BBC wanting me to give a talk, requests to edit her letters and to write an introduction to a French translation of her famous book. This was the time when feminism was reviving and people were suddenly interested in its early development. The most helpful letter came from Deborah Rogers, whom I knew, urging me to write a book about Wollstonecraft and offering to become my agent. I accepted her offer gladly.

Things moved very fast. I was already worrying about whether I could go back to the *Statesman*. I knew I would need to find a part-time nanny for Tom and I had started looking for one. I was in touch with an enterprising American girl, Gail Coté, who had, if I remember rightly, left the

US with an ex-Catholic priest she was going to marry. I saw Deborah on 4 June to discuss a possible book and hired Gail on 5 June: she would drive over several times a week to take care of Tom while I worked. Nick and I sat down and talked over the relative merits of my returning to the *Statesman* or attempting a book, and agreed that the book was worth an attempt. On 21 June I told Richard Crossman I could not go back to the *Statesman* and at once began planning my research: reading, listing libraries and museums with archives to be consulted, places I needed to visit, historians I might consult.

Deborah asked me to provide her with a synopsis. Nick and I made a quick visit to Beverley in Yorkshire to look at the town where Wollstonecraft had lived as a girl in the 1760s. It still kept the same street plan in the centre and the beautiful minster. We took Jo and Tom with us, and included a walk around Gordale Scar, carrying Tom on our backs. I managed to deliver my synopsis to Deborah on time and she negotiated a contract for the book with Weidenfeld & Nicolson. Tony Godwin was to be my editor. This was good news, because I knew he was a formidable figure, famous for his attention to the detail of the text and his energy in working with writers.

In August the lift was installed in our house while we took the children to Ireland, where Wollstonecraft had worked as a governess: I needed to see the place. In September and October, Nick was away again, in Pakistan. Tom was making steady progress with speaking, sitting and crawling.

I was able to buy first editions of Wollstonecraft's *A Vindication of the Rights of Woman*, published in 1792, and her husband William Godwin's memoir of her, published in 1798 – they were not so expensive then as they became. Few other works of hers had been reprinted and it took time to track down copies. My diary records many days of 'work, work, work', some at the British Library (then inside the British Museum), some at the Bodleian in Oxford, some at the Public Record Office, then in Chancery Lane, the Guildhall, and further afield. The 'work' entries were interspersed with notes of Tom's progress in crawling, sitting and speaking: 'Tom sitting at table says Pa Ba Ma.' At the British Library I was allowed, to my amazement and delight, to go into the stacks and work there in order to make my research easier as I looked through the many volumes of the magazine Wollstonecraft had worked for, the *Analytical Review*, which ran from 1788 to 1799. In the Print Room I went through the works of Blake and Fuseli, since Blake had known her and illustrated her stories for children, and Fuseli had been her dear friend: she was in love with him, but, although he found her interesting, he did not reciprocate her love, and besides he was married. Every week a new door into the past seemed to open and a new subject demanded attention. I knew I had at last found my vocation – late in life, but it changed everything for me. I now had a purpose and a field to explore and a good use for my brain, because biography is history, and demands wide-ranging research and precise thinking if it is to be any good. I was intensely happy.

I had no study, so I set up my typewriter, books and papers on a small table in the sitting room. In the early months Tom was often beside me in his carry-cot, sleeping or looking about, examining his hands and trying out sounds, but as he grew Gail would take him out. When we had guests I tidied away all signs of my work.

I had some bad moments. One came after I had found out there were unpublished letters by Wollstonecraft held in a Liverpool library – and yes, they would send me photocopies. They were to William Roscoe, a scholar with liberal ideas and a keen abolitionist. I thought I had a coup, but almost as the copies arrived I heard that an American scholar had got there first and was about to publish the letters in a new book. I sank into gloom. But not for long. I cheered up when I read the new book and found it very unlike what I was planning.

Then a friendly and generous bookseller gave me a wonderful present: a small book published in 1803 in London, *Eccentric Biography; or, Memoirs of Remarkable Female Characters, Ancient and Modern*, containing an engraving of a painting of Wollstonecraft which I had never seen.* The black top hat she is wearing over loose hair suggests the revolutionary thinker as neither of the other portraits I knew did. I decided it should appear on the jacket of my book.†

I was lucky to have Eric Hobsbawm as a friend I could always consult on historical points. I was also introduced

---

* The engraving is by John Chapman (*fl.* 1792–1823), known for a wide range of engraved portraits and Shakespearean scenes. The original artist is unknown.

† The two others are one from 1791, commissioned by William Roscoe, artist unknown, and John Opie's beautiful portrait made during her pregnancy in 1797.

by our neighbour Colin Haycraft to another historian, Richard Cobb, whose writing about the people of revolutionary France I admired. Richard gave me encouragement and advice, including a recommendation that, when studying eighteenth-century lives, you should walk where they walked, if possible, or go on horseback, to see the world as they did. When I was dubious about the horseback, he modified it to a bicycle.

Early in 1972 I dashed to Paris to see what I could find in the archives relating to Wollstonecraft's visit and contacts there in the 1790s. I thought Tom was ready to be weaned and would be happy with his father, Gail and his sisters, so I allowed myself three days of concentrated research away. When Wollstonecraft went, she was already a published author, famous for her radical stance and her polemical writing, especially her book making the case for the rights of women. She was due to give a paper on education in Paris and was fired with enthusiasm to see how the French were changing the basic structures of society, attacking religion and monarchy, patriarchy and marriage, even legitimizing divorce. I had read Condorcet, the mathematician and philosopher of the Revolution, who at the same time was urging that women should be treated in all respects except physical strength as equal with men. He was the first Frenchman to do so. He was also a republican, but one who advised Robespierre against executing the king and so fell out of favour. Wollstonecraft should have met Condorcet, but he was proscribed under the Terror and forced to go into hiding. Soon, hearing the house where he was being sheltered was to be searched, he fled, was arrested and died in prison, almost certainly of poison, self-administered.

Wollstonecraft witnessed the dangers and horrors of those times, saw the guillotine, and lost men and women friends to it. In spite of this, she chose to remain in Paris, even when offered a chance to leave. She knew many French politicians, and had friends among a group of British and American sympathizers with the Revolution, writers, artists, journalists, poets, all seeing the world in a new way, questioning almost everything that had been taken for granted, and enjoying themselves in the process, at least for a time. She had a further reason for staying: she fell in love, embarked on an affair – she and her American lover Gilbert Imlay agreed that the formality of marriage was unnecessary – and gave birth to a child. My intellectual heroine became tender and vulnerable, and then immersed in baby care.

I knew from her letters that her daughter Fanny was born in Le Havre in 1794. When I talked to Richard Cobb about this, he suggested I write to the archivists in Le Havre, even though the whole town had been pretty well flattened by bombs during the Second World War. There was little hope that any eighteenth-century documents could have survived, but I sent off my query: did they have any record of the birth of Wollstonecraft's daughter? Two weeks later a large brown envelope arrived for me: enclosed was a photocopy of the official declaration made by Imlay, Mary's lover, in which he declared himself to be her husband. It gave the date as it was in Revolutionary France: 'Le vingt-cinquième jour Floréal l'an Second de la république française une et indivisible', and the child's name as

Françoise. Research is mostly slow, hard slog, but just occasionally a magic moment arrives, and this was one of them. Here was something no one had looked at for two hundred years, the official notification of the birth of Mary's first daughter – the sad child who lived long enough to know Shelley and be mourned by him at her death.

❧

In March, Richard Crossman left the *Statesman* – he had not been judged a successful editor. Tony Howard took over, and appointed a new literary editor, John Gross. I was working at the Public Record Office, then in Chancery Lane, where one day I rose to my feet with an involuntary cry of triumph on turning up an unexpected piece of information, and hastily sat down again, embarrassed at interrupting the scholarly silence of the other readers. The Dr Williams's Library in Gordon Square, Bloomsbury, was another useful and agreeable place to work. Then there was the Guildhall Library, Stoke Newington Library and of course the London Library, with its open shelves and reading room. I made more visits to the Bodleian. The reading room and North Library at the British Library became a second home. I tracked down Captain Douglas King-Harman, a descendant of the Irish aristocrats who hired Wollstonecraft to educate their children, and he let me see family records and portraits which added significantly to my account of her Irish experiences.

In May, Gail had to leave – she was to be married – and Theresa McGinlay arrived, to become the great mainstay of

Theresa and Tom

the family, a sisterly companion to my girls, a friend to me, a perfect nanny to Tom, intelligent, warm-hearted, generous and always good company. Tom had to start wearing callipers during this year, which meant buckling him into metal or plastic contraptions that held him upright, caging him from chest to toes. It was believed that standing upright was good for him and no doubt it was in some respects. But I saw that he thought he would be able to walk in them, only to find he could not. It was painful to watch his distress as he discovered that he could not do what other children so easily accomplished. I became reluctant to take him to the playground. He was much happier playing on the floor and in the small red trolley he was supplied with, and wheeled round energetically. On the plus side, he started going to a nursery school run by neighbours on some mornings, which he loved: he was sociable and eager to play with other children wherever it was possible.

The 'work, work, work' in my diaries did not keep me from seeing friends too: Karl Miller, now editing the *Listener*, Tony Howard, Eric and Marlene Hobsbawm, Terry Kilmartin, David and Sue Gentleman – with two small daughters – Peter Jenkins now married to Polly Toynbee, Jonathan and Rachel Miller, John and Sheila Hale, Eric Korn, Alan Williams, John and Miriam Gross, Simon and Ann Broadbent, Julian and Margaret Bullard, Ronnie MacKeith. There were many more, from the *Sunday Times* and from our Greenwich years. Nick's half-sister Stefany Heatherwick had a baby son, Thomas, only a few months older than my Tom. My mother was with us a good deal, and we took her on holidays. My niece Claire came from Oxford to help us with Tom.

Nick was kept busy reporting. He was away in Pakistan, Bangkok and India in the autumn of 1971 and again for many reporting trips throughout 1972, when he returned to Saigon and also visited the Philippines. I worked as steadily as I could on my book. 'Mary Who?' I called it, because nobody could cope with the name 'Wollstonecraft'. I amassed notes on file cards, translating French passages and seeking help with German; checking, typing, retyping. There were no computers then. As I extended my researches, my subject seemed to me more and more like a modern woman in her attitudes and behaviour, defying convention, boldly travelling with her baby daughter through Scandinavia on a business trip, writing a polemical novel with an intelligent prostitute as a principal character, falling into depression, fighting it by working harder, and by finding herself a new partner. I was asked to give a talk on Radio Three about Wollstonecraft and women's rights, which Karl Miller printed in the *Listener.*

As I got near to finishing my book, I gave Nick a chapter to read and tactfully left the room as he did so, only to find him fast asleep with it in his hand when I crept back. We were both able to laugh. When it seemed finished, I paid a professional typist to make a tidy copy and sent it off nervously to Tony Godwin. Silence fell. After four days the telephone rang, Tony on the line. He seemed stiff and odd, and I, embarrassed, thinking he must have hated the book, tried to chat about nothing much. Then he exploded: 'What about my telegram?' What telegram? I asked nervously. More wrathful explosions – he had sent me a glorious message of enthusiasm and congratulation – only, we gradually discovered as we talked it through, to the wrong address. It had gone to 57 Gloucester Avenue, a house standing empty at that time, instead of Gloucester Crescent. It had been put through the door and was presumably still lying inside. Long explanations, cries of rage and relief. The essential point was that he loved the book, had pages of notes to give me, and was confident of its success. There would be rewrites, copy editing, proofs, illustrations and captions, but the main work was done. And we found the missing telegram in the empty house.

Nick was such a good reporter that I expected him to continue with his foreign travels, but early in 1973 he again decided on a change of direction. He wanted to write another book. The *Sunday Times* was commissioning a history of the National Theatre, and asked him if he would like to take it on. There was a good chunk of history to be investigated, because the theatre first projected in 1848 and had only now become a reality, its building still going up on the South Bank. It was a worthwhile subject, if not an obvious one for him, but he liked the challenge, agreed to take it on and started work enthusiastically.

I was busy with Tony Godwin. Much as I liked and respected him, I found some of his editorial suggestions hard to deal with. One was that I should fictionalize parts of my narrative, something I refused even to consider. I shocked him too, by telling him I thought of submitting the book for a Ph.D. since I had done original research for it. Tony responded to this with 'I won't publish your book if you do that.' I gave in and we stayed friends, although I regretted not pursuing the Ph.D. The months went by quietly: Nick was sometimes restive and was away a good deal; so were the girls, on walking holidays or abroad with friends. I was forty in June – it did not feel like a birthday to fuss over. We had a family holiday in Brittany in late August and September, in a hotel on a beach. Theresa was with us, we swam every day, played beach games in the sunshine and ate ice cream and quantities of shrimps. Nick sailed his dinghy. Tom was still supposed to wear callipers for a few hours every day and I was told he might soon need an orthopaedic operation on his legs and hips.

At home again, we settled into the children's autumn term. On Saturday, 6 October 1973, Egypt and Syria made a joint surprise attack on Israel. They chose the holiest day in the Jewish calendar, Yom Kippur, or the Day of Atonement, when fasting and attendance at a synagogue are generally observed, to start fighting on two fronts. Reporters and photographers rushed to Israel. The *Sunday Times*, knowing that Nick was at home researching a book, called him and asked if he would be willing to go. He told them he would think about it and call them back. Then he came to me and asked me what I felt. I asked him, 'Do you want to go?' 'Yes,' he replied, and I answered, 'Well, then, you should go.' 'I wouldn't go to anywhere dangerous now,' he said, 'with four children – but the Israelis know how to look after journalists and I'll be perfectly safe with them.'

So he prepared to fly out on the Monday. On Sunday evening we had a musical party with his usual wind group. I am not sure what they played, very possibly they had a go at Hummel's Wind Serenade in E-flat Major, since they often played Hummel. Difficult music, and they sometimes had to break off, laughing, but they always made it enjoyable.

The next morning, Monday, Nick must have said goodbye to the girls before they set off for school. Jo and Su usually walked over Primrose Hill to South Hampstead, Emily up Camden Road to the Camden School. By chance, his mother, Beth, was in London and due to come to lunch with us, and during the morning his father rang and offered to drive him to Heathrow, and to take Beth with them. So I saw him off with both his parents, uncharacteristically united. I remember thinking how odd that was, and nice for him, almost making a celebration of the farewell.

Life went on as usual. Nine ordinary days. I took Tom twice to Great Ormond Street Hospital for different check-ups – we had to go in the car, and it was always difficult to find a parking meter. On other days he went to his nursery group in the mornings and I worked on the proofs of my book, with my papers, file cards, typewriter and books on a side table in the sitting room, near the garden window at the back of the house. Outside, the weather was brilliantly sunny and warm. After lunch either Theresa or I took him to the park. The girls played with him when they came home from school, he was bathed and put to bed. He liked to have his toy cars carefully arranged around him in his big cot, and to hear Scott Joplin, so we played the music loudly for him as he settled to sleep. Then we older ones cooked and ate our evening meal together. There was always plenty to talk about.

On 10 October I had lunch with Karl: we met, as we often did, at a small Italian restaurant in Sicilian Avenue, off Holborn. We must have talked about our work plans – my venture with a first book, he being about to leave his job as editor of the *Listener* to become an academic, running the English Department at University College, which he was to do with great distinction and good effect. On another day I met a geriatric specialist to talk about my mother's failing powers. Jo and Susanna were both away with friends at the weekend. On Sunday there was a group report from Israel in the *Sunday Times* to which Nick contributed. Emily was ill on Monday with asthma and stayed at home. On Tuesday I had to deliver a review for the *Observer*, and Fay Godwin came to take photographs of me, commissioned by my publishers for publicity. I saw other old friends, Anne and Simon Broadbent, in Greenwich in the evening.

On Wednesday, 17 October, all three girls took themselves to school, Theresa went with Tom, he in his wheeled cart, to nursery, and I settled down to work on my proofs in the sitting room. The telephone rang: it was my piano teacher and friend, Tamara Osborn, sounding not quite like her usual self. She asked me, 'Are you worried about Nick being in Israel?' 'No,' I answered cheerily; 'he told me there is nothing to worry about – the Israeli press people are so good at looking after journalists.' I can't remember what else we said: perhaps she told me that her nephew Frank Hermann, a photographer, was in Israel too, covering the war. She left me wondering why she had rung. As I pondered, another call came from her son Tom, a friend of Nick from their schooldays. He said bluntly that he had heard that Nick had been killed. 'You must be wrong,' I said. 'I'd have heard if anything like that had happened. This is just some garbled message.' I spoke so confidently that he conceded he might be mistaken.

All the same, I picked up the telephone to speak to someone at the *Sunday Times*. It was impossible to get through.

I thought for a while, and decided to ring Charles Wintour at the *Evening Standard* to ask if he'd had any recent news. I had never done such a thing before – you did not disturb a newspaper editor lightly – but I asked for him anyway. He was in conference and came to the telephone to scold me angrily for calling him out of it. I explained that I had heard something had happened to Nick. 'I'm sure it's not so,' he answered. 'I'd have heard it.' He was cold and brusque, understandably annoyed at what seemed to him an unnecessary interruption at work. I apologized, rang off and called Tom Osborn to tell him the story was nonsense. Then I turned back to my work. More or less as I did so I heard something happening downstairs.

In our house, friends usually came in through the lower door into the kitchen/living room. Theresa was down there alone. I heard footsteps coming up the stairs, put down my work again and got to my feet to go to see what was going on. Three men were coming silently and sideways, keeping their backs to the wall, through the half-closed door from the hall into the room, one by one. I knew them all: Harry Evans, the editor of the *Sunday Times*, and two journalists, Ron Hall and Hunter Davies. As I saw them, before any word was spoken, I knew what had happened. They were the messengers of death. Nick had been killed in Israel.

I suppose they told me – a heat-guided missile from the Syrians hit the car he was driving in the Golan Heights, with an Israeli officer and several other foreign journalists. I can't remember what words they used. But he was the only casualty. He was forty-one, two weeks from his forty-second birthday.

I had now to telephone Beth, Nick's mother, and give her the news that the son she loved more than her own life had been killed. I decided I must begin with the words, 'I've got to tell you something bad,' as a warning, pause for her to take this in, and then say, 'Nick has been killed.' It was unspeakably dreadful doing this. Then to explain the few facts I had been given. Next I had to tell his father, Miles – the same words, the same realization that I was giving the worst information he could ever have. Miles came straight round and met Jo coming in – as a sixth former she was allowed to leave school early on certain days, and this was one. She remembers being pleased to see her grandfather, and then he and I had to tell her that her beloved father was dead. Miles stayed with her while I was driven, by Nick's colleague Hunter Davies, to South Hampstead School, where Susanna was fetched from a class and came running innocently out, pleased with the interruption, then struck down by what I had to tell her. We drove home, I left her with Jo, then Hunter took me on to the Camden School. It was between classes, or perhaps by now the end of the morning, and the girls were milling about – someone found Emily and told her I was there for her without adding anything further. She started screaming – I have never understood why – and she ran to me, screaming all the way, so that I hugged her and calmed her and told her the terrible news all at once. We went home. Theresa appeared to tell me she had taken Tom to our friends opposite, Sue and David Gentleman, and would remain there with him for the rest of the day. She added, 'I want to tell you now that I'll stay with you as Tom's nanny until he is five' – a promise of the greatest generosity and comfort to me, never to be forgotten, binding herself into the family, although she was engaged to be married. And indeed she was like another daughter to me after this.

I had more telephone calls to make: to my mother, to my father and stepmother in France. Nick was loved by all of them, and each time I knew I was delivering a message so painful they would struggle to take it in and find hard to bear. I failed to reach his sister Stefany before she heard his death announced on the BBC lunchtime news. It went all round the world: Alison Lurie remembers hearing it disbelievingly in Ithaca (New York) on the radio. The death of a journalist is a rare event.

Friends arrived at the house: neighbours first, then from further away, shocked and full of kindness. I felt stunned, as though I had been hit on the head myself, and hardly knew how to talk to them, or they to me. Alan Brien was a theatre critic and immediately invited me to go to the theatre in a few days' time, to see a new production of *Coriolanus*, and although I had no wish to go I felt I had to accept out of politeness. Michael Frayn heard the announcement on the news and drove straight over from Blackheath. When he arrived the kitchen was full of people and he was told I had gone upstairs to find some photographs of Nick. He ran up the stairs to find me on the landing, put his arms round me and held me.

Miles's Hungarian wife Madeleine arrived raging and asked me if I did not hate the Syrians for what they had done. I didn't know how to answer, because hate seemed beside the point when someone was killed – a heat-guided missile was like a thunderbolt. All the Gloucester Crescent and

Regent's Park Terrace neighbours gave comfort, tactfully and sweetly: Jonathan and Rachel Miller, Juliet, the Mellys, the Smiths, the Haycrafts, Ursula Vaughan Williams, the Pritchetts. Friends were a comfort but I needed mostly to be with my children, and with Beth, who soon came. And also alone, to begin to try to take in what had happened.

The hours went by. More information came about the circumstances of Nick's death. Fred Ihrt, the German press photographer who had been with him in the Golan Heights and seen him killed, telephoned me from Hamburg the next day. He told me he had heard Nick cry out '*Ich sterbe*', which means 'I am dying.' This made things worse, because it meant Nick had been conscious that he was dying, and had no one with him as he died. To die alone is terrible. No one should die alone.

The *Sunday Times* asked me to agree to Nick's being buried in Israel, where they said there was an especially beautiful setting among trees. I refused. I believed the children should see the coffin and understand that their father was in it, even if they could not see his body. And they should be able to visit his grave. Otherwise he would simply have disappeared into thin air one day – as he had done so many times over the years. Bringing him home meant he had to be placed in a lead coffin, sealed to travel. It was very expensive, but after some argument the *Sunday Times* agreed, and paid the costs. So, although none of us was able to see his body, at least there was tangible evidence that he had been killed. The coffin arrived within days and was taken to the undertakers. His parents were able to visit it. I also sat beside it alone, and thought about Nick: how gifted he was, and generous; how delightfully unpredictable and wretchedly unreliable; how much he loved his own children and how good he was with other people's; what happy times we had shared. Whatever the failings of both of us in our marriage, it felt now as though the sun had been eclipsed.

Jo was about to be seventeen, Susanna was fifteen, Emily twelve, and they all behaved so well that it was hard to know what their inner feelings were. They helped themselves to Nick's shirts, sweaters and pyjamas to wear and take to bed with them at night. That was a good thing to do. I found the sight of his suits and ties hanging in the cupboards painful yet could not resist looking at them, as though they might tell me something.

During breakfast on Monday there was a letter for me from Nick, and a postcard for Tom. Our postman came into the house with them and we all cried together and hugged each other. Later Frank Hermann, who had left Israel after Nick was killed, also came. Through him we first heard of Don McCullin's extraordinary act of courage when he heard what had happened.

Don wrote his own description of how Nick had come to him at 6 a.m. on 17 October to borrow a combat jacket because he had arranged to drive towards the front with a man from *Stern* magazine who had a Peugeot, and Nick knew how to drive Peugeots. Nick took the jacket, said 'See you later' and ran off. An hour later Don was approaching the Golan Heights when he saw a black pall of smoke rising ahead and was flagged down and told not to go further because a man from the *Sunday Times* had been killed by Syrian fire. Don at once thought it must be Nick, and that he might not be dead, only wounded; and he thought of Nick's family. He put down his cameras, pulled on a helmet and then – like a man possessed, he writes – ran to find Nick. He ran in a stooped position to make himself less vulnerable. It was a terrifying run, he told me, each minute expanding so that every step seemed to take an enormously long time, and he expected to be hit himself at any moment. There was an eerie silence and a voice in his head kept asking him, 'Why are you doing this?' He knew he must be observed but still went on and saw the car, with no one in it. There had been a spare tank full of petrol on the back seat which made the effect of the missile that hit it more deadly. He found Nick's body on the ground beside the car and tried to talk to him, 'so far gone was I with terror and grief, though there could be no doubt that he was dead'. Then he picked up Nick's glasses, lying close to him, bent and with one eyeglass blown out, the other intact, and ran back with them. He brought them to me two weeks later. Don believed that to die alone is terrible, that you need someone to be with you, and he knew that Nick had no one. How many of us would have had the courage to do as he did? I have never been able to thank him properly because no words could ever be good enough.*

🙰

Our three daughters went bravely back to school. Michael Frayn, who loved Nick and was close to me too, carried me off to Hyde Park one morning as the warm days continued.

* See *Unreasonable Behaviour* by Don McCullin (1990), pp. 190–91.

As we sat in the sun, I told him that my greatest fear was for the children, for whatever effect Nick's death would have on them. How could I best help them through this loss? Then he talked to me about losing his own mother when he was twelve – she died with no warning, and suddenly, of heart failure. He had been very close to her. He was not taken to her funeral and nobody talked about her, after his father's one cry of grief and loss. Reticence of this kind was normal then, seen as a way of protecting children and keeping their spirits up perhaps. He said the world turned grey for him for two years after her death. But he added that he now felt that the loss changed him and made him develop differently, and that he might not have become a writer had she lived. Unprovable of course, but I took comfort from what he said.

Nick was to be cremated on 23 October. Two more post-cards had come for Tom from him. Harry Evans, unfailing in his kindness, drove the girls and me to Golders Green, stopping on the way by Hampstead Heath and leading us out for a short walk, all joining hands. The weather remained as bright as it had been every day since the news came. I think we were all dazed at this point. Nick's parents were there, and a very few friends. We listened to music we had all heard Nick play so often with a Music Minus One recording, the Adagio from the Mozart Oboe Quartet in F major (K370).* The following day I drove with Nick's ashes to Great Waldingfield in Suffolk, where we had spent so much time, and his mother and father helped me to bury the ashes

---

* Music Minus One recordings provide the orchestral or accompanying parts 'minus one', allowing soloists to rehearse with them.

Nick

in the village churchyard, next to the grave of our baby son Daniel. I planted primroses and a hellebore. The birds sang above us in the high trees all the time we were there.

The children continued resolutely with their schoolwork. Jo had exams to sit, and we celebrated her seventeenth birthday quietly – the same day would have been Nick's forty-second. Neighbours, friends and family were all good to us. Ronnie MacKeith came to grieve with us. We went to a Schubert recital, to Susanna's school concert, spent a day in Cambridge – just what we might have been doing anyway. I took Emily to the theatre and Tony Godwin carried me off to Puccini's shabby shocker, *Tosca*, with the final leap of the heroine from the roof of the Castel Sant'Angelo. Michael took me to see Truffaut's sublimely funny new film

La Nuit américaine. The *Sunday Times* sent round a kind and efficient secretary with hundreds of letters and messages of condolence to be answered. I had many more and we started on the long labour of replying to them.

Karl, Terry and Michael all helped me by listening, taking me to lunch, talking good sense from their own experience. Karl had grown up with both parents absent, just a good grandmother, and flourished at school and university and in his career. Terry had to earn his living young, leaving school to go to a French family to teach the children English. Harry explained to me that the *Sunday Times* proposed to give me £100,000, which seemed like limitless wealth. I was told I must find a financial adviser to deal with it.

At home, we formed a close group, sitting together, reading, talking about Nick and making plans for the future, the girls deciding which universities they favoured – Cambridge for Jo, a mathematician, Su thought of Oxford to read English, Em was most interested in science and not yet ready to decide. They discussed life with Theresa, who was so much ahead of them, already earning her living and engaged to be married to a young photographer we all liked. And we talked about clothes and hair and make-up, and devoted ourselves to Tom and his progress. He was preserved from sorrow by not knowing what had happened, and I remember thinking that we were living through an almost idyllic phase, setting aside our grief while we supported one another. When the weather changed and turned cool, we put rugs on the floor and sat round our open fire in the sitting room on cushions, cheered by the occasional sputtering from burning coals and the changing light of the flames. That was the winter of power cuts and candlelight that made everything in the house look different.

Beth had already offered to come to help in January when Tom was to have an operation. She was always outwardly calm, easy to be with, interesting to talk to. My mother, overflowing with emotion, told me she felt Nick's death more keenly than I did. He had charmed her, and she told me that, whereas I might build a new life, she could not. Miles struggled with his grief, surely the deepest he had ever felt. My father and stepmother Kath were struck with profound sorrow. They came to London for the memorial service in December. It would be the first time my father and mother were to be present at the same occasion, and we had to make sure they did not come face to face.

Before the memorial service, something unexpected happened. John Gross, currently literary editor of the *New Statesman*, told me he was moving on to edit *The Times Literary Supplement*, and didn't so much raise the possibility that I might return to a job at the *Statesman* as command me to take over as literary editor. Tony Howard had given his editorial blessing already, and he also insisted that it would be much better for me to have a job than to stay at home. I was taken aback. It seemed far too soon to be thinking of a job. It would mean hours away from home and children, who had already lost one parent and would be losing a noticeable chunk of my time and attention if I were out of the house every weekday. I asked for a week to consider and consult with my daughters, my mother-in-law and Theresa. They were all in favour of the job. Tom was at nursery school already, and Theresa was there to look after him at home. The girls were in their teens, doing well at school, with good friends and busy lives. Maybe John and Tony were right, and a mother working at a job she enjoyed and earning money might be better for them than one at home. Others advised me strongly against, but those I trusted best told me I should. I thought hard, came to the conclusion they were right and promised the *New Statesman* I would start work in February.

Nick's Uncle Humphrey, as head of the family, invited me to lunch to talk over practical matters. We met at the Langham Hotel's restaurant, where you eat on the twelfth floor, and after a quiet meal we walked into the lift. It filled up with other diners, started down and almost at once juddered to a standstill. There seemed to be no immediate prospect of rescue. Everyone was quiet. I was frightened and I imagine the others felt the same fear. Lucky to have my back to the wall, I went through what poems or snatches of poems I could conjure up in my head: one was Keats's ode 'To Autumn', which the children and I had memorized together while driving. It took a good hour before we were winched back to the top. This was nothing more than an inconvenient mini-danger, but just two weeks after Nick's death it was a reminder that the physical world could be a dangerous place where nothing should be taken for granted.

The memorial meeting in December was held in the stately rooms of the Stationers' Hall, near St Paul's. Harry Evans and I had agreed on the speakers, whom he introduced: Paul Johnson and Michael Frayn. Alan Williams – the novelist, a good friend – read a favourite poem of Nick's, Auden's 'The Fall of Rome', and Neal Ascherson read Donne's 'A Nocturnall upon S. *Lucies* Day'. The long first movement of Schubert's String Quintet in C Major was played by the Dartington String Quartet.

I knew it would be a very large occasion, and hundreds of people came, because Nick was admired and loved as a journalist and broadcaster as well as a friend. I was uneasy about presenting myself and the children for public sympathy. Nick's death was horrifying to me. I should have been there to help him at the end. And he should have lived to follow a long and rewarding career in journalism. At the same time, I doubted our marriage would have prospered. However much I missed him – and I did miss him, and mourn for him, and long for him to be with us – I was already distanced from him. I had learnt too well that I could not depend on him. I knew I had to make my own working life, and my own independent emotional life.

I grieved. But I also thought, 'NOW!' What did this NOW mean? That I was released from a contract. That from now on I was in sole charge of my own life, of my four children, each of whom needed me in a different way; and of the house, and of all the daily, weekly, yearly decisions that have to be made. That I was to start again and live as I chose – not only could but *must* start again, and choose and make my own life. That everything was changed. That I was already standing alone, and not afraid.

The missile that killed Nick killed his mother just as surely. She was diagnosed with cancer a year later and died in May 1975. She told me she did not think his death was the cause of her illness, and she also said that, although she would have preferred not to have treatment, she felt she must, or it would look as though she wanted to die. I took her for a week's holiday to the Engadine in Switzerland in February 1975. I asked her where she wanted to go and she chose Switzerland because she remembered a happy holiday there with Nick when he was a boy.

We had to get permission from her surgeon for the holiday and he gave me a precise date when she could go, to be fitted in between treatments. She was not allowed to fly, so we took the boat from Harwich – she lived in Suffolk – to the Hook of Holland. We shared a cabin and she took off her pretty wig to show me the scant hair left by her treatments, laughing about it with her usual spirit. In Holland we took the flashily named Rheingold Express train on to St Moritz.

At our hotel in Sils Maria, we watched elderly German couples dancing with perfect precision after dinner. We talked over all our meals, and in the daytime we were able to go out, warmly wrapped, on big sledges, to be driven over the snow along the high valleys around Sils. The air was clear and crisp and we breathed deeply. One day Beth said, 'You feel you could live forever in this air.' Then later, 'You can't believe in your own death. You may know intellectually that you are going to die soon, but it has no meaning for you, the person alive thinking about it.' She was a remarkable woman, brave and truthful, and I learnt from her courage and clear-headedness.

All too soon the week ended. I took her home and went to see her as often as I could in the following weeks, bringing her the brightly coloured flowers she liked to look at when she was too weak to do anything else. In April she was taken into hospital and on 6 May she died. I wrote to my father on the 13th: 'Everything here is in abeyance because Beth died last Tuesday . . . it has been a harrowing process, made worse by the sense that she was dying of Nick's death and the circle is now closed. Yesterday was the cremation and her husband asked me to speak about her, which I felt I had to do but which was an ordeal.' I was there with my daughters, and in what I said I mentioned Beth's adventurous years as a young woman in London – she had left Miles Tomalin and taken up with the actor Miles Malleson, also married – and as I used the words 'a wild colonial girl', I saw her younger son Conrad's head lift sharply. But he knew I loved and respected her. It was true that, as I researched Katherine Mansfield later, I did see resemblances between Beth, daughter of a university professor in Winnipeg, and Mansfield, whose father was a New Zealand banker, when they found themselves on their own in London, full of energy and ambition and ready to take risks. She told me she had had an abortion when she became pregnant with another child after Nick, and now grieved for it, having lost him. Happily she had made a good and steady second marriage which gave her Conrad, her beloved second son. Like Nick, she was admired and courted for her high spirits, and given a certain licence by the Tomalin family to behave unorthodoxly. All the Tomalins came to her funeral.

Beth had asked for the same oboe music we had at Nick's cremation to be played, and for her ashes to be buried next to his. A week later we took them to the Waldingfield churchyard and dug them in under the trees. Mother and son were together.

Working Mother

I was back in the *New Statesman*'s tall building in the corner of Lincoln's Inn Fields to take up my new position as literary editor in February 1974.

Following John Gross was daunting. Katharine Whitehorn teased me, saying, 'You *do* take culture seriously . . .', and I did. I believed that critical discourse mattered, that discussion and controversy are an essential part of any culture, and that an intelligent review is the best tribute that can be paid to a book, a film or a play. I wanted brainy critics to educate me and all our readers, and to entertain us at the same time. In trying to bring this about, I enjoyed myself. Looking back on that time years later, I wrote:

> I felt free and busy and full of energy and hope when I was forty, working for the *Statesman*. It was like having the best of a woman's life and a man's too. The children all seemed to be happy and secure in spite of all, and although Tom had every sort of problem, family life was good. I chose and bought my own car, I knew all the writers, and enjoyed that. Yesterday evening, walking from Holborn Underground through the back streets to Theobald's Road – Red Lion Street, where I used to lunch in cheap Italian

restaurants – I was overcome with nostalgia for that bit of my life. Well, I'm sure it wasn't all wonderful, but what really struck me last night was that I remembered it as my *youth* [letter to Émile and Kath, January 1996].

I made my first lead a page-long poem by Clive James, a witty verse letter to fellow poet John Fuller. Clive took culture so seriously and made jokes so easily that within weeks he published his 'tragedy in heroic couplets', *Peregrine Prykke's Pilgrimage*, a satire on the current literary scene in London. Clive understood that satire is a form of flattery and put in portraits of poets, reviewers, television personalities and literary editors: Klaus Mauler, Terry Towelling, Professor Chris Rix, Marvin Grabb. Clara Tomahawk got a mention, although I knew I had not earned my place yet.

Neal Ascherson told me that literary editors are those who prevent their friends from writing books by getting them to review other people's. He was right, but in spite of it he took on a book on the Warsaw Rising of 1944, and later another on German history. I wanted to get historians to write – a political magazine must keep its eye on history – and extracted reviews from historians I admired: Blair Worden, Richard Cobb, Christopher Hill, A. J. P. Taylor, Keith Thomas, James Joll, Peter Stern, Eric Hobsbawm.

V. S. Pritchett was our grand old man, and he gave us his deep critical responses to the books he chose to write about, from Saul Bellow's *Humboldt's Gift* to Michael Glenny's translation of Bulgakov's *Country Doctor's Notebook*. Being a neighbour, I often collected his copy from their house and admired his wife Dorothy as she prepared dinner, laying out the silver on the dining table while he worked on upstairs. I invited them both to an office party at which they held court. He wrote afterwards to say how much they had enjoyed the 'good food, good drink, everyone clever', and went on indiscreetly, 'I was once asked to a political editorial lunch about 30 years ago; and never asked again and never would have gone – total boredom.'

Some of the clever people he talked to at my party would have been Marina Warner, Alan Ryan, Shiva Naipaul, Hilary Spurling, Paul Theroux, Craig Raine, Victoria Glendinning, John Naughton. John Carey and John Bayley, stars of the Oxford English faculty, were not there but I did persuade them to deliver occasional reviews. Jonathan Raban shone among the new generation. Brigid Brophy wrote for us on animal research, Alethea Hayter on Samuel Palmer, A. S. Byatt on Browning. I was always eager to find women reviewers.

The *Statesman* had a tradition of publishing new verse, and we printed poems by Hugo Williams, Derek Mahon, Dennis Enright, Roy Fuller, John Fuller, Fleur Adcock, Clive James, Craig Raine and George Mackay Brown. I extracted one poem from Ted Hughes, none from Philip Larkin, but at least he consented to review *The Young Thomas Hardy* for us in 1975 – Hardy was a poet he admired and studied.

The most brilliant and versatile young writer on the *Statesman* was Francis Hope. He could edit, turn out a leader or a general essay on any subject, review any book or play, devise a competition, write a poem. In my first month at work he was killed in a plane crash, leaving a young wife and daughter and a host of mourning friends. Coming so soon after Nick's death made it worse. The memorial, held in the same rooms in the Stationers' Hall, was grimly sorrowful with our awareness that two of the brightest journalists of our time had been lost.

But the *Statesman* was only one part of my life. Tom was always in my mind, his health and his education. My mother-in-law's illness also preoccupied me, and my own mother was becoming more dependent. We were still a big family at home, the three sisters, with many friends and intellectual worlds opening to them, Theresa more like a fourth elder sister than a nanny, and Tom our cherished little one, to be played with, encouraged, delighted in as he learnt to talk, struggling with some sounds, and wheeling himself about in his red chariot. We were lucky to be able to spend weekends in Suffolk and Sussex, where aunts and uncles had their cottages, and holidays in France with my father. Our old car was falling to bits, so I asked advice from the people who wrote about cars in the *Sunday Times*. They recommended a Volvo estate car, given that I had four children, a nanny, a mother and a mother-in-law, plus a few cats and soon a wheelchair to be moved about. The car salesmen showed me a brilliant orange car so cheerful and reliable-looking that my spirits lifted at the sight of it. I bought it at once, my first major purchase with the money I had been given, and loved it for all the many years it served us. That July I drove it fast and happily to Vence and back with the children.

Jo had won a scholarship to my old Cambridge college, Newnham, and was going up in the autumn to read Mathematics. We took Tom with us when I drove her there and stayed with her as she found her room, met friends and unpacked books, enjoying the excitement of the day with her. The next morning, over breakfast at home, Tom asked me, 'Is Jo dead now?' He had made a logical deduction, based on his memories of his father's departure. I explained that she was alive and would be returning. But it was a moment of melancholy, and going up to her room I thought how soon a big family house can empty.

In September 1974, my book *The Life and Death of Mary Wollstonecraft* was published. A first book is like a first child, a source of pride and anxiety in equal amounts. I had rejected the beige jacket proposed by my publisher and asked David Gentleman to take over, and he designed a strikingly handsome one, using the contemporary portrait of Mary looking fierce in her top hat. My publisher, George Weidenfeld, told me that the only biographies that sold were those of famous people. All the same, he was giving a party for me. The day before, he rang and said, 'Do you mind sharing your party with Edna O'Brien?' Pure George – and luckily I admired Edna. It was a good party, and the book got many reviews, some good, some attacks. Film rights were sold. I was asked to give a talk in Lewes, my first experience of standing up in front of a strange audience. I began the talk by contrasting Wordsworth – who visited France during the Revolution and fathered a child on a French girl, a fact he kept concealed as he became a revered poet in England – with Wollstonecraft, who also had a child in France during the Revolution, brought her daughter back to England and was vilified. As I reached this point, a man in the audience broke into my talk and started attacking me for being rude about Wordsworth. He was persistent, I took him on as best I could, the audience managed to shut him up, and I continued. It was a startling initiation into public speaking, but I had learnt to hold my nerve. After that, I heard I was to be given the Whitbread Prize for a First Book. Better still, I noticed two separate women on the Underground reading it one day. Not so good was Weidenfeld's having printed only 2,000 copies; it sold out fast and could not be reprinted until after Christmas. Tony Godwin, who had such faith in it, had moved to New York, and would be publishing the American edition. Robin Denniston, not seen since I was seven, at boarding school in Hertfordshire, was now my editor.

On New Year's Eve that year I took all my daughters to hear *Meistersingers* from a box at the Coliseum. We sat above the brass, getting the full benefit. Then we went on to a party at Ron Hall's house in Hampstead, and danced for several hours more.

❦

Tom was doing well but he sometimes stammered. He told us about a friend, 'The boy in my mouth', with whom he talked privately. I had heard of imaginary friends and took an interest: this one was important to Tom for several years. He never gave the boy any name other than 'The boy in my mouth' or attempted to explain him, simply referred to him as a normal part of his life, and we accepted his existence. So much so that I sometimes thought I might see the boy if I looked hard into Tom's mouth.

At four he started at the Franklin Delano Roosevelt School in Swiss Cottage. It was for children with disabilities and he, like all the pupils, was collected every weekday morning and brought home in a bus at teatime. He had his first standard wheelchair then. It was a magnificent school in almost every way. The children were cared for kindly and efficiently. Not much was expected of them in the way of intellectual development, perhaps because the range of disabilities was so wide. They said he had no need to learn to write since he could use a keyboard. I insisted on the importance of writing, useful for notes to yourself and others, for lists, for labels – and keyboards are not always to hand. So he learnt handwriting and became an excellent and prolific writer. Soon he asked me to teach him to read and learnt easily; but he never became enthusiastic about books. He told me later there were just too many of them about the house when he was a child. Terrible to have put him off the enjoyment of books, since reading is such an obvious resource for someone who has difficulty in moving about. But his passion was for trains and travel.

He loved going to school, hated missing a day. He made some good friends. One was Yasmin, a sweet and cheerful girl with several brothers who were interested in football, supporters of Ipswich. Yasmin told Tom to support Ipswich too – they were doing well at that time – and he became a fan, so enthusiastic that he has never wavered and now, forty years later, still goes regularly to Ipswich matches. She was allowed to come to stay overnight with us, and I asked her mother if it was all right for the two little ones to sleep in the same bed. Yes, it was. So I tucked them up together and they chatted and laughed until they fell asleep, and got up happily together in the morning. The next night, when Yasmin went to her own home again, Tom was as inconsolable as Romeo. He cried and cried for hours, and refused to be comforted. He saw Yasmin at school again, and their friendship remained strong, but somehow there was never another happy night together.

Paul was another of his friends, also loved. He was beautiful and as ethereal as an angel, and he never complained although he was suffering from cystic fibrosis, which made it hard for him to breathe. I had no idea how bad his condition was when I invited him to spend the day with us one Saturday. He and Tom played and ate together, and I did my best to keep him comfortable – he needed thumping on the back regularly to help his lungs. In the evening I took him home to his family, where I met his young Irish mother and old grandmother who sat coughing and complaining in a corner of their sparsely furnished flat. A few days later the school let me know that Paul had died. I could hardly believe it. I explained to Tom and we grieved together. I took some flowers from our garden to his mother and asked if I might go to the funeral. I couldn't help hearing, as we spoke quietly together, his old granny grumbling loudly that, with the death of her grandson, the telephone would be taken away from them. I realized what a sheltered life I led, not knowing that you got a phone if you had a mortally sick child, and were likely to have it removed after the funeral.

The next day I went to Kensal Green. I didn't take Tom. It was a short Catholic service, after which we went outside and stood around the grave. All at once there was a movement as Paul's mother threw herself down into the grave, howling in her grief and misery. It was appalling yet I knew it was right and true: she had given death its due, given her child the passionate tribute she needed to bestow on his dead body. I have never seen anyone else throw themselves into a grave, and I shall never forget Paul's mother. Tom has never forgotten Paul either, and he still gives money to help find a cure for cystic fibrosis.

I learnt through Tom's experiences. I don't know whether the telephone was taken away from Paul's family after his death. The school told me they did not mention death to their pupils, and I had to explain that I had naturally told Tom that Paul was dead, so he at any rate knew.

I was seen as an odd mother, but kindly tolerated. I asked the school not to give Tom sweets, which they handed out frequently and freely to all the children. One day when I happened to be there I heard a teacher say, 'Now there will be a sweetie for everyone except Tom Tomalin, whose mother does not allow them.' He did not seem to mind at all, and he has never needed a filling in his teeth.

At the office I had a new young reviewer, Martin Amis. I met him first in January 1974, inviting him to lunch when he was working for *The Times Literary Supplement* and I was about to start at the *Statesman*. His first novel, *The Rachel Papers*, had cheered me in my sorrows and made me laugh, and I intended to ask him to review for me. Of course he was the son of Kingsley, so born into literary grandeur, although his childhood had not been easy after his parents divorced, and he said he had read nothing but comic books until his stepmother Elizabeth Jane Howard introduced him to Jane Austen. But with that he had gone to Oxford and become a star.

We made friends. He was twenty-five and I was forty and we surprised one another. He said, 'I thought you'd be fat,' and I had not expected quite such assurance. We were about the same height, so that if I wore high heels I was just taller than him. As I got to know him, I noticed that his hands shook in the morning, making him seem vulnerable. But the solidity of his presence belied that, as did the confidence of his pronouncements. He stood out in any group. He wrote well because he thought well. He rolled his own cigarettes and drank a good deal. And he had a seriously intelligent face, a neat and expressive mouth and blond hair, like my Tom's blond hair. Perhaps I saw Martin as an older son, one who shared my love of books. From the start he liked to put his arm round my waist and hold it there, standing beside me. I liked it too. And, although I did not care for cigarette smoke, I succumbed to the charm of his smoker's voice, so deep that it made him sound older than he looked. It was the voice of a man of the world, which he was not, but soon would be.

In my first Spring Books number I let him review *The Sacred and Profane Love Machine*, Iris Murdoch's latest novel. At this time Iris Murdoch was at the height of her fame, winning prizes and producing annual bestsellers. His review was an elegant, polite and devastating put-down. He was right, because the story she told was

banal – the man with a pure wife and an exciting mistress –
and, worse, it was far too long, and had needed to be cut
and edited. An established author as intelligent as Murdoch
should have seen she was expected to do better. With this,
Martin stepped fully armed into the literary arena. Tony
Howard and I agreed that he was a prodigy and must be
brought to the *Statesman* as soon as possible. I asked him
if he would become my deputy and he started in February 1975.

Tony also brought Christopher Hitchens to the *Statesman*. Hitch was a born journalist and the office became an
increasingly diverting place as the poet James Fenton also
joined the staff – here were three young men with brilliant
futures, each looking for the territory he wanted to mark
out for himself. Martin says he and Hitch set out to explore
the lower Bohemia together. They were best friends:
neither was gay, although Hitch sometimes behaved as
though he were in love with Martin, and kept a watchful
eye on me.

Martin knew nothing about opera, so I took him to
Covent Garden to hear *Rosenkavalier*, Strauss's great account
of the love between an older woman and a very young
man. I may have been giving myself a warning. Opera did
not speak to Martin. My brief love-affair with him began
in the summer of 1975. I was a widow, he a bachelor, and
we did not keep it secret. There was much holding of hands
under tables and kissing. Terry Kilmartin mocked me
affectionately, telling me I was pretending to be the heroine of a French film. He was right in that the whole
experience was intoxicating and did not seem quite part of

the real world. My mother, finding Martin in the sitting room at home one day, waiting to take me out, looked at him with undisguised disapproval. But he made himself part of the family. He was always especially nice to Tom, and he and Susanna got on so well that we joked about being close to the situation in Turgenev's play *A Month in the Country*, in which the tutor is involved with both mother and daughter.

It was an exceptionally hot summer and we made up a party one sultry evening early in August to go swimming in the Hampstead Ladies' Pond after dark – my three daughters, Valerie Grove, Martin, Hitch and a few others. We drove up to Hampstead and climbed over the gate into the pond enclosure easily. The swim was deliciously cool and we parted company chastely at the end of the evening. Only Hitch misbehaved, ringing a newspaper and putting a story into the gossip column.

I went with the children for two weeks' holiday in Sussex, where Uncle Humphrey let us use a cottage on his land. Tony Howard and Martin came down for lunch and Martin stayed on for two more days. In October he took me to Oxford for the weekend: we stayed at the Randolph and spent the evening with Craig and Li Raine. Craig thought Martin and I should get married, an idea neither of us ever entertained. Then Martin invited me to spend the weekend with his father and stepmother Elizabeth Jane in their house in Barnet. It passed decorously – drinks and dinner, separate bedrooms, a walk through the suburban countryside on Sunday morning. Afterwards Martin wrote to me saying they had expressed amazement that I had a daughter at university. Perhaps they also advised caution.

He sent me charming letters when he went to visit his mother in Spain. We had no quarrels, but after a time I began to realize that what I thought of as a love-affair was more like membership of a club. Martin was attractive to many young women, and he was ready to enjoy the situation. That did not work for me. Our affair ended and I was sad. My daughters were probably relieved. Friends cheered me up, and he and I remained good colleagues. He edited the pages very well when I was on holiday. In the summer of 1976 we celebrated his twenty-seventh birthday with a merry lunch together, something I'd forgotten about and found mentioned in a letter to my father in which I praised him for his hard work and added, 'There is no doubt he is cleverer than his Dad.' I knew Martin could take over my job easily and do it very well.

I found it difficult to make up my mind about my own future. I loved editing, yet I had accepted commissions to write a major biography of Katherine Mansfield and a short life of Shelley, as well as compiling an anthology. This was a lot of work to fit round an office job. I wrote to my father, 'No nearer to making up my mind about my future. I do so enjoy the editorial life . . . I am really frightened of what I might sink into if I gave up overwork and tried to take up the solitary life of the writer again.' Yet it became increasingly difficult to deal with the conflicting demands on my time. In 1977 we asked Julian Barnes to become our television critic and he was an immediate success, a born essayist and a welcome addition to office life. So I left the *Statesman* to work on my various commissions, Martin became literary editor and Julian his deputy: a pretty good team, I thought. But it was not a good move for me.

❦

Not long before I left the *Statesman* I had an unexpected visitor: Maurice Kaufmann. He asked me to meet him at a café and told me he had some terrible news for me: that his cousin, my old schoolfriend Auriol, was dead. She had been in a car crash – or rather something worse: he suggested that it was not a random accident but a deliberate act. He did not want to say more and I was too shocked to ask. She and I had kept in touch, although with gaps that grew longer with the years. She had told me about her grim experiences with a boss who made her pregnant, a late abortion and then a second pregnancy. Then, thankfully, I heard she was married. I had not seen her since her marriage and the birth of a son, but her letting me know this good news had made me think she was secure and happy, and I had planned to see them. I asked Maurice if I could now go and at least meet her child? No, he said, because the father was taking him to New Zealand and intending to settle there – and that he was severing all contact with the Kaufmann family. There was nothing I could do. Maurice did not linger. He wrote to me later apologizing for being so abrupt, recalling my old friendship with him and the family. I failed to respond. I was shocked by the thought of what might have driven Auriol to such a fate – whether the hysterical outbursts I had seen years before should have been taken much more seriously – but I put it aside, not wanting more useless grief. Auriol had deserved much more from life, I knew, but now it was too late to make anything right for her. I still think of her, and our friendship and laughter, and of her son growing up on the other side of the world.

※

There were changes at home. Theresa married in September 1975, and Tom and I rejoiced at the wedding. The young Frenchwoman who replaced her was not a success. She taught Tom nothing, and we discovered that she was disciplining him by locking him in the dark larder. I dealt with the situation by appointing an unconventional new nanny. His name was Christopher Reid. He was just down from Oxford and he wrote poetry – I had no idea then how celebrated a poet he would become. In the summer of 1976 he came into the *Statesman* to see Martin – they'd been taught together at Oxford – and heard me talking, saying that I was having trouble with a bad nanny and needed to find a new one. Chris said, 'I could do that job.' I paid no attention, as he recalls, but I must have taken in his words because some weeks later I rang him and asked, 'Were you serious?' and he said, 'Yes.' So I invited him to come and meet Tom over Sunday lunch. Tom was just six, he took to Chris at once, and we agreed Chris should move in and look after him.

Jo was mostly away at Cambridge now, Susanna preparing to take university entrance exams, Emily in the sixth form at Westminster School with an early intake of girls – she rode to school daily on a moped and planned to become an engineer.

Emily

Chris, who by his own account came from a conventional family and had no sisters, says he warmed to the Bohemian aspect of life in Gloucester Crescent and especially liked moving into a house of young women with strong characters. He enjoyed our dinner parties too: Kenneth Clark came to one, and Chris questioned him about his patronage of Stanley Spencer, which had surprised him. Kurt Vonnegut came to another; and at various times Paul Theroux, Jim Farrell, Alison Lurie, Dennis Enright, Eric and Marlene Hobsbawm, Jeremy Isaacs. And since the life of the Crescent was sociable and informal, Chris got to know all my old friends, and a new neighbour, Mary-Kay Wilmers, who took the Mellys' house when they left. Her sons Will and Sam played football in the street with Tom and other local boys, and Sam became Tom's best friend.

Chris helped Tom to get up on weekday mornings, saw him on to the school bus and was then free until the bus brought him home at 3.30. Tom liked Chris so much that he very soon preferred to be put to bed by him. He called him his nanny, by agreement. One day, when they were in a shop in Camden together, Tom looked up at a very tall bearded man and asked him, 'Why don't you shave?' – and, getting no answer, remarked, 'My nanny shaves,' at which the man left the shop rapidly.

Chris was the first of a long line of male helpers I found for Tom. It seemed a good idea for a boy who had neither father nor brother, and it worked well. Some I arranged privately, some through organizations that specialized in putting volunteers into families. They came from all parts of England, from Wales, Dublin, Belfast, Germany and Switzerland. I learnt that young men needed a great deal more food than girls of the same age and I had to double the amount I prepared. Otherwise they were interestingly various, and almost without exception likeable, committed to helping Tom, and kind; and some became friends for life.

Jo flourished at Cambridge, and in December 1976 Susanna won a scholarship to read English at Oxford. Everything

In the garden with Tom and Ian, friend and helper

went well for her. She brought home Adam, the model boyfriend every mother rejoices to meet, gifted, high achieving, modest, friendly and good-looking. He was in his last year at Cambridge, also reading English, and they became a steady couple: everyone liked him. She put in some work experience at the *New Statesman*, then took herself travelling in America, sending home cheerful and detailed accounts of her enjoyment of Boston and Harvard, and of the West Coast. She arrived back in time for the first night of Michael Frayn's play *Donkeys' Years*, and I remember her reassuring him during the interval, when he looked doubtful as playwrights often do, telling him that she and everyone else in the audience was having a good time.

Chris Reid left us, to be replaced by Ian MacKenzie from Edinburgh, who offered to work with Tom for a year. Ian was a graduate and an intellectual, preparing to take a further degree; he quickly became part of the family. In October 1977 Susanna went up to Wadham in Oxford, where she had many friends already; she was writing stories and poems, and started on her studies enthusiastically. Later in the month we celebrated Jo's twenty-first and my mother's eightieth birthday together.

In November, while I was investigating a leaky pipe in the attic, I found a trunk of Nick's old papers. I decided to sort them out, and wrote an account of my response to my father. 'Judge my amazement when I found many packets of impassioned love-letters from a whole series of women, some known to me but mostly not. What an extraordinary man he was . . . I'm glad I didn't find these letters at the time of his death.' I threw them away and quickly stopped thinking about them. I had too much else to worry about.

I realized that if Nick had lived he would have made sure I did not come across such things, and that it was another result of the catastrophe of his death that they turned up. This helped me to be more tolerant. And now I understood better that many men are programmed to be pursuers. I found that being a young widow brought me a great many admirers, consolers, wooers, romantics and would-be seducers. Most of them were charming. I think they convinced themselves that a woman alone in her house, or with fatherless children, must need looking after, and their intentions were good. I lost count of the friendly men who insisted on examining the wiring in the house, declared it unsafe and offered to fix it for me. I remember that it was fixed several times. I laughed a lot without explaining why as I gave my thanks each time.

※

Having left the *Statesman*, I found myself still leading the literary life. I reviewed for the *New York Review of Books* one day and *Punch* the next. I wrote a script on Virginia Woolf for German television. A publisher suggested I should write a short history of feminism, which I considered, talked over with them, and decided against. I judged the Whitbread Prize and agreed to become a Booker judge. I did many four-week stints on Radio Three's programme *Critics' Forum*, which meant covering a play, a film, a book, an art show and a radio or television programme each week, to be discussed with other critics. Its formidable editor, Philip French, gave all his contributors crash courses in how to have a good argument on air: listen to the others, he said; don't just worry about getting in your own good remark. I wrote some pieces for the *Radio Times*. Harry Evans let me know I could review for the *Sunday Times* whenever I wanted to, and I did a little, particularly pleased to be invited to write about the great Elizabeth David's *English Bread and Yeast Cookery*. It's on my kitchen shelf now, well floured.

Michael Frayn took me to a charity show to which he had contributed a short farce that showed actors backstage. Afterwards I lost one of my contact lenses and we were obliged to crawl round looking for it, an incident that found its way into *Noises Off*, which was the extended version of the short farce played that night. And, while I am claiming credit, I'll add that I suggested the cactus.

I was invited to make an official cultural visit to the Soviet Union, agreed to go, and visited Moscow and Leningrad (as it still was). I asked to see one of the Baltic states but was told that was impossible and sent instead to Yerevan in Armenia, where I met the proud translator of Galsworthy's *Forsyte Saga* into Armenian. I had told the organizers in advance that I intended to raise the names of imprisoned writers at the formal dinners, and did so at every opportunity. The chief difficulty was avoiding taking too much vodka as toast followed toast.

The contents of my suitcase were investigated by our guide while I was out of my hotel room at the opera in Leningrad. I knew what she had done because I found a paper that was clearly hers lying among my folded dresses. She did not turn a hair when I offered it back to her the next morning in the taxi on the way to the station, simply took it and said, 'Good, we could not make our journey today without this.' She was a beautiful young woman, a knowledgeable guide through the Hermitage and Tretyakov galleries, and no doubt doing her best to survive and flourish in a society where a false step could be disastrous. She was tough too, and when we said our farewells at the airport, she rather airily suggested I should not take 'things' too seriously – meaning, I suppose, the imprisonment of writers. Clearly she was doing well under Brezhnev's rule – she wore a splendid mink coat. A few years later I saw her in London, looking as beautiful and well dressed as ever.

❦

I became a committee person in the Seventies too, first with the Royal Literary Fund, which helped writers in need. I felt it an honour to be invited. I was also curious to see how things were done in what was at that time a predominantly masculine group – the only other woman member then was Janet Adam Smith, who like me had been widowed young, and also edited the back half of the *New Statesman* in the 1950s while bringing up her children. John Lehmann was the chairman, and there were about twenty male members of the Committee: publishers, journalists, editors, agents and successful writers. The Fund's long history dates back to the 1790s.

We met once a month, in the Stationers' Hall, and discussed applications by writers and occasionally writers' widows, who were also entitled to ask for grants. At one of my earliest meetings, as we looked at the case of one widow, an acerbic Osbert Lancaster demanded, 'Why must we waste our money giving assistance to all these dreadful widows?' There were coughs and murmurs; Janet and I exchanged smiles. Debates about how much we should or could give were sometimes fierce. We had disagreements too when, no longer able to afford the Stationers' Hall for our meetings, it was proposed we should hold them at the Garrick Club: how could we meet at a club that excluded women, I asked? My objection was overruled, and I had to give way. The porters at the Garrick were always exquisitely polite to me.

Our Committee was always short of money and one of our duties was to try to persuade fellow writers who were doing well to make contributions. I remember writing begging letters to friends who were said to have been paid large advances, asking for small donations, and I never got a refusal. I learnt that most writers earn very little, that they can't afford to be ill, and that life becomes increasingly difficult for them as they age. Some who had moved abroad to live cheaply found themselves stranded when they needed the health service. Some ran up debts and faced bankruptcy. The use of credit cards especially led to such disasters. Our job was to read the work submitted by applicants and assess its literary merit, which we were inclined to be generous about; then we discussed how best to help. We could hand out lump sums or small pensions.

I thought then – and still think – that the RLF is one of the most worthwhile committees on which I have served, because it is entirely practical, giving help quickly to writers facing disaster and supporting those who can no longer help themselves by providing them with pensions. The difficulty in the 1970s was that our funds were simply too small to allow us to give as much help as was needed. Everything changed in the 1990s, when A. A. Milne's huge bequest came to the Fund, and since then it has acquired its own premises, extended its activities and been able to give substantial help whenever it is needed – thanks chiefly to Winnie-the-Pooh.

Another committee on which I served, first in 1975, was that of the London Library. I'd been a member and regular user since the Sixties, and become a Life Member in 1973 when I was widowed, thinking that, whatever happened to me in the future, I could spend my days in the Library. I believe I was put on the Committee because there had been a row about all its members being rich and privileged people. Bamber Gascoigne took me to lunch with the chairman, Michael Astor, and I passed muster as someone neither rich nor posh. Over the years I was on and off the Committee, and the one good thing I did came in the 1990s, when Rupert Christiansen and I decided we would press with all our might for some evening opening hours, and after a struggle we made it happen.

I was also persuaded on to a non-literary body – this is my second most worthwhile committee – the Silver Jubilee Committee on Access for the Disabled, established in 1977 by Alf Morris, the stalwart Labour MP who set himself with Jack Ashley to change things for the disabled, and succeeded. What he achieved was of immediate interest to me in bringing up Tom, because I had many battles to fight, from persuading the council to lower a few kerbs so that he could wheel himself along the street, to getting him into a regular school. We put out a report headed 'Can Disabled People Go Where You Go?' in 1979, and Alf co-opted me on to a further committee looking at restrictions against disabled people (CORAD) that reported in 1982. Both these were chaired by Peter Large, a civil servant disabled by polio who worked with Alf. I did little but turn up and support their ideas. Their persistence brought in the mobility allowance and forced a new attitude to the built environment. They are heroes to me because they changed the world for disabled people and their families: I met parents who told me they kept their disabled children hidden out of shame and fear of how they might be treated. We must never revert to that situation.

⚇

The books I was supposed to be researching and writing were not making the progress they should have been. The Katherine Mansfield biography was the one I found most difficult, possibly because I had not chosen her but been asked to take her on, and I had not yet found a way of engaging with her. I was invited to visit New Zealand where she was born and lived her early life, and was tempted, but decided it was too far and meant leaving Tom without a parent for too long. It was the right decision but it became part of a general difficulty I had in building up the necessary closeness to my subject.

For the short book on Shelley there was no problem: the complex patterns of his life make him an irresistible subject, threaded with ambiguities, rich in foreign travel and friendships (Byron, Keats, Peacock), engaged with politics, crammed with sex, love, betrayal, tragedy – and out of this came some great poetry. I wanted to argue against the dismissal of his poetry by Eliot and Leavis, by quoting from *The Masque of Anarchy*, 'The Two Spirits', 'The cold earth slept below' and other powerful short poems and fragments to make my case. Exploring the inconsistencies and puzzles of his life was not too difficult because so much of his correspondence and that of his circle was in print. He was an idealist and yet selfish, born into privilege but unable to keep his life in order. He believed in the power of love but was unable to be monogamous and made his wives miserable. There are still unsolved mysteries about his behaviour. All this made the process of thinking and writing about him challenging. Susanna was a particular help to me, taking an interest and offering to make the index for the book, which indeed she did. She was a good companion too – we often went swimming together in Hampstead, and for walks on Primrose Hill and in Regent's Park. I noted in my diary her reading aloud to me from another poet we both loved – Hardy – his poem about the birds and time, 'Proud Songsters':

> The thrushes sing as the sun is going,
> > And the finches whistle in ones and pairs,
> And as it gets dark loud nightingales
> > In bushes
> Pipe, as they can when April wears,
> > As if all time were theirs.
>
> These are brand-new birds of twelve-months' growing,
> Which a year ago, or less than twain,
> No finches were, nor nightingales,
> > Nor thrushes,
> But only particles of grain,
> > And earth, and air, and rain.

With all the children and Humphrey Tomalin in Sussex

She was writing poems herself, as I had done at her age. Hers were better than mine.

In 1978 Jo moved to Brighton to take a higher degree in education. Emily won a place at Cambridge to read engineering, Su was at Oxford. I rented a house in Tuscany and took a group of my children and their friends for a holiday. Su's boyfriend Adam was one – he knew Florence well – and Em's friend Imogen, preparing to go to Oxford. We lived on pasta, spent days in Florence and Siena, celebrated Tom's eighth birthday. Enjoying Italy with them was good, but I felt a weight of anxiety about the work I had taken on. Home again, I cut through my difficulties by deciding to abandon the Mansfield book, in spite of all the notes I had made and research done. I paid back the advances to the British and American publishers and felt a surge of relief. But I still had to earn. I tried to find part-time teaching, without success. I managed to complete work on the anthology, only to have it turned down by the publisher on the grounds that he had wanted a heart-warming book and the pieces I had chosen were too gloomy. I had not realized how low my spirits were until he pointed this out, and they sank further. I stumbled through another month doing the *Critics' Forum*.

My mother was ageing, and needed care and attention, which I tried to give by visiting her often and having her to stay; but it was never enough and I could see that she would soon need more than I could give. That was a worry. Then news came of the death of our doctor Ronald Mac-Keith. He was only sixty-nine; it was unexpected and I had no chance to say goodbye. He had looked after all my children except Su, who was never ill. The knowledge that I would never see him again was painful. A close bond is formed between the mother of a sick child and the doctor who takes charge, and I loved him for his skill and kindness. I thought of how he had crossed London, arriving at Gloucester Crescent one day to remove Emily's asthma inhalers himself, having decided they might be dangerous. And of the evenings he had sat with me in Guy's with baby Tom. Full of sorrow, I went to his memorial service in Conway Hall and sat at the back digging my fingernails into the palms of my hands to stop myself from sobbing aloud. I dare say there were other mothers doing the same thing. He was a doctor like no other, not to be forgotten.

Harry Evans was still keeping an eye on my progress,

and now he told me there might be a job on the *Sunday Times* – that is, as long as the long-running dispute with the printers did not mean the paper folded.

I managed to deliver my Shelley book with Susanna's help. Not wanting to rely on Harry, and hearing that *The Times* was looking for someone to edit its book pages, I applied formally for that job. I was interviewed in September 1979 by the opera critic and editor of the arts pages, John Higgins. Two days later a call came, telling me I was not wanted at *The Times* – but would I like to become literary editor of the *Sunday Times*? And could I start in November? This was of course Harry's doing. He had already signed up John Carey as a regular lead reviewer, and now he also appointed Julian Barnes to be my deputy. Things could hardly have worked out better for me – as long as the dispute with the printers was settled. I braced myself for another change of direction.

I can only describe and not explain what happened to my daughter Susanna in 1979 and 1980. Her first year at Oxford seemed a progress of happiness and achievement, during which she wrote poetry and short stories, enjoyed the company of her many friends and the continued love of her boyfriend, who was taking a higher degree at Cambridge; she did outstandingly well in her exams. A change began in her second year. She met and admired an undergraduate who was gay and had a brief sexual relationship with him. She brought him to see me and we took him for a picnic in Kew Gardens. I was friendly towards him, since Susanna brought him to me. He was not easy to talk to. I found him guarded, and I thought he seemed pleased with himself. Their sexual relationship was soon over – he infected her with pubic lice – and he made clear to her his preference for male lovers. She told me this much. He then called on me and told me he thought she might kill herself on his account, a suggestion that seemed to me so absurd I thought he was trying to impress me with his own importance. But even if I had believed him it would hardly have changed things.

Something happened to her, whether in her mind or through an outside agency, or both, that made her turn away from everything she had loved and known and sub-ject herself to darkness and despair. She drove away her former boyfriend with cruel and false accusations. He still loved her, grieved and hoped to help. But there was noth-ing he could do. In the summer of 1979 she joined an experimental theatre group run by her gay friend and trav-elled with it to Edinburgh. She was brought home to me without any prior warning in a state of visible distress by a young man I had not met before who simply said she needed to be at home and left.

The transformation in her was unfathomable. I had thought of her as my invulnerable child. How wrong I had been. One of her tutors who knew her well wrote to me later, describing the last supervision she gave her before she fled from Oxford:

> The change in her was much greater and much different from anything I had expected . . . I wish that I had some better understanding of what had happened . . . It seems to have overcome everybody's powers of explanation. I keep thinking of her in her first year at Oxford. She was certainly the brightest student I ever taught, but I am not thinking of that so much as of her pleasure in things . . . her lovely communicativeness . . . Even the last day when she had become so much more tentative and unsure . . . I wanted to tell her that she must trust her own thoughts, that they were real. But she had stopped trusting her intel-lect, and something else also, I don't quite know what. I wish that I had known something to tell her that day, or that someone else had (letter from the late Nora Bartlett).

I had the same helpless feeling. The child who had amazed and delighted me for twenty years seemed as though she had been wrung out until almost nothing was left but a small husk of herself. Nothing in her life had prepared us for the change. Susanna had always delighted in the world and expressed her joy in every discovery she made, whether it was a new landscape or a new food, a freshly encountered poem or a painting. Now she seemed almost to have forgotten who she was or how to be. Yet she remained kind to Tom and me. She played with him, she and I went for walks and to the London Library.

At the beginning of October 1979 she told me she was going to visit Jo in Brighton. It seemed a good idea. I rang Jo to make sure she had arrived, and Jo said she was not there. I went upstairs, found one of the bedroom doors locked, broke in, found Su unconscious on the bed, rang for an ambulance and went with her to the Royal Free Hospital. I sat beside her in the intensive care ward, watching the graph that showed she was coming slowly back to consciousness, willing her to live, passionately relieved as I saw her recovering. Then the nurse who was caring for her took me out into the corridor and told me not to rejoice. 'She will do it again,' he said. So I was warned.

Now I know that warning was not enough. I have seen other parents go through the same problems and sorrow, and it seems obvious to me that in all such cases there should be a plan for treatment, clearly set up and explained to the whole family and carefully monitored by doctors and nurses.

Susanna came home from hospital full of guilt for wasting the resources of the health service. She refused whatever distraction or supposed treat I tried to interest her in: it might make me feel better, she said, but would have no effect on her. She dressed herself in drab clothes. Yet she offered to make the index for my short book on Shelley, and did it well. She took Tom to a wheelchair clinic. We made bread together. She made a brief visit to Oxford, where she was no longer considering pursuing any studies. Her closest friends saw her and did all they could to restore her confidence and spirit.

Tom started at Westminster Cathedral Choir School, Emily left school and planned to travel to India during her gap year. I delivered my Shelley book and other promised work, agreed to be a judge for the Booker Prize in 1980, wrote reviews and – I see now – took on far more than I should have done. I was also by then preparing to start working at the *Sunday Times*. A day came when Su got up on to our high roof, and Jo managed to coax her back into the attic again with loving patience. Another time, she took her bicycle into the London traffic and apparently tried to ride under a bus. Emily was sent for and brought her home. In April 1980, I took Tom with Susanna and a mild Oxford friend of hers to Cornwall for a holiday. Her mood was so dark it seemed almost tangible to me, as though she were surrounded by black air, and on our return I made an appointment for her with Charles Rycroft, the most respected and experienced psychiatric doctor I knew of. After seeing her, he told me she was the most depressed person he had ever seen – I remember these surprising words clearly. He said he would take her as a patient if she agreed, but that he did not think she would agree. In a letter he said that those in her condition sometimes made sudden recoveries.

Meanwhile, he said, she must be treated in hospital. She did not want to see Rycroft again, and I took her back to the Royal Free, where she was given drugs and made to sleep a great deal. She seemed to be recovering in some ways towards the end of May, and took an interest in other young patients with anorexia. She sent cards and letters to Tom, odd and fanciful and strangely written, but delightful because something of the familiar Susanna was in them. Emily left for India. Then, early in June, Susanna began to feel like a real person again. She wrote a long letter to her grandparents in France, telling them that she had been 'a stone', unable to write, until

suddenly, about ten days ago, something happened which felt like a weight falling off my back – or a switch being turned on, and I am now – not just a happy person or an active person, but a Real, Living Person, with the capacity for expression instead of just making marks. My doctors, not knowing how I usually am, think I'm a bit high, and the phrase 'manic depressive' gets cautiously and quietly mentioned. I am on lithium, a mood stabilizer, and will be for six months or more, or possibly for life. I'm more worried about the outbreak of any more depressive spells than being affected by drugs . . . I'm an in-patient in the psychiatric ward here, which is no stigma either – of the company, some highly interesting, some tedious, and some downright awful. A bit like real life, in fact, that strange area of experience to which I will be returning in – a month? Perhaps. The fact that I fear certain elements is better than stony-not coming.

The relief was wonderful, although that last sentence, with its 'stony', sounded a warning. Then she let me know that her gay friend had visited her in hospital and told her he had a First. I saw that she was distressed by his visit. He had not asked me if it was all right for him to visit her, or made any contact with me.

A week later she was allowed home. Friends came to see her – her loyal and loving friends – and we went to the theatre and to art galleries. A day came when I was able to describe her in my diary as 'cheerful'. At supper with Tom she shared 'pop music and tables' – multiplication tables. When the Shelley book was published in July, I was proud of the fact that she had made the index, and hoped she was too. The hospital doctors told me she was well enough to go on holiday with me to her grandparents in France. I managed to deliver my shortlist for the Booker Prize by reading a book a day, and waking myself at 2 a.m. to read another in the night. We left for Vence in August 1980 with Tom and Ian, his carer, who was also a good friend to Susanna.

She was given many pills to take and I supposed they were having an effect. This could perhaps be the beginning of a return to normal life, I thought. We slept in small hotels on the way, bought ourselves picnic food – bread, ham, tomatoes, cheese, peaches – and found shady places to eat. We looked at butterflies, played car games with Tom – 'Who am I?' or 'Something beginning with A', and there was football talk. He was just coming up to his tenth birthday and his fair hair was darkening. Ian was good at making running jokes with him. He was also a comforting presence to me and a brotherly one for Su. We were welcomed in Vence by Kath and my father, and spent our time there much as usual, swimming in the pool and reading beside it, scrambling down to the river, strolling round the familiar streets of Vence, being driven by my father to village restaurants in the mountains. In one, we celebrated Tom's tenth birthday.

For the journey back, we put the car on the train from Avignon to Paris. We reached home late at night. Susanna said she would sleep in the attic room. I went up in the morning with a cup of tea for her and found her lying on her back on the floor, her face calm. I knew she was dead and ran down through the house crying out. I rang for an ambulance. It came but when the ambulance man saw her he said they could not take her and I must send for the police. I found a very small note on the floor near her, a few words saying she was sorry, 'but it would get worse'. I supposed she had saved up the pills she had been prescribed for depression and taken them all. How could such a risk have been taken, and why had I not made sure she was taking her pills?

Jo came at once to see her sister. A young policeman arrived, looked round and said I must send for an undertaker. Ian, whose mother had invited him to take Tom to Edinburgh for a few days, set off with him quickly. Emily was unreachable somewhere in India. Neighbours and Su's friends appeared and I must have telephoned family, but I remember nothing of that. Michael came to grieve with me.

None of the warnings I had been given were enough. Clearly she needed much more care than we were able to give her, and to be watched over in a way that I had not done, nor perhaps would I have been able to. Now I know we should have protected her fiercely, and that had we been given more and better advice, we might have saved her.

⚝

Police, undertakers, coroner's court, newspapers, inquest. I tried to go to work and was sent home firmly. For many days we could not track down Emily and had to postpone the funeral, and in the end she did not arrive back in England until the day afterwards. I went back to work in October.

Letters came, reminding me of Susanna's energy, her joy in the world, her beauty, bringing her to life as she had been. Her Aunt Stefany wrote, 'There is a glorious picture in my mind of a Christmas charade – I forget the word enacted but remember Susanna, you and your mother crawling into your sitting room wearing woolly rugs and bathmats to represent sheep, everyone in fits of giggles . . . lightness, wit, inventiveness, hilarity and a sense of celebration was transmitted from Susanna in particular . . . When the news of her death was given to my children the first thing that came from both was – Oh! wasn't she the *jolly* one? The one who played games with us!'

I could have expected a formal note of sympathy from her headmistress at South Hampstead, but something quite different came from her: 'She was one of the most intensely alive people I ever met: in fact the *very* first to emerge from the mass of South Hampstead pupils as a [very forceful] individual, for on the very first day I was there, in January 1975, she came to protest on feminist grounds that we were to sing "Let Us Now Praise Famous Men" at Prizegiving!'

Among so many others, Tony Howard's description of her was written with old-fashioned formality: 'I shall always remember her as the marvellous, cheerful, sparkling girl who came to the *New Statesman* [for a holiday job] that summer – and whom I later saw in the full bloom of her youth, success and confidence outside Blackwell's in Oxford, surrounded by admirers but still ready spontaneously to greet (and insist on talking to) an old figure from the past like me. She had that day such charm and animation – and if I had known anyone in my generation remotely approaching her in sheer appealing, unspoilt brightness I should have counted myself the luckiest lad in Oxford.'

Something else came from her close friend, Katie Mc-Ewen: 'I wish she hadn't succeeded but it was the one thing that she really wanted to do – though that isn't the whole truth, just a part of it which became overwhelming.' Katie understood Susanna's darkness because she felt some of the same despair, and her life too ended in tragedy. So many families have been through this desolation.

The people at Golders Green wept when I collected her ashes. I took them to Suffolk to be buried under the tall trees beside her father, her grandmother and her baby brother. The churchyard is next to her Aunt Eliza's garden, where she played over the years as a child, a place of many memories. Susanna seemed born to give and receive happiness, I thought as I sat beside the grave; yet cruel and inexplicable blackness had descended on her.

I remembered her as she was born, so small that she was like a little bundle of sticks, but soon and ever after sturdy and strong; her hair curly or straight at will (it seemed). I remembered her blue eyes looking at me from the high chair when she discovered that she could pour the entire contents of her mug of milk down on to the floor, and could not resist doing it again and again. Her cartwheels, part show-off, part pure pleasure in movement. Her shyness and curiosity mixed: during the visit of a Hungarian cousin she came down to the sitting room in her nightdress, aged about four, I suppose, watched him from a big armchair and presently, to hide her face, stood on her head so that her nightdress fell over it, revealing the rest of her to his slightly startled but delighted eyes. I thought of her generosity: like her father, she was a marvellous present-giver, taking great pains to give pleasure, wrapping her gifts always in bright colours and with labels and ribbons. She wrote excellent letters and whenever I saw her handwriting I knew there would be something worth reading. Her jokes; her temper, which could be alarming and spread a pall of gloom over the house. I feared her disapproval and anger, which I sometimes merited. I also leant on her kindness. She took other people's troubles to heart; it was part of her generosity of spirit. She seemed to me, until the last year, supremely fortunate: she was lovely, she was exceptionally clever, she was as good a companion as one could find, she knew how to enjoy poetry, music, painting, food, nature, friendship, work, love. She was brave, setting off cheerfully alone for America, and for France with a bicycle. And when everything else went her courage remained.

She lit up our lives with her intelligence and generosity. She is not forgotten by her friends. I don't think there has been a day since her death when I have not thought of her,

Susanna

her blue eyes and her high spirits. I should have protected her, and I failed. The system failed too, badly and inexplicably, and so she was lost.

12

Sunday Times

Grief has to be set aside, but it does not go away. It arrives each morning as you wake, lies in wait in the familiar routines of the day, takes you by surprise. You may not lose the power to enjoy the pleasures offered by the world but you stand in a different relation to them, in some ways more intense because you now know how fragile they are. The best things I saw, heard, read, felt, often brought me to tears because they came with the knowledge that my daughter was never going to return to share them. She had gone forever. She would have no children. I looked for her in old photographs, none offering what I was trying to find. Her writing – letters, poems, fragments of stories – were a reminder of how alive she had been. Her clothes and books, all the reminders of how she had lived, were there, saying too much but also not enough.

I carried Wordsworth's sonnet with me, in which he remembered his dead daughter after a burst of joy:

> Surprised by joy, impatient as the wind,
> I turned to share the transport – O! with whom
> But thee, deep buried in the silent tomb,
> That spot which no vicissitude can find.

Love, faithful love, recalled thee to my mind –
But how could I forget thee? By what power,
Even for the least division of an hour,
Have I been so beguiled as to be blind
To my most grievous loss? . . .

I knew I had to return to ordinary day-to-day existence. Jo and Emily were both away at college for much of the time, each with her own sorrow. Life at home had to be organized, and Tom's care and education. He never spoke his sister's name and his new carers knew nothing of her. I decided to say nothing to my mother rather than try to explain what had happened to her, and she seemed to accept the blankness. Comfort came to me from Susanna's friends, with whom I was able to talk and share sorrow. My neighbours, as always, helped me greatly. Michael was a steady support – he had loved her and thought her greatly gifted. He and I both knew that work has to be the healer. He was busy writing, and a job was waiting for me at the *Sunday Times*.

For the next five years I worked as the paper's literary editor, in a big, squarish, ugly building in the Gray's Inn Road. My fellow journalists were all shaken by the year of closure they had endured and eager to get back to work. I was grateful to have an occupation that kept me busy and needed close attention. I usually bicycled to work – probably the first literary editor to do so – and those parts of the day were important to me, giving me time when I was unreachable and could think my own thoughts. My route – through Camden, along Bayham Street, round Somers Town, across the Euston Road, Judd Street, past Coram Fields and into the Gray's Inn Road – became so familiar that I could do it while hardly noticing the world I was pedalling through. When the traffic became particularly menacing, I took it as a challenge, scrambling round lorries and getting along so much faster than the cars.

A writer friend marvelled at the power I was to have, commissioning reviews that would be going out to something like a million readers each week. I knew that literary pages are supposed to make bestsellers, but I wanted mine to cut across the bestseller culture, to draw attention to the unexpectedly good, the unknown writer with something new to say, the odd, the difficult but worthwhile. And whatever passion was left in me, I was passionate about making our book pages the best in the business.

I started as the paper came to life again after its year out. As though to mark the end of an era, Raymond Mortimer died in January 1980.* He had been joint chief literary critic of the *Sunday Times* with Cyril Connolly for many years – Connolly died in 1974 – and both had written elegant and influential reviews. Harold Evans, our editor, had already invited John Carey to write regular reviews, to my delight, since I believed Carey's distinctly different voice was going to become more powerful still, as indeed it has

---

*Raymond Mortimer (1895–1980), critic and literary editor of the *New Statesman* (1935–47).

done. My ambition was to print at least one piece every week that would attract readers not usually interested in the book pages, and I saw John as the sharpest critic in the business and most likely to draw them in. I wanted a new tone for the book pages, and I also set out to bring in young contributors to enliven the paper. Julian Barnes came from the *New Statesman* to be my deputy and was as congenial a colleague as I could have hoped for. He was also happy, just married to Pat Kavanagh, the formidable and beautiful literary agent, and about to publish his first novel, *Metroland*.

We worked on the fourth floor, with windows looking west. The windows had been fixed shut because we had air conditioning, and were wrenched open by our colleagues, who preferred the air from outside. I liked that, and was also pleased to discover that the mansion flats next door had been lived in by Katherine Mansfield, whose biography I was again supposed to be working on. She was there from 1909 to 1911, when she was writing for magazines and published her first book, and living on the fourth floor, so I had the same westward-looking views.*

Inside was the familiar sight of book parcels piling up on the tables, catalogues, proof copies, letters from publishers. The Literary Department shared a large open-plan space with the Arts Department, but the literary editor was still obliged to have a lockable room in which to keep the books. It was not meant as a retreat, although I found it useful as one, but was provided because, if the books were not locked up, they would be stolen at a great rate by the other

---

* Both buildings have since been demolished.

journalists, all enterprising and curious people. Many of our journalist colleagues liked to come by for a chat and to turn over a book or two, but since they reported the real world of politics, foreign affairs, wars, crime, finance and fashion, they viewed us with condescension. We were not proper journalists, we were told, but dilettantes, inhabiting an ivory tower.

Hard-working dilettantes, we were. I was my own secretary for very many months because the union troubles at the paper meant I had only occasional and inefficient help. I had to stay late almost every evening to keep up with things. It was a comical situation, since callers wanting to speak to the literary editor almost always assumed he was a man, so when I answered the telephone I was regularly taken for the secretary – which of course I effectively was, in addition to being literary editor. I learnt about real secretarial skills from Sarah Forman, who worked for the arts editor John Whitley. She told me that an earlier boss, Godfrey Smith, used to take her to lunches at which they would get through two bottles of Sancerre, then go straight back to the office, where he began dictating letters to her. Those were the heroic days of journalism. She was tall and elegant, and so much admired that one of the art critics used to arrange for galleries to be specially opened in the evening to allow him to escort her to a private view. She became a friend and support to me. She knew the traditions of the paper and how to get things done, and she also understood that we all had to juggle with the difficulties of life outside the office.

The journalists' part of the building was awkwardly joined at the back to another, older building, where the printers worked. Since the two buildings were set at different levels, we had to go down a short flight of stairs when we took copy to the printers – going on to the stone, it was called. It was a great space, noisy with machinery, where the time-honoured process of hot-metal printing took place. The printers were men: women had always been excluded by the unions. They had all served six-year apprenticeships, with two extra to work on a London paper, and they were proud and touchy as well as highly skilled. They feared the coming changes in technology with good reason. I had to be reminded that I must not touch the type under any circumstances – even picking up a piece dropped on the floor was likely to make the men walk out *en masse*, because they claimed total control over every aspect of their work. They could be friendly, but sometimes turned difficult, sulky and unhelpful if they thought I was asking for too many changes on my page proofs. The management lived in fear of strikes, and we were all obliged to be careful never to offend a printer. Even Harold Evans looked nervous, I noticed, if it looked as though they were taking offence at some inadvertent remark or gesture.

Our week started on Tuesday, when the editor held a conference and department heads offered their ideas for next Sunday's paper. They might be encouraged, argued about, sometimes put down. When Frank Giles was editor in 1983, he objected strongly to my proposal that John Carey should review the manifestoes of the three parties at the time of the election. He said he did not want politics on the book pages. I fought back, arguing that Carey would not be writing about politics but about style. The deputy editor, Hugo Young, came to my defence, and Frank gave way. Carey did it so well it made me think it should be done more often.★

For the rest of the week we put together our pages, planned ahead, talked to publishers and writers, wrote headlines and captions, even did some reading. All the books had to be unpacked and entered into a ledger with their publication dates, prices, who they were sent out to, how long a review we had asked for and when it was due. This was the secretary's job, when there was a secretary, and in the absence of one Julian and I got used to doing it ourselves. When the copy arrived, we read it, edited it and took it to the printers; then proofs came back and were sent to the critics for their corrections and second thoughts, which they usually telephoned in. It was a leisurely procedure compared with the way things are done now.

We looked through the new books with the critics who came into the office, discussing which they might take away, going through their copy, exchanging gossip. I relied on Victoria Glendinning and Marina Warner to write regularly and to choose books they found interesting. Paul Theroux made unpredictable and welcome appearances. Alan Ryan took on sociology and politics with an easy, authoritative sweep. Christopher Ricks gave occasional inspired scholarly insights into poetry and poets. Adam

★ His piece can be found in his collected reviews, *Original Copy: Selected Reviews and Journalism 1969–1986* (1987), a book that gives a good idea of the range of his writing in the paper.

Mars-Jones embarked on his career as a critic with a tough and original voice. Richard Cobb wrote sublimely but always at twice the length I had asked for, so that I had to perform major surgery. John Mortimer usually meant meeting for lunch, with a bottle of wine and no hurry: 'Are you doing anything this afternoon?', but of course a literary editor was not free in the afternoon. A few critics wrote on the premises. I don't know how they did it. I remember Ian Hamilton settling at a typewriter and in under two hours, with all the office noise about him, producing a well-thought-out review ready to go to the printers.

I invited John Keegan to review after reading his *The Face of Battle* (1976), a fine book that looks at the detail of Agincourt, Waterloo and the Somme through the eyes of the common soldiers, and he became another regular. John Carey almost always delivered his copy in person, travelling from Oxford and very occasionally bringing his small sons with him. He barely needed editing, although I remember once taking courage to ask him to tone down the ferocity of an attack on Virginia Woolf. Another contributor from Oxford, Nick Shrimpton, was the first to send copy by fax. Fax seemed like magic to me, but at that time we had to send a messenger to Paddington to pick up the fax, so it was quite slow magic.

I asked John Coleman to review crime fiction for us. His column was always entertaining and his gifts as a critic were never in doubt, but his drinking habits meant there were weeks when he failed to deliver anything. I knew this from working with him at the *Statesman*, where he reviewed films, and I forgave him regularly because he was worth keeping: he made entertaining copy out of all the crime novels he reviewed. During a sober period he gave me an account of the cycle of his drinking. After a collapse came a period of remorse and abstinence, helped by pills that made him vomit if he took alcohol. That was humiliating, and presently he persuaded himself he didn't need them and could handle the occasional drink. This was the period of greatest happiness, he said. With a few drinks he knew himself to be clever, a real writer, a charming man and irresistible to women. He had affairs with some attractive and clever ones, and married a beautiful and gifted wife. But the drinking never stayed at the light stage. It built up steadily until he lost control, drinking all day and keeping a bottle by his bed for first thing in the morning. Then the crash came again. He knew it would, and could do nothing to change it. But he was a fine critical writer.

There was a particularly good period in 1983 and 1984, when I was able to alternate Carey's leads with the historian John Vincent's. Vincent described Michael Foot as fighting the 1983 election 'with the party points of the 1930s and the campaigning style of 1910'. Reviewing a study of Oswald Mosley that suggested he might have become a British Pétain, Vincent objected, 'hardly, because so many others wanted the job'. And the first volume of Robert Skidelsky's life of Keynes, which revealed its subject's compulsive promiscuity as a young man, led Vincent to suggest that 'In Vol. 1 Keynes does in bed what in Vol. 2 he will do in economic theory.' I treasured Vincent's wit, but after eighteen months he decided to give his energies to other work. I did my best to persuade Jonathan Raban, who never wrote a dull piece, to become a regular lead reviewer, and failed – he wanted to keep his freedom.

The book pages had to be finished on Friday, so unless there was a literary obituary we did not need to go in on Saturday. It left plenty of time for reading. Commissioning obituaries could be delicate: Noel Annan agreed to write about Isaiah Berlin on condition that his words remained anonymous. I had to write about the shortlisted books for the Booker Prize and W. H. Smith Literary Award, usually with little notice, which meant some very fast reading and writing. Once I was established, I decided to run my own short weekly column recommending the current books I thought most important or entertaining. It meant I could keep plugging a work I particularly admired for many weeks. One was Andrew Hodges's *Alan Turing: The Enigma*, a biography published in 1983, and possibly the most influential book published during those years. Salman Rushdie's *Midnight's Children* in 1981 was another. I also brought in a paperback column.

Harry was a great editor. He had run campaigns that made a difference to the world, with the most famous one bringing compensation to the victims of thalidomide; he was afraid of no one and pretty well revered by most who worked for him. I wrote about him in an earlier essay:

Working under him was like being at the court of Louis XIV. When he beamed his attention fully on any one of us, we were all, men and women, a little in love with him. 'Let's make these headlines a bit sexier,' he would say, coming into the Literary Department on Thursday afternoon and putting his arms round us. We wanted to please him. If he liked a review, he took the trouble to write to the contributor, and to make him feel as if he were part of the family. Not many editors do this. Harry was loved, even if we sometimes swore at him when his attention was distracted or his favours divided. I had no fights with Harry, who upheld my view that the book pages should represent the best in critical judgement.

He was the best ever, and things were never the same at the *Sunday Times* after he left us to edit *The Times* in 1981. I missed his enthusiasm and energy, his eye for detail, his responsiveness to a particularly interesting review. But the job remained absorbing, and working with writers is never dull.

At the end of that year Julian bowed out too in order to devote himself to his writing full time, with the results we know. A few months before he left, in September 1981, he sent a holiday postcard to me and the Literary Department from Rouen that reads:

Our quest for literary and artistic landmarks is getting steadily more esoteric: today, in the Rouen Medical Museum, we saw the stuffed parrot which Flaubert borrowed to help himself grasp the essence of parrothood when writing *Un cœur simple*. Claire – you were quite right about the hotel in Sancerre – love Julian.

This was the first inkling of *Flaubert's Parrot*, published in 1984, a book critics and general readers alike fell on with joy for its wit in sending up the absurdity of the way we sometimes choose to remember writers we revere.

In November 1982 I had my only direct exchange with our proprietor, Rupert Murdoch. I invited him to review a book called *The Life and Death of the Press Barons* by a respected historian, Piers Brendon. In reply, he wrote,

> Dear Mrs Tomalin I am afraid that I am quite unable to review the Press Barons book. I found it a great gossipy read until I came to the part referring to myself which is outrageously defamatory to say the least. If I were to do a signed piece it would certainly make an event of the publication.
>
> I am sorry if I am letting you down but I hope I can meet you again soon when I am in London, if only to tell you how consistently excellent your pages are.

It was worth a try, and it would indeed have been an event – a coup – to get a review from him. But I never had a proper conversation with him, although I had reason to think he went on approving my pages.

Our department played no part in the ludicrous drama of the Hitler Diaries. We merely watched the excitement and subsequent dismay and humiliation from the sidelines. Murdoch, tough as always, insisted that the mistake raised the circulation of the paper and that it remained higher thereafter – so that was all right. Hugh Trevor-Roper, who had endorsed the authenticity of the fraudulent diaries, suffered the humiliation, and Murdoch took the occasion to sack our editor Frank Giles, who bore no responsibility for the giant fiasco.

⚘

When Julian Barnes left, John Ryle came from *The Times Literary Supplement* to be my deputy. He was an anthropologist who had worked among the Dinka in Sudan and also run a brave small literary magazine, *Quarto*, and he brought new ideas and contacts. He had also been commissioned to ghost Mick Jagger's memoirs, but that project foundered, partly because Jagger was unable to remember much about his own life. There was a lot of laughter in the office with John. One day I told him I was fed up with the pictures of half-dressed young women pinned up around the building, and asked him if he would bring me a few gay magazines with photographs of young men seductively posed. He brought them and I pinned up the best of the pictures around the Literary Department. Soon there was a steady stream of journalists and printers arriving in our office to take a look. Some found it hard to believe I could have done something so shocking. Since I also ran a no-smoking department, I probably annoyed several of my tough associates. By then we had acquired a secretary of great charm and sweetness, Zori Amini. She was not shocked.

One of my fellow journalists involved me in a ludicrous incident. In 1983 he sent a letter purportedly by me to Auberon Waugh at *Private Eye*, inviting him to review *Mae West is Dead*, a collection of lesbian and gay stories edited by Adam Mars-Jones, and instructing him to write a favourable review. If Bron had paused for even a moment, he must have realized how unlikely it was that I should have written such a letter, but instead he wrote a piece in *Private Eye* denouncing me as a foolish and corrupt literary editor. It attracted a lot of attention and a good many people believed I had written the letter. I felt it as a direct attack on my reputation as a literary editor and went to Andrew Neil, by then our editor, to discuss what action could be taken. He immediately said the paper would sue *Private Eye* on my behalf – it was a good opportunity, I realize. Bron then published another piece inviting readers to send in any dirt they could about my private or professional life.

I did some detective work at the office and discovered that the forged letter came from the typewriter of a colleague, one I hardly knew. Plainly this was a joke between two public school boys, and a misogynistic one aimed at someone neither of them had any reason to attack. When I met the lawyers, they said I was likely to get large damages because Bron had accused me of lesbianism. I protested that I did not think it wrong to be a lesbian, so did not feel damaged by it. This brought disappointed looks from the lawyers. As the case dragged on, I wrote to the perpetrator telling him I did not think he had acted in malice but that he had wasted a lot of people's time and that he could save distress and more time by owning up. He chose not to, and Bron went on writing rude pieces about me in the *Spectator* and *Eye* to stir things up. I risked nothing financially, since the paper was paying the legal costs, but it was still tedious, and I was warned that I might face a hard time being questioned in court. To my amazement we won the case without my having to go into the witness box.

Large damages were awarded – in the region of £20,000. I had said from the start that I would give any damages to charity, and I did so. Some went to Tom's school, some to the Royal Literary Fund. As I wrote to my daughter, 'Who knows, Auberon Waugh may need it one day?' He and I saw life in different terms, and I was glad to have defeated him in legal combat. But that was the end of our fight. Bad feelings and vendettas are damaging to everyone involved in them, and later we exchanged reasonably friendly letters.

One of the lighter duties of a literary editor is to give lunch to their reviewers. At the *Sunday Times* I found that this was a grander affair than it had been at the *Statesman*, where we tended to go for cheap Italian or Greek. Sarah explained that the Savoy Grill was the place, and I duly invited my lead reviewer, John Carey, to meet me there one day. I turned up in good time, installed myself at a table, ordered some water and took a preliminary look at the menu and the wine list. Ten minutes went by; the waiters hovered. Mobile phones were not then invented. I sat, and sat. I felt pitying looks coming my way. More time went by, extremely slowly. I told myself not to consult my watch or check my diary. After forty minutes I apologized to the head waiter, paid for my water and left. When I managed to make telephone contact with John, he was a little frosty.

What had happened? He had sat in the foyer of the Savoy, expecting me to meet him there, while I sat at our table in the Grill Room. After that we agreed that the smart life was not for us and abandoned any further attempts to eat grand lunches together.

I tried again with another guest, Vidia Naipaul. I had met him several times and admired his writing, and I thought I might be able to persuade him to contribute something to the paper. I wrote to him after reading *Among the Believers*, praising him for his reporting, which made things I had not understood before comprehensible to me. He answered with a short note: 'I telephoned you at the paper, but I was told that you were on holiday, travelling about France. That sounded very glamorous. I will telephone again. We might have lunch one day.' On my return, I invited him to the Savoy. The day came, and as I made my way from the office I realized I was feeling wobbly. I resolved to take no notice and things started well. We chatted and surveyed our menus. I chose fish, and even as I ordered it I knew it was a mistake. We talked on; I felt my stomach heave. I knew Vidia to be the most fastidious of men. What should I do? I rose carefully to my feet, excused myself in a calm voice and said I would be back in a moment. I managed to make my way without haste to the door of the Grill Room and once through it I ran as fast as my feet would carry me along the corridor to the Ladies, where I threw up with great violence. I washed my face in cold water, combed my hair, powdered my nose, gave myself a shake and returned.

Vidia looked at me and said, 'You did that very well.' Then he summoned the waiter, cancelled all our orders for food and asked for a pot of tea and a jug of hot milk. 'It must be hot', he said. 'We are not going to eat anything,' he told me. 'I shall make you feel better with tea and hot milk, and then we shall go out and walk by the river together.' And that is what happened. I did feel better after the tea with hot milk, we did walk by the river, and we talked and parted company in the most friendly fashion. I have no idea what we talked about, but I decided Vidia was not only one of the great writers of his generation, he was also the kindest of men.

One more lunch to be described was with Woodrow Wyatt. I invited him for one reason only: that I wanted to end his retainer as a reviewer for the paper. He suspected as much and turned on his charm, telling me about his service in the war, when he had fought heroically across Normandy, and his experiences as a young Labour MP – taking part in a mission to India in 1946 and serving in Attlee's 1951 Cabinet. He had become a different creature since then: now head of the Tote,* a *bon viveur* and, although I did not know it, a close friend of Murdoch. He did not mention that, but after entertaining me with stories of his radical past he put on a performance of pathos, saying how much it meant to him to write the occasional piece and begging me to keep him on. I'd like to say I took no notice and sacked him, but instead I gave way weakly. I warned him that I should have very little to offer him, and it was left at that. He wrote two or three reviews of no significance for me after that, no

---

* The Tote was the Racehorse Betting Control Board, government appointed. It was set up in 1928 and privatized in 2011.

more, I think. He also took to inviting me to dinner parties. At one I was seated next to Edward Heath, who turned to me and said how much he had regretted the death of my husband, to which I responded suitably, after which he closed his eyes and to all appearances remained asleep throughout the rest of the meal.

Andrew Neil was brought in by Murdoch to edit the paper in 1983 and announced to the assembled journalists that he intended to be an editor in the mould of Harold Evans. It did not feel like that to us. He was only thirty-four, ambitious and undoubtedly able, and, like most new editors, determined to make his mark and impose his ideas on the paper.

The deputy editor, Hugo Young, left in 1984 after many disputes with him about political coverage, and Ron Hall, who had founded the Insight team and been a leading force in the paper for twenty years, was sacked by Murdoch in the same year. Both were my friends and their departure made the paper a less congenial place. On the plus side Sean French became my deputy, proved outstandingly efficient and hard-working, and made my life much easier. He asked his Oxford contemporaries and friends, Andrew Graham-Dixon and Kate Kellaway, both of them destined for literary success, to write shorter notices; Nicholas Shakespeare and David Sexton also contributed short reviews we were proud to print. In my arguments with Andrew Neil, who was always pressing me to use famous names, I said the paper could and should make famous names by discovering and promoting talent.

Early in 1985 I came into the office one day to find Neil had called back one of my pages and removed a review by Hugh Brogan, a distinguished academic historian, of a book by a *New York Times* reporter that gave a highly critical account of what the Americans were doing in El Salvador. I asked if there were factual mistakes in the review, Neil said no, he just wasn't having that sort of thing in the paper. I asked if I could run the piece next week and he said no, it was killed. So I wrote to him saying the glory of the paper was that it published strong pieces by people who knew their stuff and that unless he let me run the piece next week I'd have to resign. Neil said he wanted time to think and was off to New York where he was due to see Murdoch. He would tell me his decision when he got back next Thursday. I replied okay, but that I stood by my letter. I thought he would give way, but a tense time followed before he did. He said I could print the review on condition I got Brogan to write in some explanatory sentences, which was easy and did not change what he had already written. Of course Neil had every right as editor to do as he liked, but I was glad to have fought him on that. I was touched by the support given me by Zori, who told me she would leave if I went, adding that she did not ever want to work for a man.

There were times when things were calm and Neil and I were friendly enough, but then he would have another go at me. In July 1985 he sent me a memo saying my pages were the only bit of the paper that had resisted his will and that I must make them more popular – by using famous names, he said yet again, and printing gossip about publishers – and that I must come into line with the rest of the paper. I see from my records that I was about to print a poem by Hans Magnus Enzensberger in the next issue, and another by Christopher Reid in a later one: two fine poets, although possibly not to Neil's taste, although Enzensberger's name was already famous – he wrote perfect English as well as German – and Chris Reid's would win fame when he won the Whitbread Prize for his wonderful elegiac volume of poems *A Scattering* in 2009.

Not long after this I asked if I might cut down my working hours, and was allowed to. Neil may have seen it as a hopeful sign that I was thinking of resigning, although that was not then my intention. I knew Sean was more than capable of editing the pages in my absence, and I wanted time to get back to my Mansfield book, and to start reading for another book I had in mind: 'Wonderful to get into archives again,' I wrote to Jo in December; 'I'm spending every bit of spare time working on Dickens and Ellen Ternan; deeply fascinating renewing my Dickens reading.'

I had thought about the story of Dickens's relationship with a young actress for years – since my undergraduate days in the Fifties – and my interest was encouraged when our editor was called on by a man who claimed to be among the illegitimate descendants of Dickens, banished to Australia. Neil asked me to look into the matter. I went over to the Dickens Museum to consult with the curator, who confirmed my belief that the claim was bogus; but after talking it over with him I told him I wanted to write about Ternan. He said, 'I can't tell you how many people I have told not to do that . . .' Then he paused, looked hard at me and added, 'but I think you might be the right person to do it.' And with that he promised to give me every assistance. I was eager to start on it as soon as I could make time, but for the moment there was no chance.

Neil launched another attack on the Literary Department when he decided to intervene by sending a secretary to make a computer printout of the names of all the books coming in from publishers so that he could make sure I chose the right ones to review. She had to copy the titles by hand, transfer them to a computer and print them out for him to go through. Since there were hundreds of titles, and I naturally arranged most of the reviews well in advance, by the time she came in to note down titles it was too late. In any case no instructions ever came down from the editor and the arrangement lapsed. Another row came in January 1986: 'Dreadful week at the office, fighting with the editor and deputy editor [Ivan Fallon], who want to put the bestseller list right across the top of the page,' I wrote to Jo. We fought that one off too. I also realized I must learn to use a computer myself, although I did not acquire one until I had left the paper.

Did our pages have any effect on book sales? Marginally perhaps. We drew attention to the best and most original fiction: Anita Brookner's earliest novels, Milan Kundera's *The Unbearable Lightness of Being*, Alice Munro's *The Progress of Love*, Martin Amis's *Money*. Also to biographies: Hilary Spurling's of Ivy Compton-Burnett, Cathy Porter on Alexandra Kollontai. To history: *The Invention of Tradition*, ground-breaking essays edited by Eric Hobsbawm and

As literary editor for the *Sunday Times*

Terence Ranger. To memoirs: Edward Blishen detailing the horrors of teacher training, Norman Podhoretz's version of the literary/political scene in New York, cruelly well assessed by Raban. John Carey hailed Clive James's *Unreliable Memoirs* with 'his exuberance with words seems as natural as sun-tan'. Carey's exuberance also, I thought.

As literary editor, I received many requests to talk and conduct interviews. One of the worst occasions was when I was asked to give a talk on John Updike's novels at the Institute of Contemporary Arts. The people there told me they wanted something seriously informative and, after I'd agreed to do it, added the terrible rider, 'We expect you to talk about *all* the books.' Fortunately I had read most of them: three of the Rabbit books had already appeared, *Couples* was his best known, and my personal favourite was *Of the Farm*, which tells of a man taking his second wife and her son to visit his mother, living alone and still running her farm: it's short, lyrical and sharp. I should have said no to talking about *all* the great big ones of course – it was a ridiculous task. Instead I obediently put together my comprehensive survey as best I could, with warm words for almost everything and only a few reservations. At the very last minute I was told that Updike himself was going to be present at the ICA. And there he was, comfortably seated and looking straight at me as I rose to my feet to hold forth about his work. A nightmare. He was polite afterwards, teased me for having left out one book, and we got through a cordial enough exchange. The questionable value of the enterprise must have struck him as forcibly as it did me. To my relief he was borne off rapidly to other events by a bevy of publicity girls.

Three days later fate brought me an encounter with another great American novelist, Saul Bellow. This was at a PEN meeting in the Purcell Room, where I was introducing Peter Ackroyd, who talked about his newly published life of T. S. Eliot. Bellow was in the audience and afterwards he came into the green room, where I was alone, resting. He was talkative and charming, and I listened to him and chatted happily, having read and admired all his books, and relieved that no one had ever asked me to sum up his achievements. I wrote to my daughter Jo a few days later, boasting of having met the two American greats, Updike and 'Saul Bellow, with whom I discussed death, D. H. Lawrence and other writers, and who told me I had beautiful legs: so much for the literary life – but actually he is a very interesting and attractive old man, I really liked him.'

In 1985 I did some television filming for a programme about Dorothy Wordsworth, which I was to present. It began with a scene for which I had to stand on the ice in Lake Ullswater for several hours, doing my best to talk animatedly to the camera while my feet froze. I liked and respected the people I worked with, and we had good times following in Dorothy Wordsworth's footsteps in Somerset and Norfolk; but I developed doubts as to whether television can present the complexities of people's lives as well as the written word. Andrew Neil told us books were a sunset industry; I thought they would survive.

In another letter to Jo I told her Neil and I were destined not to see eye to eye, and the wonder was that I had lasted so long. 'I shall be sad if I go because I do think I have an exceptionally good team of reviewers, and I wonder how long they will survive without me – John Carey says he will leave in any case if I go.' Things worked out differently, and with the move to Wapping I left and John decided to stay, after being assured that his copy would not be tampered with. We remained friends.

Murdoch sprang the closing of the Gray's Inn offices and the move to Wapping on us skilfully, acting with all the brutality he had found necessary to defeat the print unions. Their own intolerable behaviour had brought this on them, and cost them the support of the journalists. The journalists were summoned to a meeting, offered rises of £2,000 a year and membership of a private health insurance scheme if they turned up the next day at Wapping. Otherwise they would be sacked. A majority went, many reluctantly. This was in January 1986.

All the secretaries were sacked summarily. They were told they might reapply but would not be taken on on the same terms, i.e., with the benefits they had enjoyed. Zori wrote to tell me she was not reapplying, and Sarah Forman also left.

Sean and I remained in our office to think things over. Going in the following day, we found that our proofs for the next week's paper had been removed during the night by Penny Perrick, who had come from the *Sun* to take over our book pages at Wapping. By Friday almost all the *Sunday Times* journalists had gone to join her. I was asked again to go by the management, but in such a manner – one thing they demanded was to film Sean and me walking into Wapping – that I responded with my resignation. Sean was told that Penny was now the literary editor and that his job had gone to Nigella Lawson.

I wrote a formal letter of resignation to Andrew Neil, pointing out that the house agreement had been broken in that there had been a promise of consultation and negotiation with the journalists before any move to Wapping, and there was neither. I went on:

> You yourself personally assured us all that you were in favour of peace and an 'evolutionary approach' to resolving the industrial problems associated with the introduction of new technology only ten days before you instructed us all to go immediately, without negotiation and on pain of losing our jobs, to Wapping. Clearly this is not an acceptable way of dealing with a team of journalists whom you claim to hold in high regard. The effect on almost every one of us, including those who did go to Wapping on Tuesday, was to make us feel we had been betrayed and humiliated by our own editor; that instead of leading us . . . and fighting for our interests, you had become a mouthpiece for a ruthless and bullying management . . . The sense of shock, bewilderment and grief that passed through your journalists on Monday is something I shall certainly not forget. Some went willingly – a few eagerly – to Wapping; many more went with ashes in their mouths, saying they were going simply to pay their mortgages while they sought other work as quickly as possible.

> I feel the greatest warmth towards and sympathy with all my colleagues, and I deeply regret not being able to join in the real excitement of using the new technology, to which I had been looking forward keenly. But I cannot in conscience continue to work under an editor who, in my

view, has ceased to be a leader and an inspiration to his
journalists.*

There was nothing heroic about my resignation. It was
fired by indignation at what I saw happening to my colleagues, journalists and secretaries. It may well be that
Murdoch's methods were the only way of dealing with the
print unions: if so, it was a case of one monster taking on
another. A good many of the journalists accepted the situation cheerfully, the papers kept going without a break,
things settled down at Wapping, the new technology took
over. I could not stomach Murdoch's mixture of bullying
and bribery, which has not in the long run been good for
the press. I also knew that I was lucky to be able to face losing my job, because I had ideas for books I wanted to write
and a publisher ready to pay me advances.

A group of us talked about trying to set up a new paper
and made lists of possible editors, but the practical and
financial difficulties were too much and the project made no
progress. I went to picket once. It was not much fun, until
Nigella Lawson came into view, when even the sternest
printers on the picket line gave lecherous groans mingled
with cries of appreciation at the sight of her beauty. Sean,
whose job she had taken, was one of the nine journalists
who resigned from the paper. One hundred and twenty-
eight remained. Some hated it; others settled down without
much grief; still others just got on with their work. I never
regretted leaving. I felt confident that I could manage. I also

* Neil has found his métier since on television.

had a great many letters of support, from strangers as well as friends. Only Paul Johnson chastised me for leaving, in the *Spectator*, saying I owed it to English Literature to remain. But English Literature kept going pretty well.

※

While I was still with the *Sunday Times*, I was invited to join an Arts Council poetry committee. I said yes, not because I thought myself particularly qualified to pronounce on poetry but because I knew that Philip Larkin, the greatest English poet then alive, was on the Committee. I had exchanged words and postcards with him on several occasions, and I decided that the prospect of meeting him again and hearing him talk about poetry was not to be missed. Charles Osborne, the Australian critic, poet and journalist, was the chairman and the other member was Michael Schmidt, poet and publisher. Osborne liked to gather his team over a luxurious lunch, and in October 1983 he arranged for us to meet at the Caprice. It was not a very good choice, because Larkin was so deaf that it was hard for him to hear what was said over the noise of the restaurant, and in any case he ate very little.

Among other now forgotten topics we discussed a proposal from Judith Chernaik, an American scholar and writer long resident in London, to have poems posted up in the Underground trains; she was backed by poets Gerard Benson and Cicely Herbert. Osborne and Schmidt were both against the idea and ready to dismiss it. I said I thought it was a good proposal and we should back it, that I knew

Judith and that she was a gifted and serious person. Larkin, after some hesitation, supported me, although he was worried that the proposers might have a 'left-wing agenda'. As we talked the others came slowly round, until, helped by the good wine Charles had ordered perhaps, we arrived at some sort of agreement that we should give the proposed scheme our support. The others appointed me to keep an eye on any left-wing agenda. I promised I would, keeping a straight face as best I could.

The next day I telephoned Judith and suggested she should write to Larkin to explain the project. She did so, and he replied,

> I found your idea more original and more attractive than subsidizing the production of one more unread magazine or anthology. I have always liked the Wayside Pulpit placards ('Don't Put Your Wishbone Where Your Backbone Ought To Be'), and think it might be equally inspiring to be able to read on a tube journey poems that served as a reminder that the world of the imagination existed.

He also explained that he was undergoing 'tiresome medical tests', and that he was not in a position to *do* anything; and further, that the situation at the Arts Council suggested that 'this project, or any alternative, is not high on anyone's list of priorities'.

He was wrong about this. The first poems went up in 1986. He never saw them, though, because he died in December 1985. The medical tests had been a warning. But the scheme he had encouraged, cautiously yet effectively, became one of the great cultural features of London life and goes on bringing unexpected pleasures to travellers every day. It has been copied in other cities. I suppose that every now and then someone is alerted to poetry who has never memorized or even read any before, and finds a new interest opening up before them. I like to remember how Larkin, tired and ill as he was, spoke up for that world of the imagination he himself inhabited and offered to his readers.

13

Other Lives

I was fifty-three when I left the *Sunday Times*. It was my last job, and I was going to spend the next thirty years as a writer. I once described working at home as 'silence, hard slog, loneliness, old clothes', which was only partly true. I did miss the feeling of perpetually renewed excitement, of belonging to a band of brothers and sisters who care about the same things – books, reviews, journals, who's said what, who's writing where. But research is not all done silently at home, and is not always lonely. I had learnt something of what it involves from the two books I wrote in the Seventies, on Mary Wollstonecraft and on Shelley, both profoundly enjoyable experiences, and I was now embarking on the happiest time of my professional life, examining the histories of women and men who interested me and doing my best to make sense of their struggles and achievements. The effort kept me challenged, absorbed and entertained. It also widened my experience in many different and sometimes unexpected directions.

Working on a biography means you are obsessed with one person and one period for several years. Another life is bound up with yours and will remain so for the rest of your own life – that at least is my experience. You have gone in too deep to cast them aside. You have looked into the context of their lives in every aspect, examined their family backgrounds, their beliefs, their tastes, their eccentricities, their friends and enemies, their ambitions, achievements and failures, their quirks and mysteries, their betrayals and unhappiness, their political allegiances, their medical histories, their finances, their children, their reputations both in life and posthumous. You will have been surprised by them, maybe disappointed, amused, amazed. Your interest is so strong it can be called a passion.

You will have approached them through archives and libraries, photocopies and microfilms provided by universities and archivists all over the world. You will have studied letters and portraits, wills, newspaper cuttings and caricatures. You will have walked in their footsteps and travelled where they travelled. You will have compiled chronologies, filled file boxes and computer files. You will have talked to a great many people, a few discouraging, most helpful; just occasionally one will have something extraordinary to tell you or be persuaded to show you. You will have setbacks and gloomy times. I cannot remember being bored, although I sometimes felt desperate, asking myself whether I should ever have embarked on so difficult a task. You will have done your best to live mentally in another period and with other sets of values. You will have tested the patience of your family severely.

What was my family now? I lived with Tom and his helpers, who came and went at irregular intervals, and among my friends in Gloucester Crescent, including new neighbours Mary-Kay Wilmers with her sons Will and Sam, who moved into the Mellys' house when they left. Sam became Tom's best friend and Nina Stibbe, his helper, was popular with us all long before she became the chronicler of life in NW1. Alan Bennett had also moved into a house opposite and the lady in the van was a feature of all our lives. My daughters were no longer at home: Jo settled in Sheffield on her return from Mozambique, taught maths and gave me my first grandchild, Rosa. Emily took a degree in engineering at Warwick University and went on to work in renewable energy projects with water, sun and wind turbines in Wales.

The biggest change in my life was that Michael and I were now living together. Our long friendship, in which we talked and confided in one another about our lives, had turned to love. It was an overwhelming experience. It also caused pain and difficulties for everyone. We tried to give up our relationship more than once, and never could. The situation was resolved very slowly through the generosity of his wife and his determination to keep an unbroken and close relationship with his three daughters, which he achieved.

Middle-aged love proved stronger than anything I had known before, and enduring. We were able to settle down to a life together, both working as writers, reading each other's efforts, travelling together, sometimes to see his plays put on in New York or filmed in Los Angeles, sometimes to follow a piece of my research or his, sometimes to give talks or go to conferences – and also simply to experience countries we already loved, some we wanted to know better.

We knew we were lucky to have found happiness together, and when we reached sixty, in 1993, we were married. Michael's eldest daughter, Rebecca, brought her twin sons Finn and Jack, tiny babies, to bless the occasion, and my little granddaughter Rosa was our bridesmaid. My father and stepmother Kath came from France. The June sun shone warmly on us, and at the height of the festivities my 88-year-old father took my arm and said, 'You never cease to surprise me, Claire.'

❧

My first task on leaving the *Sunday Times* had to be to finish the biography of Katherine Mansfield I had partly written, given up on, renewed, redrafted, despaired of. I got out my files and folders and set to work again. Among the notes were ones that I had made after driving to Gloucestershire to see her only surviving sister, Jeanne Renshaw, then in her eighties, a charming and elegant lady with an overpoweringly genteel speaking voice. French and German phrases were sprinkled through her conversation and a great many dears – dear Father, dear Mother, dear Katherine. No trace of a New Zealand accent, and sweetness where dear Katherine was sharp. She was generous with her time and eager to be helpful, although she had been too young to know Katherine at all well; but her pride in her sister's reputation was touching and she had written down André Maurois's tribute as he kissed her hand with the words, '*Madame, quel grand honneur – vous êtes la Sœur de K. M. – Seulement trois personnes – Chekhov, Maupassant et K. M.*' After our meeting she took the trouble to write me several letters: 'Don't forget we as a family did love one another' and 'My Mother was <u>so</u> clever

with Men! My dynamic Father adored her!' 'We Beau-
champs came over to England in 1066,' she told me more
than once, and 'K. M. could not help being a genius.' K. M.
might have smiled at some of this.

My visit to Mansfield's closest friend, Ida Baker, was a
different matter. She was about to be ninety when I met her,
living alone in a somewhat dilapidated cottage half hidden
among the trees of the New Forest. Peter Day, a literary
enthusiast who had befriended her through his interest in
Mansfield, and persuaded her to write down her memories,
asked if he might bring me; she agreed, and he took me
there and introduced us. She had very poor eyesight and
difficulty in hearing but told me she found my voice easy to
catch, and we talked at length about Mansfield, her character and her illnesses, their friendship and their life together.
We paused at intervals to let her rest. She spoke quietly and
simply, and I found her account of the past, with all its difficult times, sickness, jealousies and sorrows, as well as her
great love for K. M., moving and credible.

Her belief that Mansfield had suffered from the effects of
gonorrhoea sent me to the Wellcome Library to research
the illness, its effects and its treatment in the early twentieth
century. I could have written a treatise about what I found
out about the neglect suffered by women of that time,
when such things were not talked about.* Mansfield had

---

* Newly married women were frequently infected by their respectable
husbands, failed to seek treatment for their symptoms and became infertile as a result. Women doctors were determined to do something about
this situation by talking, writing and educating the public.

surgery, became infertile and suffered pain and ill health for the rest of her life. Miss Baker was straightforward and impressive at our meeting – amazingly so, considering her age and the years that had gone by since the death of Mansfield in 1923. I was fortunate to be able to talk with her, and I was just in time, because she died only a few weeks after my visit.

I finally delivered *Katherine Mansfield: A Secret Life* early in 1987, and it was published later in the year. In my foreword I laid claim to being better qualified than a male biographer to deal with my subject: 'I can't help thinking that any woman who fights her way through life on two fronts – taking a traditional female role, but also seeking male privileges – may have a special sympathy for such a pioneer as Katherine.' Not all my readers found my portrait sympathetic. French devotees of Mansfield were shocked by my account of her – one told me it felt like '*une douche froide*' (a cold shower), which was not how I intended it. It was better liked in England and America and translated into German, Spanish and Japanese as well as French. The response that most pleased me came from my friend Victoria Glendinning, who knew how I had struggled to get the book done. She wrote to me, 'No one if you didn't tell them would ever dream that it was begun, put down, taken up again, rejigged, finished, etc. It reads all in one breath, all in one piece, and as if written in high spirits. Which it can't have been, always.' Praise from someone who works in the same field and faces the same problems is the best there is – Victoria was writing her own books, skilfully researched and narrated

with élan, while bringing up her four sons. We were
sisters-in-arms.

❧

Mansfield, like Wollstonecraft earlier, had led me into
medical research. What I found out at the Wellcome
Library was invaluable, because it set Mansfield's illness in
its social as well as its strictly medical context. Virtually
every biography has a medical aspect to be investigated,
and I was back at the Wellcome when I wrote about Pepys
a decade later. He gives his own account of the pain of a
kidney stone suffered throughout his childhood and youth,
and how the stone moved into his bladder and made his life
so difficult he resorted to surgery, and I needed to put this
in context and understand what the surgeon did. I found all
the information I needed at the Wellcome, and something
more: a print from a surgical treatise of the seventeenth
century showing the operation to remove a stone being
performed, with the patient bound and held down by four
strong men as the surgeon probes. I knew as soon as I saw
it that this would make an illustration that every reader,
and perhaps especially men, would find compelling, even
as they shrank from it. No one forgets it. Pepys made a
good recovery from his ordeal, but at the end of his life his
bladder gave him serious trouble again, and the autopsy
carried out after his death by three of his friends from the
Royal Society (one was Hans Sloane) listed seven irregular
stones in his kidney, a gangrenous bladder, a septic gut and
the old wound opened again. It makes you think again

about what he had gone through in the course of his life, recognize how much pain he had to endure, and admire his courage the more.

Causes of death in the past are often uncertain, and Jane Austen's has been attributed to a variety of illnesses – most recently to an overdose of sedative by the doctor, without which she would have got up and returned to work.★ I doubt that one. Posthumous diagnoses of her death by doctors include Addison's disease, a tuberculosis of the adrenal glands or a lymphoma, but we have to accept that we cannot always know. When I visited the modest house in College Street, Winchester, where she died in a small first-floor room, I thought how confined it must have felt in the hot summer weather, and how inconvenient for those nursing her – chiefly her sister Cassandra. Characteristically Jane made a joke of things, calling herself 'a very genteel, portable sort of Invalid'. And, as her brother Henry reported, her courage was with her to the end, for she kept writing, with a pencil when she could no longer manage pen and ink.

When I came to look at Thomas Hardy's death, I found it was a beautifully simple one. He was eighty-seven, he could no longer work at his desk as he had done for many decades, and he took to his bed. It was midwinter. He asked for and ate his favourite breakfast of kettle broth – chopped parsley, onions and bread cooked in hot water, a Dorset speciality. Offered a rasher of bacon, he refused it. Then he asked, 'What is this?' as death arrived and his heart stopped.

★ Helena Kelly, *Jane Austen: The Secret Radical* (2016).

In one of his last poems he had joked to his wife Florence that he would be less trouble to her once he was dead:

> It will be much better when
> I am under the bough;
> I shall be more myself, Dear, then,
> Than I am now.

But, as things turned out, the trouble came after his death – an irony he would have appreciated. There was a dramatic disagreement about where he should be buried. It led to the surgical removal of his heart, the cremation of the rest of his body and two separate funerals, one in Westminster Abbey with every sort of grandee carrying the coffin containing his ashes, the other in Dorset as he wished, so that at least his heart was placed 'under the bough' and close to his family and first wife.

Dickens's death created difficulties too. He wanted to be buried in a country churchyard near Gad's Hill, but his family and closest friends decided that his body should be taken to Westminster Abbey for a private funeral. On the following day the crowds arrived, queuing in thousands with their flowers, which perhaps justified their decision. Dickens also said he wanted no memorial statue, yet he now has one in Portsmouth. Should we have respected his wishes? I think so. He had already appointed his own biographer in the shape of his closest friend, John Forster, who had known him through half his life, and with whom he shared his most intimate secrets. Aside from that, Dickens thought carefully about how he wanted to be remembered, and wrote down his wishes in one simple and memorable sentence: 'I rest my claims to the remembrance of my country upon my published works, and to the remembrance of my friends upon their experience of me.'

❀

Travel comes with the job for a biographer, and Michael sometimes took time off to go with me. These are good memories. When I was working on Jane Austen in the mid-Nineties I naturally spent many long hours in the archives at Winchester and Maidstone, but there were days when he walked the Hampshire countryside with me, and we admired together the green lanes with double hedges that have persisted since Austen's day. We also visited some of the houses she knew together, one being the Vyne, the beautiful home of the Chute family, well known to the Austens. William Chute was their MP; he and his younger brother Tom Chute hunted with James and Frank Austen, and Tom played cards and danced with Cassandra and Jane.

We also went together to another famous Austen site, Lyme Regis. We were there in November in warm sunshine which, we were told, is normal at Lyme. So we climbed on to the Cobb and walked in our shirtsleeves along the dramatic coast, past 'the green chasms between romantic rocks'. And we travelled further afield, to the Landes in south-west France where we searched for the château in which Austen's cousin Eliza de Feuillide lived for two years with her French husband. After consultations and wandering through wild woods and over heathland, we succeeded: there it stood, remote, turreted and empty, the one sign of life some white plastic chairs on a terrace. Later I made contact with the owners and, at their request, I sent them the French edition of my book on Austen.

※

Mansfield was the last book I wrote on a typewriter. I bought my first computer – an Amstrad – in 1987, and learnt to use it with WordPerfect software, which was indeed perfect for writers, only to be driven out by other less good systems. With this new technology I began to research a long-planned book on the twelve-year relationship between a young actress, Ellen – Nelly – Ternan and Charles Dickens.

In December 1988 I spoke about Mansfield in Rome for the British Council. Michael went with me, and I went with him to New York ten days later for the opening of his Chekhov adaptation *Wild Honey*. I took the opportunity to work in the Pierpont Morgan Library, going through their Dickens material and making my own pencilled copy of the Dickens diary for 1867, which he had lost on his second American trip. This was a crucial document because it gave a record of how he divided his life between his official home at Gad's Hill, his office in Central London, where he also sometimes slept, and Slough, where Nelly was living – dramatic evidence of an energetically maintained secret existence.

The story I wanted to tell was what it was like to be a young actress in the mid-nineteenth century – you were not respectable even if your behaviour was spotless – and how Dickens and Ternan were perfectly matched: he a middle-aged man drawn to young girls and with a passion for the imaginative world of the theatre; she a lively, literate and hard-working girl bred to the stage, fatherless, penniless and pretty.

This was the scene I had to set. The central section of the book told what it could of their relationship: how they risked exposure and scandal and managed against the odds to keep it secret. So successful were they that none of their letters to each other survives, and there is a period about which very little information is available. I acknowledged this and offered my conjectures as conjectures only. I myself believe the testimony of Dickens's two most intelligent children, daughter Kate and son Henry: that there had been a love-affair and a child who died, and indeed there is much circumstantial evidence to support this.

The climax of the story I was telling came after the death of Dickens, when Nelly decided to re-create herself, phoenix-like, by taking ten years off her age and appearing as a young woman of twenty-one. It was a brilliant deception, worthy of a Wilkie Collins novel. She was no Little Em'ly, who accepted that her life had been ruined when she was seduced by a gentleman, as happens in *David Copperfield*, Dickens's – and Nelly's – favourite among his novels. Nelly showed herself to be the direct opposite of Little Em'ly: a coolly determined woman who made the world do as she wished by skilful lying, and did not allow society to destroy her. Her own sisters colluded with her, and Dickens's sister-in-law Georgina remained her discreet friend. She got everything she wanted: a young clergyman husband, a respectable middle-class life, a son and a daughter.

While I saw a narrative emerging that opened fresh light into the past, I ran into trouble with Dickens scholars and devotees who objected to my writing about Ternan's twelve-year relationship with Dickens. Many saw him as a man of near saintly character and objected to my supposed spoiling of his image. I was accused by an Oxford English don at a conference on biography of merely peddling gossip. On the other hand I was fortunate that Dr Graham Storey, who was editing the Dickens letters, and had known me since my Cambridge days, approved and assisted me. When I delivered my completed book to my editor in March 1990, he was enthusiastic. I wrote to a friend, the literary scholar Edward Mendelson, in New York that month, telling him,

> I am feeling pretty good because I have finished my book. Three years' hard labour, the last six months very hard indeed, but now it's done, footnotes and all. I even dare to have moments of being quite pleased with it. Michael thought of the title, 'The Invisible Woman' (it's about Dickens's Nelly Ternan). It led me into lots of odd bits of research which I enjoyed, and it's come out as one of those mixed books, not biography or lit. crit. or social history or detective story or family saga, but a sort of amalgam of all those things.

In writing *The Invisible Woman* I thought I might change, however slightly, my readers' view of the past. It was very widely noticed and discussed, and perhaps was part of the reason why I was invited to become a trustee of the National Portrait Gallery in 1991. I was surprised by the invitation, which came from the prime minister, John Major, and I asked the chairman, the Reverend Owen Chadwick, to explain to me what was expected of a trustee. He knew me because he had conducted my marriage to Nick, and he replied, 'Well, my dear Claire, it means you are responsible for the pictures – you own them.' This was daunting information, although I realized that the other trustees had not been deterred by it. There is no point in insuring the portraits because they are priceless, so not even the richest trustee could hope to make up for any losses. Part of our job was to work with the curators; another part was to commission portraits of the living.

The National Portrait Gallery is an institution at the heart of the Establishment, and what makes it exciting is that part of its job is to look outside the Establishment for its portraits. The royal family is very fully represented, but in the 1990s we put alongside them Germaine Greer, Alan Bennett, Tracey Emin, digital drawings of the pop group Blur and others who challenged Establishment values – and mostly became part of the Establishment themselves soon enough. I was responsible for getting two group portraits done. One was 'The *Guardian* Women' (Posy Simmonds, Polly Toynbee, Liz Forgan, all highly distinguished, as were Jill Tweedie and Mary Stott, both now deceased). The other was the Lindsay String Quartet, based in Sheffield and with a world reputation. We had them painted from life as they performed. Music was somewhat neglected at the Portrait Gallery, as were the provinces, and this struck a blow for both.

In 1993 I was one of the small group of trustees asked to interview applicants to become the new director. There was some fierce disagreement before we brought in Charles Saumarez Smith, but he proved an excellent choice and under his direction the Gallery flourished. Visitor numbers rose to more than a million a year. Charles was adventurous and effective in setting up exhibitions, and he also embarked on major changes to the structure of the building. We had a lecture theatre installed and enlarged the space for the great seventeenth-century paintings on the top floor. A group of us went up on to the roof and agreed we should build a restaurant there. It was swiftly done, and offers diners one of the best views in London, over Trafalgar Square and beyond.

When I first knew the Gallery you sometimes found yourself alone in one of the rooms; today that is unlikely. I served for ten years and felt proud to be connected with such an extraordinary place. I still feel part of it and go in often to enjoy the permanent display and the special exhibitions. It is a treasure house, one of the glories of Britain, and entry is free.

❧

While I was at the Portrait Gallery my book *Mrs Jordan's Profession* came out. It was a study of one of the greatest of the Regency actresses, Dora Jordan, known as the Comic Muse (Mrs Siddons was of course the Tragic Muse). Mrs Jordan, without interrupting her career, bore ten children, five sons and five daughters, to Prince William, Duke of Clarence, the third son of George III. My book tells how she was ill used by the royal family and their advisers, including bishops, and driven to exile and death; and how William, once he became king in 1830, overcome with remorse for his treatment of her, commissioned a life-sized statue of her from England's leading sculptor, Francis Chantrey. William set down that he wished to have the statue of Dora placed in Westminster Abbey 'beside the monuments of the queens'. His words can still be read, although someone struck them through later. All this was written out of official history. It made a story thrilling to research and horrifying in what it revealed. Lord Longford, after hearing me speak about it at a public occasion, came up to me and said briskly, 'You made all that up, didn't you?'

As for the statue of Mrs Jordan, which shows her seated with a baby in her lap and an older child beside her, it was long kept out of public view, first by her youngest son and then by later descendants, and is now by an irony of fate displayed in Buckingham Palace. A guide to visitors there came to a talk I gave at the Portrait Gallery, at the end of which she told me she had been offered no information at all about Mrs Jordan at the Palace, and learnt of her history for the first time that day from me.*

Yet I was given every assistance and kindness when I

* The fifth Earl of Munster, descendant of Mrs Jordan and William IV, bequeathed the statue to the Queen, and after consultation it was accepted and installed in Buckingham Palace in 1980.

worked at the Royal Archives in Windsor on material relating to her. Many of Mrs Jordan's descendants also helped me, producing letters to and from her children that had been kept shut away in boxes or folders for nearly two hundred years. I found that Bushy House, the mansion in which she had lived with Prince William from 1797 to 1811, bearing and bringing up his children, was closed to visitors, having become the National Physical Laboratory, and I was told there was no possibility of a visit, but I persisted and wrote to the director, Peter Clapham. He at once invited me to spend a day there, made me warmly welcome with his wife, and I was allowed to go through every room, which gave me a very good appreciation of what life there must have been like. What a perfect place it had been in which to bring up children, with its own parkland and farms, horses to ride, cricket, boating on the river, coursing and fishing.

During my research I came upon so many portraits and caricatures of Mrs Jordan that I began to think of an exhibition. I decided that Kenwood, which already had a fine portrait of her as Viola in *Twelfth Night*, would be the ideal place for it. I consulted Jocelyn Stevens, chairman of English Heritage, who saw the point at once and gave me the go-ahead. I started work on it with a curator at Kenwood, Ian Dejardin. We had a gloriously busy time assembling paintings and drawings, Gillray cartoons, song sheets, letters and memorabilia. The life-sized Chantrey statue was the obvious centrepiece, and we were dismayed when the Palace refused to lend it on the grounds that its weight made it too difficult to move. Sir Oliver Millar, one time surveyor of the Queen's pictures, known to me from the Portrait Gallery, told me to insist. 'Write another letter, ask them again!' he urged me, and I dare say he put in a word. I did write again and this time permission was given for us to have a plaster cast made, as long as we ensured that there would be no mess on the Palace carpets. Trevor Nunn generously donated the cost and Keith Taylor made the magnificent cast, and without damaging the carpets. It was a happy day when she arrived at Kenwood.

The exhibition was extremely popular and ran for three months in 1995. Princess Margaret came to see it and stood by the piano visibly enjoying Ian Dejardin's performance as he sang one of Mrs Jordan's songs to his own accompaniment. At dinner I sat beside the princess: she scolded me for being rude about King William IV, and I replied that I thought I had dealt kindly with him, considering what he did. At this she opened her beautiful blue eyes wide but we went on conversing amicably. I failed to pluck up my courage enough to ask her to have a search made in the basements of the royal residences for a cast of one of Mrs Jordan's legs made by the sculptor Anne Damer. I still hope it will be found one day.★

I was involved in another exhibition in 1997, to commemorate the death of Mary Wollstonecraft in 1797 and the

★ Mrs Damer (1749–1828) was the first successful woman sculptor in England. She was born into an aristocratic family, hired a surgeon to help her study anatomy, travelled in Europe and made a career for herself after being widowed. She lived in Twickenham and was a friend of Horace Walpole. She made busts of Napoleon and Charles James Fox, and is believed to have made a cast of Mrs Jordan's leg, which belonged first to Joshua Reynolds and then the Duke of Clarence. A search has now been made in the Royal Collection, but sadly the leg has not been found. I am told that items relating to royal mistresses are rarely preserved.

With Robert Woof in the National Portrait Gallery

birth of her daughter, who became Mary Shelley. I worked with the super-energetic Robert Woof and his wife Pamela, who had set up the Wordsworth Museum at Dove Cottage on Grasmere, making it a cultural centre to which scholars travel from all over the world, a rare achievement in so remote a spot. Robert spent his life doing the impossible, which made him just occasionally exasperating and generally magnificent and inspiring. We produced a fine, full catalogue, and the exhibition opened at Dove Cottage and moved on to the Portrait Gallery in November.

❧

The third late-eighteenth/early-nineteenth-century woman I chose as a subject was Jane Austen, who wrote so well and wittily that people in London were inclined to believe her work must be that of a man. I saw her in the context of my earlier books, knowing she had seen Mrs Jordan act, and was aware of the existence of Mary Wollstonecraft.

I also knew that anyone setting out to write about Jane Austen must be aware that they are treading on ground that is both sacred and extremely well trodden. The prevailing view of her when I began to research my book was that she was a ladylike person perfectly at ease in the world of the gentry into which she was born. This seemed not quite right to me. Her parents ran a small boys' boarding school in the country vicarage in which she grew up. Her mother had some aristocratic connections of which she was proud, but the boys in the family knew they would have to earn their own livings, and the girls, Cassandra and Jane, sewed their brothers' shirts and helped with the cooking.

Their father had been orphaned young, and his sister Philadelphia sent to London and at fifteen apprenticed to a Covent Garden milliner for five years, which must have tested her strength and her virtue, after which she managed to get to India, where husbands were easily found, and there married a businessman. His second sister, Leonora, effectively disappeared from view in London and is never mentioned in surviving Austen family letters: very possibly she was handicapped.* Jane's brother George, unable to

---

* Leonora died, aged fifty, in 1784. Deirdre Le Faye speculates in a *Jane Austen Society Report* for 1998 that she may have been brain damaged at birth. Her sister's husband calls her 'poor Leonora' (Hancock to Philadelphia, 17 January 1770).

live a normal life, was sent away to be cared for permanently away from home. It was necessary to be tough, and the other sons each had to make his own way: to college, in the church, or into the army, as a banker; the two youngest went into the navy. Only Edward was lucky enough to be given an easy path, adopted by rich cousins and moved into a different social world of privilege, with foreign travel, a large guaranteed income and a wealthy bride. Jane was always loyal to her family, yet when she went to stay with Edward and his wife she did not make friends with her sister-in-law but with the governess, Anne Sharp, poor and clever, to whom she afterwards sent copies of all her books, asking for her critical response. I saw in Austen someone who questioned the behaviour of the privileged and distrusted conventional views.

When I consulted Brian Southam, a leading Austen scholar, about some small point, almost his first words – we were speaking on the telephone – were: 'You will of course join the Jane Austen Society.' He was the chairman of the Society, and he spoke with such authority that I immediately obeyed his instructions. It must be the most remarkable of all literary societies, founded in 1940 by the modest but determined Dorothy Darnell and her sister in order to raise money to buy the small house in Chawton where Austen lived for the last eight years of her life. They could not at first raise the £3,000 asked but in 1947 the money was given by Thomas Carpenter in memory of his son John, killed in the war. The house was saved, repaired and opened to the public in 1949, and in the same year the Society put out its first annual report. Since then it has grown so that there are associated branches in most parts of the world, and the annual reports are necessary reading for anyone interested in Austen studies. When I have a spare moment I often browse through early ones and am always rewarded – most recently by the transcript of L. P. Hartley's talk of 1965, in which he makes the case for *Sense and Sensibility* being at heart a tragic novel.

From living Austens and other scholars I had cheerful assistance. Alwyn Austen, great-grandson of Jane Austen's brother Frank, befriended me, went with me to Godmersham and talked through facts, theories and ideas with me – he was an extremely jolly companion. Robin Vick told me of his discoveries about Philadelphia's apprenticeship. The Austens' bankers, Messrs Hoare, allowed me to study the family's account in their archives. I came to them again when working on Pepys, who had also banked with them in the late seventeenth century. I doubt if there is any other bank that has been in business for four hundred years and opens its records so freely to researchers.

As I worked on Austen, my own family life was eventful. My grandson Raphael was born in August 1996 and I just managed to deliver my completed text to my publishers in May 1997, the month in which we helped to organize two family weddings of our respective youngest daughters, my Emily and Michael's Jenny. Both weddings were a good deal larger and noisier than the wedding of Austen's niece Anna, which I noticed was without flowers, friends or music, and with nothing fancy to eat except for the cake. We had flowers, music and dancing as well as cake.

Jane Austen: A Life was published in October 1997. Another biography was published simultaneously, but the market was able to bear both. I noted then that the critical literature devoted to Austen ran to thousands of volumes, tens of thousands of critical articles and hundreds of doctoral dissertations; that was twenty years ago as I write now, and I dare say the numbers have doubled since then. Today there is what can be called a Jane Austen Industry worldwide. How much this helps people to understand her writing is an open question.

When the idea that I might try to write about Pepys came to me, I was still working on my Austen book, and after it came out I had to spend much of 1998 giving talks. At the same time Michael's play *Copenhagen* became a major success in London, New York and Paris. We had a busy year, and only in the autumn was I able to get down to serious work on Pepys, familiarizing myself with a century I had not yet written about. One thing I was sure of already was that the seventeenth century is the most interesting period of our history, when we got rid of the king, lords and bishops, only to bring them all back.

How does one choose a subject? Often it arises from a discovery made while working on an earlier book, as it did for me with Mrs Jordan, whom I met while researching Ternan. This was not the case with Pepys. He simply imposed himself on me through his diaries. They were being published in the first complete edition through the years 1970 to 1983, but I started buying them only in 1980. The first two volumes I bought to give my daughter Susanna, hoping she would be drawn into reading something that might distract her by presenting an entirely different world, and so help to carry her out of her depression. It failed to do that – she would not look at them. After her death I took up the first volume and found myself quite unexpectedly at home in 1660. At times it felt more real than the present.

I was working as a literary editor then, and always busy, but I gradually acquired all the volumes of Pepys and kept one at my bedside, making his acquaintance slowly, reading whenever I could. Each volume as it appeared cost £25, which seems a bargain now. They were rightly seen as a great publishing achievement, because for the first time the text of the diary was complete and unbowdlerized, the transcription was first rate and supported by an exemplary apparatus of notes.* Yet it struck me that, even with the notes and comments, it was still often difficult to follow all the twists and turns of his crowded life easily, or to remember the names of his numerous friends, family, professional contacts and pick-ups. I began to read books about him, and to delve into seventeenth-century history. I even made an attempt to master the shorthand myself but found it more than I could manage. Years went by before I decided to attempt to write something about him.

It happened when the complete diaries with index and companion, eleven volumes in all, were published in

* The publisher was Bell & Hyman. Robin Hyman was a true Pepys scholar.

paperback in 1995. The *Guardian* asked me to review them. I was eager to have the paperbacks – I do not write in hardbacks but allow myself to annotate paperbacks, and I wanted to be able to do this with Pepys – so I agreed. Richard Ollard, a respected Pepys expert whom I knew, wrote me a very kind letter about my review. This gave me courage to think of attempting to write a biography of Pepys. From the start I knew I wanted to lay stress less on the naval administrator and more on the Renaissance man of multifarious interests and talents, as curious about himself as about the world around him.

Pepys's Cambridge college, Magdalene, to which he bequeathed his library containing the six volumes of his diary, made me welcome from the start. Richard Luckett, Pepys librarian, and Aude Fitzsimons, his deputy, became the best friends I could have wished for. I would take the morning train from King's Cross, then bus, then walk across the river into Magdalene, across two courts and up the single flight of stairs to the door of the library. I sometimes spent a night in College and was once given the rooms which Pepys reputedly shared with fellow students.

I went to Huntingdon, where Pepys was at the grammar school. I walked the idyllic path between his uncle's house at Brampton and Huntingdon many times, alongside the meadows in which Pepys heard the milkmaids singing as they brought in their cows, and past Hinchingbrooke, the great house of his cousin Edward Montagu. Montagu, a close friend of Cromwell, raised a regiment in his cause, and served him in government and at sea; his good and gentle wife Jemima became the model of what a woman should be for Pepys. Pepys's father hailed from East Anglia and lived off Fleet Street, a tailor whose clients were mostly London lawyers; while his mother was a Londoner born who would have preferred to stay in town even during the plague rather than be safe and bored in the country. All Pepys's London dwellings were close to the river, the central artery of London life, until his last years in Clapham. St Olave's Church, built in the fifteenth century, which he attended during the years of the diary, and where he put up a bust of his wife Elizabeth after her death, and chose to be buried himself, was saved from the Great Fire of 1666 and survived the Blitz of 1940–41, though much was then burnt and rebuilt.

Walking through the City and by the river between London and Greenwich, a journey Pepys more often made by boat than on foot, became another of my pleasures, shared with Michael. Enjoyable as the walking was, as I progressed with my research I sometimes felt I was carrying so much information in my head that it was like a physical weight – I can remind myself of that by looking at the notes at the end of the finished book, where for Chapter One alone there are forty-two notes covering four and a half pages. But it was never dry work.

Pepys: The Unequalled Self was published in October 2002, the same year that Michael's novel *Spies* appeared. I was the first person to read *Spies*, and I remember that once I started reading I could not put it down until I came to the end of the last page. I knew it was destined for every sort of success. What I did not know was that our books would be

With Michael on a train, photo by his daughter Rebecca

shortlisted for the Whitbread Prize and become rivals. When this happened, we became news. We were interviewed by journalists, caricatured, profiled and even invited to be photographed hitting one another over the head with our respective books (we declined). We laughed, and the publicity sold both our books. When mine was announced as the overall winner, Michael celebrated with me and I would have done as much had *Spies* won.

I was given other prizes for Pepys: one from the Royal Academy, another from the Pepys Society, a large and beautifully engraved medal. The occasion at which I was awarded it, in May 2003, three hundred years after the death of Pepys, with trumpets playing exuberantly and the sun shining into St Olave's, made the connection with the past seem very close.

☙❧

For years I had thought of writing about Thomas Hardy. I began to enjoy his poetry as a child. My interest grew when I first visited Dorset with my mother in the late 1940s. I was enchanted by the landscape and the coast, Studland, the villages and towns, the challenging hills and many rivers, Corfe Castle. I began to read his novels, and to look out for whatever was written about him.

I especially liked his detail, in poems and novels: the dust fallen into the folds of a working man's collar; the 'silver-bright' soles of Giles Winterborne, whose feet are kept walking all day in the woods; the way the colour of a striped dress changes at night; how thistle seeds are picked up by a woman's long skirts as she walks through fields; moonshine on snow lighting up ceilings, where window curtains are left open. Auden wrote of his 'hawk's vision'. Hardy kept the lyric tradition alive, and he became for me one of the indispensables among the English poets, with his great lifespan, 1840 to 1928, and his poetry a long-running conversation with himself kept going to the very end.

In his novels too he had an eye for the strange, the odd and unexpected. In *A Pair of Blue Eyes*, a young man slips from a cliff edge and is hanging on for dear life as the young woman with him strips off all her layers of Victorian underwear from under her dress and tears it up to make a rescue rope. It bears out Irving Howe's suggestion that

Hardy used chance to show what later writers attribute to the workings of the unconscious: the chance slipping of the man led to her undressing.

In *The Hand of Ethelberta* the servants in a Kensington house are shown playing a boisterous silent game in the drawing room, chasing each other and leaping from sofa to sofa as their employers are being served formal dinner in the room below. The game is obviously an expression of class hostility and I have never read about it anywhere else. I guess Hardy had it described to him by his cousin Martha when she was a lady's maid in Kensington.

His novel of 1882, *Two on a Tower*, was found shocking and even 'repulsive' for depicting sexual passion between a middle-aged lady and a young boy from the village. In the early stages of their love she watches him asleep and snips off a lock of his hair to keep – a reversal of the standard male/female role which no doubt upset people. When *Tess* was published, it led to broken friendships and family rows between those who were shocked and those who sympathized with the heroine. Hardy struggled against the nineteenth-century English insistence on keeping sex out of literature, and to be allowed to 'demolish the doll of English fiction'. If he did not entirely succeed, he still did better than any of his contemporaries.

I finished writing the Hardy biography in February 2006. Like most books, it set off further demands. One was from my publishers, asking me to prepare a short anthology of a hundred Hardy poems, with an introduction, to be published alongside the biography. They allowed me only one week to prepare this, but I thought it such an attractive idea that I took a deep breath and did it. And it was such a success that I was allowed to follow it up with a similar Keats anthology, another labour of love. I should have written a life of Keats had there not been so many good recent ones, and this at least allowed me to spend time with him, rereading poems and letters and retracing the terrible final months in Rome. After that I produced a small Milton – a contradiction in terms perhaps. I was happy to read Milton again – but I confess my anthology hardly sold a copy.

Another demand relating to Hardy came from the *South Bank Show*: Melvyn Bragg was planning a film about him to which I was to contribute. He and his team were so relaxed and friendly that it was more like a holiday than work as we filmed under a June sun in Cornwall and Dorset. I enjoyed every minute. Then we were in London, at the Athenaeum Club, where Hardy had been a member. We filmed while it was closed at the weekend, and when I was about to leave I noticed two pretty young women peering through the glass entrance door. I opened it and said, 'I'm afraid the club is closed.' 'Club?' asked one of the girls eagerly. 'Do they want any dancers?'

I was sorry when the filming was done, but I had to return to proofs. Michael had a book due to be published in September, a philosophical work, *The Human Touch*. It was greeted with good, intelligent reviews: happiness for me, because the response to a book by your spouse makes you as anxious as to your own. After this my son Tom needed surgery to remove a kidney. I was told he would have to be in intensive care but the surgeon was so good, and Tom so tough, that he was able to skip intensive care and come home sooner than expected. Once he was recovered, I hurried to a conference on biography in Salzburg I had promised to address. My granddaughter Rosa started at Cambridge. I spoke in Cheltenham, did *Start the Week*, then a short tour in Yorkshire – the book and the anthology appeared on 19 October. On the 22nd the *South Bank* film was shown. Then talks in Belfast, Dorset, Oxford, Ely, Blackheath, Cambridge, much signing, and off to San Francisco to start an American tour.

❦

In the spring of 1862, Hardy, aged twenty-one and newly arrived in London, went to hear Dickens giving public readings. Dickens was at the height of his fame, and Hardy admired his writing and was curious about him. One day he was in a small coffee shop in the Hungerford Market and saw the great man perched on a high stool at the counter. Hardy resolved to speak to him and went and stood at a vacant place next to him, but Dickens was fussing over his bill and took no notice of him. Hardy had no idea that Dickens was going through a period of crisis caused by his break from his wife. He had only eight years more to live; Hardy had his writing career ahead of him and had not yet met the young woman who would become his wife. What might they have said to one another? What advice could Dickens have given Hardy? But he was too shy to speak and the moment passed. I left this small episode out of my Hardy biography, but I often thought about it, and the fact that Hungerford Market disappeared soon afterwards, knocked down to make way for Charing Cross Station. As an American friend pointed out to me, a biographer is lucky to live in London, where every street speaks of the past.

My next biography was of Dickens. How did that come about? Over the years people asked me why I had chosen to write about Ellen Ternan rather than Charles Dickens. I usually replied that Ternan's story was a good one and needed to be told – and that there were too many biographies of Dickens already. But I found that once you are drawn into his orbit, it is not easy to escape. He is as hard to resist posthumously as he was in life. His engagement with the world was so intense, his character so complex, his friends so various, his travels so extensive (and brilliantly recorded in his own words), his activities so surprising, his books so open to different interpretations – the list can go on, and once you find yourself thinking about all the questions raised you are already in danger of wanting to sort out your responses and set down your own account.

I was caught like this, partly because I stayed in touch with Dickens studies, and kept rereading his work. And also, as the volumes of his letters were published one after another, I was invited to review them, agreed and found myself getting in deeper with each one. The number of thick, handsome books on my shelves, clad in their yellow dust-jackets, each many hundreds of pages long and usefully indexed and annotated, grew. It grew, and they challenged me.

Unbelievable as it may sound, it had not occurred to me when, in 2007, I told my editor I had decided to write about Dickens that we were approaching the bicentenary of his birth in 1812. But my editor knew, and responded accordingly. I was now set firmly on my course for the next five years.

14

Surprises and Discoveries

Throughout these working years, life at home changed constantly. The young men who came to work as Tom's helpers came from different parts of England and from Ireland, Scotland, Wales, Germany, Switzerland. The first days with each of them could be disconcerting for everyone. Allen from Belfast found our English accents incomprehensible and we had the same difficulty with his Northern Irish speech. His parents travelled to London to see whether I was a respectable person and to my relief – I brought out my best china to serve them tea – they decided I was. Within a few days, as I was walking near home, I heard laughter round the corner – and there were Tom and Allen chatting and laughing together, evidently well able to understand one another. No one could have been better than Allen, and then when Peter arrived from Heidelberg we had another very happy year, and then another with Ian from Edinburgh. Each of them came to seem to me like surrogate sons, and elder brothers for Tom. And they helped him to grow into the independent person he now is.

Tom was often ill, needing to be hurried to hospital for quick diagnoses, and in and out for longer investigations. Hydrocephalus was again suspected, worryingly but wrongly, and he had more surgery on his hips. His life was

318

Tom

changed for the better by learning to use a catheter, which meant he no longer had a problem with continence, and he was able to start confidently at a state secondary school, William Ellis in Hampstead.

He was the first, and I fear the only, pupil to use a wheelchair there. He was always eager to go to school, although he was bullied, had his medical equipment stolen from his bag, chewing gum pushed into his hair and regularly kicked. He never lacks courage and he took it all in his stride. As the years went by, a few of his fellow pupils in the French group showed some friendliness, and the arrival of girls on the scene at sixth-form stage made the atmosphere gentler. I asked him later if he thought William Ellis had been a mistake and he said no – adding wryly, because at least nothing could ever be so bad again.

As Tom fought to be able to live as near a normal life as possible, my mother's strength and brainpower were failing. I fetched her from Welwyn to stay with us as often as I could, but seeing to her requirements became more and more difficult. I decided I could not have her to live permanently with us while I had also to arrange for Tom's needs and helpers. I found a private care home nearby in Hampstead and arranged to take her to meet the matron, who welcomed us with real kindness and showed us round. It seemed a happy place, and well organized. As I drove my mother back to Gloucester Crescent, she looked out of the window and said thoughtfully, 'My daughter Claire used to live near here,' to which the only answer I could make was: 'She still does, Mummy, she still does.' She refused adamantly to consider going to live in the home.

The next sad stage came when she fell ill and was taken to hospital in Welwyn. She was well cared for and recovered, but she was becoming more confused. As the consultant told me, 'Your mother is a charming old lady but she is completely –' I think he said bonkers, but he may have put it more elegantly. He added that they could not keep her in hospital. No care home in Welwyn would receive her because she was incontinent, which seems extraordinary.

The Hampstead one I had liked was now unavailable and I had to search for another. I settled for one in Finchley.

The whole process of moving her was heart-breaking. She did not understand what was happening or why she was in unfamiliar surroundings. My wish to take her home with me for weekends was strongly discouraged by the staff. She was now eighty-six, most of her old friends were dead, and few of those who were still alive were able to visit her. She was unhappy and I was unhappy for her. She became withdrawn. After six months she was taken into hospital with an unspecified illness – old age, I suppose. I remember the matron speaking her name gently but clearly in her ear – 'Muriel' – and turning to me to say, 'What we are seeing is the approach to death.' I was able to give her sips of water and stroke her hair, once so thick and beautiful, now pitifully thin. The television blared out its idiot noise at the end of the ward. I knew I had failed her.

She died in May 1984. Her grandchildren, my daughters and my nieces gathered for the funeral, and both my sister and my father flew to London from France to be with us. He had not spoken to her for over forty years. As he walked towards me, I saw an expression on his face I did not recognize. He stopped, made a gesture with his arms outheld and spoke: 'She was wonderful!' he said. The intensity of feeling conveyed in those words was so great that, for the first time in my life, I saw plainly how much he had once loved her – and not only loved but admired her. My perspective on my parents and the past shifted.

I wrote a note to myself: 'People are spurred to write by the death of parents, as though they felt suddenly they must catch it now, before things fade too far into the distance.' I failed to write anything down then, but I did something much more important. I collected all my mother's music, her published songs and her manuscripts, put everything into large file boxes and took them home to store safely.

❧

I had some professional dealings with my father also. In the late 1990s a French publisher, Henry Dougier, commissioned a translation of my book on Jane Austen. I went over to Paris to see him over an informal breakfast in the rue Jacob, where he ran his firm, Autrement, and found him congenial and charming. The translation was to be made by two women scholars, one of whom had been my father's pupil, and he at once volunteered to take part in the translating process. He was now in his mid-nineties, but he read, checked and corrected every page of their work. They may have had mixed feelings about having it vetted by a near-centenarian retired professor, but they took it in good part. He consulted with me on points of detail and made his own suggestions, and the result, published in France in 2000, is good. This was probably the nearest we came to intimacy, through my written words.

By then he had published his memoir with the story of my conception. I never asked him about it, and I cannot explain why I failed to. I may have felt there was nothing more to say about such an appalling story – but the fact that I failed to, and fail now to remember what I thought when I read it, disquiets me.

❧

My mother's music was still in boxes at home. In 2000 a music producer at the BBC, Bill Lloyd, persuaded me to talk about my mother on air. Bill had been taught by her as a boy singer and remembered her with admiration and affection, and he recorded Richard Lloyd Morgan singing five of her songs for the programme. It made a small stir. Bill and I kept in touch, but it was not until 2008 that I started to go through all the manuscripts, encouraged by enquiries from other musicologists as well as Bill.

Something quite unexpected happened. I pulled out a group of manuscripts and saw that they were dated 1914, 1915, 1916, 1917, some with the day she had finished the song, and with Liverpool addresses, before she went to the Royal College of Music in London to study composition with Stanford. They were written in the neat hand of a young girl. As I went through them, I could see, even with my slight musical education, that they were of interest. I took them to the piano to get a better sense of them and thought they were good: settings of Herrick's 'To Daffodils', Blake's 'Love's Secret', Southey's 'How Beautiful is Night', Christina Rossetti's 'Mirage'.

Because I was a late child, born when my mother was thirty-seven, I had known her only as a middle-aged woman. Now suddenly I was face to face with the work of a young woman. It was an experience like no other in my life, as though I were travelling back in time and looking into the heart and mind of an unknown girl. I could see that a strong creative gift had been at work in her. I asked myself why she had never sung these songs or shown them to me. I wished I had been able to talk with her about them

My mother at her piano

and the circumstances in which they were written, because I knew they had not been easy. I felt humbled. How hard she had worked, and how well.

Bill studied the manuscripts and sent copies of the songs he liked best to the pianist and composer David Owen Norris. He came for a session in which he played them and insisted on my doing my best to sing. I had long since lost my singing voice but I made a huge effort – to such effect that the next day my throat had seized up and I could not even speak. He asked me if she had accompanied herself; I told him she had. 'She must have been a remarkable pianist,' he said. As indeed she was.

Bill now persuaded James Gilchrist and Ailish Tynan to record a group of the songs with Owen Norris as accompanist. In May 2008 I met with Bill and the three musicians at a recording studio in Monmouthshire and for three days was with them as they rehearsed, talked and recorded. I was high with the delight of hearing them bring the songs to life, many of them for the first time even for me, and I had to blink back tears at the beauty of the performances, and thinking how much it would have meant to my mother to hear them. I drove home across England, rejoicing, still high. The recording was made, Bill edited it, Linn Records published it. The British Library agreed to take my mother's manuscripts to catalogue and keep. Since then BiblioFox Music Publishing has published many of her songs, making them easily available to be bought on line.

I will not exaggerate her importance. She produced only a small body of work. The style in which she wrote her songs is out of fashion. She did not expand her musical ambitions as she might have done, rather reduced them when childcare, the war, divorce and having to earn her living by teaching made it hard for her to keep composing. None of this matters. The music she wrote is original and beautiful. Now and then I hear of a concert at which it is performed, or a broadcast. It speaks to many people and deserves to be valued for what it is, and kept alive. Richard Stokes has listed ten of her songs in the 2016 *Penguin Book of English Song*: half of the ones he has chosen were unpublished, three James Joyce settings – the ones she sang for him in Paris in 1928 – also Herrick's 'To Daffodils' and Masefield's 'Tewkesbury Road'.

With my father and stepmother in Vence

My father lived to be nearly ninety-eight, clear in his mind and only getting physically weaker in the last year, 2003. That was a busy year for me: we were moving house, I was giving many talks about Pepys following the publication of my book on him, and I had started research for a life of Thomas Hardy. I flew out to see my father in January, in May, in August. During one of our talks he said, 'You have had a hard life . . .' and stopped short. I was surprised, since he so rarely said anything personal. He avoided it, I think, because he had always blamed his mother, and my mother also, for displaying emotion, which he found burdensome and suspected of exaggeration and falsity. On this occasion I was able to assure him that my life was now happier than it had ever been, through my marriage and my work as a writer.

I took his continued existence for granted, but I did realize that there is something unusual about having a living parent when you are yourself in your seventies. I told him we were all expecting to celebrate his hundredth birthday in 2005. He replied with a yes, but not a very affirmative one, and went on to say that he had expected to live to be a hundred but now felt tired and was ready to give up.

He was comfortable, cared for by Kath at home, supported by daily visits from nurses and doctor. The flat was quiet, with the mountains behind, and from the windows of his bedroom he could see the sky and look down towards the Mediterranean. When I was there in August a nurse came every morning to give him breakfast, after which he settled down on his pillows again. I stayed for a week, talking with him and Kath and going for short solitary walks along the mountain paths. On the day I was due to leave he asked a little anxiously if I would be back soon, and I said yes. Indeed I meant it. I was going home for Michael's seventieth birthday and the opening of his new play, *Democracy*, at the National Theatre.

A few days after I left, my father took his breakfast and lay back on his pillows as usual. The nurse was an experienced one. She looked at him and quickly called Kath and my sister from the next room. She must have seen something that told her he was dying. They were able to be beside him as his life ended.

I arranged with my children for us all to fly out to the funeral. This was the day before Michael's birthday and two days before the opening of *Democracy*. Death, birthday celebrations, funeral arrangements and a first night all demanded our attention. The play was a triumph, with

Roger Allam giving a flawless and devastating performance as Willy Brandt, and Conleth Hill comic and tragic at
once as the spy Günter Guillaume. We had little time to
rejoice before setting off next morning for Vence, where
the family was gathering. The flag of the Légion d'honneur
was brought and laid over my father's coffin. The next
morning we drove along mountain roads in the September
sunshine to the crematorium. I was deputed to speak. I
spoke of his career, intelligence and breadth of knowledge,
and gave an example of his quick wit: how, when I read his
history of the Delavenay family going back to the twelfth
century, I praised it, then added, 'You have established
only the male line –' to which, without a moment's hesitation, he answered, 'I was leaving the female line for you.'

After the funeral we returned to the flat for food and drink.
The youngest children of the party, four great-grandsons,
took themselves into the biggest bedroom to play. When I
looked in to make sure they were happy, I saw a wonderful
sight: all four of them jumping up and down energetically on
the bed in which he had died, and where the coffin had been
lying a few hours earlier. It was a perfect moment, as life reasserted itself with the unstoppable force of the young.

❦

For Kath it was the end of sixty years together, of that long
conversation which makes the climate in which a couple
lives at ease and mutually reliant. So we sorrowed especially for her. For his children and grandchildren his death
was less a cause for mourning than a realization that this

was the end of an epoch. He had held the family together, researched and written its history, made sure we kept in touch with each other, entertained us, celebrated birthdays, offered us festive and memorable meals, allowing all the English part of the family to partake of French pleasures. With age he had mellowed enough to be able to have fun with grandchildren and great-grandchildren.

I thought of my mother's last year during which I had failed to keep her happy. The contrast was painful. When I thanked Kath for her care of my father, she said, forthright as always, 'No one will do it for me.' She was right. She lived into her nineties, growing less steady on her feet and weaker, and obliged to take the massive daily doses of pills insisted on by French doctors. We had her to stay in England and went out to see her often – Tom was especially devoted to her. I was away in India when she had a stroke, after which she was cared for in a clinic, comfortable and well run, with a private room, and more quantities of pills. Each time I visited her she let me know how eager she was to die. I loved her and wanted to help her but was not able to hasten her death. I know she tried to starve herself, and was bullied to eat. We need to learn better ways of helping people when their lives become unbearable to them.

When you have seen many of your friends and family die, it is not so hard to think calmly about your own coming death. You will be following the path they have already taken. You need no belief in an afterlife to feel comforted by that thought. I am happy to think of being 'Rolled round in earth's diurnal course, / With rocks, and stones, and trees.' With Wordsworth, I see the world as 'the place where, in the end, / We find our happiness, or not at all!' And I know how lucky I have been to find happiness as well as tragedy.

Until now my books have ended with the death of the main character. This one has to be different. I have reached eighty-four, longer than any of my subjects except Thomas Hardy, who got to eighty-seven. He went on writing to the end, and I intend to take a lesson from him and begin on another book if possible when this one is finished.

I know that I have led an exceptionally privileged life. England kept me safe from the worst horrors of war when I was a child. In some respects its effects were even good for me: the year I spent in Cumberland when the Lycée was evacuated there introduced me to the happiness of solitary communion with the natural world, the fells and lakes, trees, rain and open skies. I grew up in a country that seemed safe and gentle, and I enjoyed almost all my experience of school. My mother gave me unconditional love and showed me that music and poetry are essential pleasures. I learnt habits of work from both my parents – it was something they had in common, although in other ways so unlike.

Through my parents too I took the sense that I am a European and that the lessons learnt from the history of Europe are essential to understanding the world we live in now. My father's early interest in the League of Nations and later years with the United Nations in New York and UNESCO in Paris led me to think about the importance of international cooperation, however difficult, and however uncertain and disappointing its effectiveness. We have to keep trying.

Michael and I have six children and ten grandchildren between us, who do extraordinary things, surprise us and make us occasionally anxious but for the most part proud. My youngest is Amy, blessed with gymnastic skills, a witty tongue and a warm heart. My indomitable son Tom is an inspiration to me as he lives his life independently and takes himself travelling alone, making light of the many problems he has to deal with.

My harshest regret is that our generation is not leaving the world in a better state than we found it, either politically or ecologically. Global warming and, in England, prison reform, both need urgent attention. If the nations could give up their insistence on economic growth, get rid of nuclear weapons, see the danger and folly of crude nationalism, empty prisons of all but the uncontrollably violent – the list is easy to make – we might see an improvement. But it may be that human nature will never allow these things to be brought about, and that the lessons of history are never learnt. The horrors brought to us by men who murder indiscriminately in the name of ideas no sane person could entertain force us to realize that peace is fragile and never to be taken for granted.

So far my seventies and eighties have been easy. I have been working at books, giving talks, tending our garden, travelling with Michael, enjoying his writing. We began 2016 in Italy, staying with friends, and since then we have made working trips to Bulgaria, to America and to Moscow, and taken the Eurostar to Avignon for a holiday in Provence. Michael went back to Moscow for the opening of his play *Democracy*, and we both spent a few days in Warsaw seeing another revival of *Noises Off*. We encourage one another to keep walking and working. We grieved together over Brexit, despaired at the American presidential election, worried about the Labour Party and rejoiced at its return to favour.

We still enjoy music, go to concerts, Proms, opera live or on film. Glyndebourne gives us particular happiness, although we now miss George Christie, the best of friends for so many years as well as a provider of so much joy. Like my hero Samuel Pepys, I believe that music is 'productive of a pleasure that no state of life, publick or private, secular or sacred, no difference of age or season; no temper of mind or condition of health ... renders either improper, untimely, or unentertaining. Witness the universal gusto we see it followed with, wherever to be found.' If I had to describe perfect happiness, I might say it is hearing the first bars of the overture to *The Marriage of Figaro* as the orchestra starts to play at the beginning of the evening. Even writing the words brings a smile.

Acknowledgements

My daughters Jo and Emily and my son Tom have helped me to recover memories of the past, as have my nieces Claire Sparrow, Jenny Rogers and Anna Fay-Barnett. Friends have also been patient with my enquiries, especially David and Sue Gentleman, Neal Ascherson, Anthony Barnes, Stephen Haskell, Christopher Reid, Sean French, Sarah Forman, John Ryle, Julian Barnes and Jennifer Hales.

Nora Bartlett, whose letter of 1980 I quote from, and who talked to me while I was writing the book, very sadly died in August 2016.

The *Sunday Times* kindly allowed me to access their archives and I am particularly grateful to Peter Kemp for his help in bringing this about.

My father provided me with an unexpected aide-mémoire by keeping almost all the letters I wrote to him from the age of eleven until his death in 2003, and my step-mother passed them on to me.

David Godwin is an ideal agent, always there when I need him, full of good ideas and backed by a terrific team, to whom my thanks also.

I am grateful to Tony Lacey and Venetia Butterfield for excellent editorial advice. Donna Poppy has once again proved the ideal copy editor and my warmest thanks go to her.

My husband Michael Frayn has shown himself patient as

334 *Acknowledgements*

I struggled to write, helped me by discussing my doubts and problems, distracted me with treats and holidays and kept me going when I was close to giving up.

I have drawn on the following books:

Témoignage d'un village savoyard au village mondial (1992), my father Émile Delavenay's memoir
Nicholas Tomalin Reporting (1975) by Ron Hall
Anne and George at Prawls: A Memoir (2004), a short account of his parents by Anthony Barnes
Unreasonable Behaviour: An Autobiography (2002) by Don McCullin

CLAIRE TOMALIN

THE LIFE AND DEATH OF MARY WOLLSTONECRAFT

'There is no better book on Mary Wollstonecraft nor is there likely to be'
J.H. Plumb

Witty, courageous and unconventional, Mary Wollstonecraft was one of the most controversial figures of her day. She published *A Vindication of the Rights of Women*, lived through the Terror in France, had an illegitimate daughter and married the philosopher William Godwin before dying in childbirth at the age of 38.

Claire Tomalin's first book inaugurated a glittering career, and brought to life one of the great figures in the history of women.

'A most intelligent and sympathetic biographer, aware of her subject's many failings, yet with the perception to present her greatness fairly' *Daily Telegraph*

'A vivid evocation of how women lived in the second half of the eighteenth century' *Evening Standard*

'Gripping. Illuminates Mary's courage and pioneering political foresight'
Sunday Times

CLAIRE TOMALIN

MRS JORDAN'S PROFESSION:
THE STORY OF A GREAT ACTRESS AND A FUTURE KING

The story of the love between a prince and a famous actress.

Acclaimed as the greatest comic actress of her generation, Dora Jordan played a quite different role offstage as the mistress of one of the sons of George lll. Dora bore him ten children, and they lived in quiet happiness in Bushy Park on the Thames until the unexpected news arrived of his ascendancy to the throne as William lV at which point he was forced to abandon her.

Claire Tomalin vividly recreates the political, theatrical and royal worlds of the late eighteenth century. The story of how Dora moved between stage and home, of how she battled for career and family, makes for a classic tale of royal perfidy and womanly courage.

'Wonderfully readable. As gripping as the best fiction' Jan Dalley, *Independent*

'The strangest and most sensational story Tomalin has written so far'
Hilary Spurling, *Daily Telegraph*

'A compelling story and Tomalin tells it with clarity and warmth'
Lucy Hughes-Hallett, *Sunday Times*

CLAIRE TOMALIN

CHARLES DICKENS: A LIFE

Charles Dickens was a phenomenon. His novels are read the world over and he enriched the English language. He mocked power and greed while speaking up for ordinary people. His public readings brought adoring crowds, and he was seen as a cheerful family man. Yet there was a darker Dickens whose demons drove him to reject his wife, fail his children, break with friends and conduct a secret love affair in his last years. In *Charles Dickens: A Life*, Claire Tomalin gives us the best account yet of the man, his works, his times and, most of all, his extraordinary genius.

'Tomalin has captured Dickens, in sun and shadow, with all the full-hearted exuberance, generosity and keen wit that he merits' Boyd Tonkin, *Independent*

'Powerful and remarkable. It is a celebration of a great genius. No question: you put Tomalin's book down knowing that you have met a living author' Miriam Margolyes, *The Times*

'Tomalin brings this energetic, complicated, life-affirming, monstrous man so vividly to life that, when he drops dead, it is like a light going out' Jeremy Paxman, *Country Life*

CLAIRE TOMALIN

THOMAS HARDY: THE TIME-TORN MAN

Paradox ruled Thomas Hardy's life. His birth was almost his death; he became one of the great Victorian novelists and reinvented himself as one of the twentieth-century's greatest poets; he was an unhappy husband and a desolate widower; he wrote bitter attacks on the English class system yet prized the friendship of aristocrats.

In the hands of Whitbread Award-winning biographer Claire Tomalin, Thomas Hardy the novelist, poet, neglectful husband and mourning lover all come vividly alive.

'Another triumph for a biographer who goes from strength to strength' Melvyn Bragg, *Guardian, Books of the Year*

'Tomalin provides an object lesson in how to write a life' *Economist*

'A moving story, and Tomalin tells it vividly, with as great a fund of sympathy and sense, as can be imagined' *Daily Telegraph*